Communication under the Microscope

D0978560

If communication is central to many aspects of human life, how important is studying the process? What can be learned from the detailed analysis of interpersonal communication?

Social interaction in recent years has become the focus of systematic scientific research in a wide variety of academic disciplines. In *Communication under the Microscope*, Peter Bull shows how communication has become an object of study in its own right, which can be dissected in the finest detail through the use of film and recording technology. In so doing he provides a clear and valuable introduction into the theory and practice of microanalysis.

Bull argues that microanalysis is both a distinctive methodology and a distinctive way of thinking about communication. He then focuses on the two principal elements of face-to-face communication: speech and non-verbal behaviour. Communication in particular social contexts is also addressed with related chapters on gender and politics. Finally, the practical aspects of microanalysis are discussed.

This unique and thorough review of microanalysis integrates different approaches and draws together research literature which is often diverse and disparate. Presented in a clear and focused style, this book will be of interest to psychologists, social scientists and all students and researchers in the field of communication.

Dr Peter Bull is a Senior Lecturer in the Department of Psychology at York University. He has over 40 academic publications, principally on the detailed microanalysis of interpersonal communication.

Thanks to Ann for suggesting the title.

Communication under the Microscope
The Theory and Practice of Microanalysis

Peter Bull

First published 2002 by Routledge
27 Church Road, Hove, East Sussex, BN3 2FA

Simultaneously published in the USA and Canada
by Routledge
29 West 35th Street, New York, NY 10001

Routledge is an imprint of the Taylor & Francis Group

Typeset in Sabon by Mayhew Typesetting, Rhayader, Powys
Printed and bound in the UK by Biddles Ltd, Guildford and
King's Lynn

British Library Cataloguing in Publication Data
A catalogue record for this book is available from the British Library

Library of Congress Cataloging in Publication Data
A catalog record for this book is available from the Library of
Congress

ISBN: 0-415-04688-2 (pbk)
ISBN: 0-415-04687-4 (hbk)

Contents

Preface

Communication is of central importance to many aspects of human life, yet it is only in recent years that it has become the focus of systematic scientific investigation. Such research has been conducted in a wide variety of academic disciplines, most notably social psychology, psychiatry, anthropology, linguistics, sociology, ethology and, of course, communication. Despite substantial disagreements and differences in emphasis, there is also sufficient common ground between scholars to discern distinctive similarities in approach. In particular, the key feature is the belief in the value of studying the fine details of social interaction through the detailed analysis of film, audiotape and videotape recordings. Because such research is based on the detailed ('micro') analysis of both speech and nonverbal behaviour, it will be referred to as the microanalytic approach.

Thus, the theme of this book is the microanalysis of interpersonal communication. Despite many differences and disagreements, it seeks to show that modern communication scholars do also share a number of common assumptions. In the cut and thrust of academic debate, differences tend to be sharpened, points of contact overlooked. But points of contact are also important, in this context they have come to represent a novel way of thinking about communication. This is the perspective that makes this book distinctive.

The first chapter seeks to outline the different modes of thought that have contributed to the microanalytic approach. Chapters 2 and 3 seek to present some of the main findings concerning the two principal elements of face-to-face communication, namely, nonverbal behaviour and speech. In Chapters 4 and 5, two examples of microanalytic research are discussed: gender and political communication. The final chapter seeks to evaluate the practical significance of microanalysis.

There must be – at the very least – tens of thousands of publications concerned with communication. Hence, by its very nature, any review of this kind is inevitably selective. Each of the six chapters could merit a book in itself; there could easily have been twice as many chapters; many other topics could have been discussed in depth: communication in organizations, health communication, new communication technologies, relational communication and interethnic communication, to name but a few.

But this review is intended neither to be comprehensive nor exhaustive. This is not a handbook of communication research. Rather, it is intended to present an argument. Microanalysis represents a novel and distinctive way of thinking about communication. This new way of thinking has produced not only valuable insights into how we communicate, but is also of considerable practical significance. To review this distinctive intellectual and social movement is the aim of *Communication under the Microscope*.

Peter Bull
York, 2001

1   Microanalysis of communication

Microanalysis represents not only a distinctive methodology but also a distinctive way of thinking about communication. Undoubtedly, the detailed analysis of film, audiotape and videotape recordings has facilitated discoveries that otherwise simply would not be possible. Indeed, the effect of the videotape recorder has been likened to that of the microscope in the biological sciences. Without recorded data that can be examined repeatedly, it is simply not possible to perform the kind of highly detailed analysis of both speech and nonverbal communication characteristic of the micro-analytic approach. But microanalysis did not develop simply as a consequence of innovations in technology. Film technology had been available since the beginning of the twentieth century; two of the earliest pioneers of cinematography, Muybridge and Marey, had a particular interest in analysing and recording movement patterns in animals and humans (Marey, 1895; Muybridge, 1899/1957, 1901/1957). The extensive use of this technology in the study of human social interaction has only really developed in the past few decades; its use reflects fundamental changes in the way in which we think about human communication (Kendon, 1982).

The aim of this chapter is to outline the ideas that characterize micro-analysis. There are three main sections. The first outlines the changing modes of thought that led to the extensive use of recording technology in communication analysis. The second section gives an account and evaluation of the different intellectual traditions that have contributed to the microanalytic approach. In the final section, a comparison is made of these different intellectual approaches. Points of disagreement are discussed, while the central features of what is regarded as microanalysis are specified in order to show how it can be regarded as a distinctive and novel way of thinking about communication. The main headings and sub-headings are listed below:

Section 1. Early influences on the development of microanalysis.

Section 2. Approaches to the analysis of communication:
the structural approach

the sociological approach:
  Goffman
  conversation analysis
Speech Act Theory
discourse analysis
ethology
communication as skill: a social psychological approach.

Section 3. A comparison of different approaches to communication
analysis:
points of disagreement
central features of the microanalytic approach.

Early influences on the development of microanalysis

The intellectual history underlying the use of recording technology in communication analysis has been discussed in depth by Adam Kendon (1982). The development of the main assumptions underlying the modern approach to the study of social interaction are reviewed below.

The importance of social interaction was recognized in the earliest days of sociology and social psychology by writers such as Georg Simmel. In his book *Soziologie* (Simmel, 1908), he urged that the study of social interaction should be considered central to the discipline of sociology. 'Society,' Simmel wrote 'is merely the name for a number of individuals, connected by interaction' (Simmel, 1950, p. 10). From the 1920s, Simmel's work became available to American readers (Kendon, 1988). It had an important influence upon the development of the Chicago school of descriptive sociology, which focused particularly on behaviour in face-to-face situations.

Parallel and closely related to this development was the emergence of symbolic interactionism through the writings of Cooley (e.g. 1902) and later George Herbert Mead (1934). Mead argued that the individual's sense of self is in itself the product of the process of social interaction. He proposed that people come to internalize a conception of themselves, as a result of the way in which they are treated by others. Mead's thinking was highly influential. Of particular importance was the value he attached to studying interpersonal processes, rather than the actions of people in isolation from one another (Kendon, 1982).

This interest in interpersonal processes was taken up by certain psychiatrists, in particular, by Harry Stack Sullivan (Kendon, 1982). Sullivan was especially interested in schizophrenia, which he believed should be understood in terms of interpersonal processes, rather than as an organically based disorder. His basic premise was that interpersonal relations should be the principal concern of the psychiatrist. This mode of thought directed psychiatrists to the study of the interaction; interest became focused on the patient–therapist relationship, which some psychiatrists began to analyse in detail. Hence, it is perhaps no surprise that many pioneering studies of interaction were carried out by psychiatrists, and that their discipline played an important role in the early development of the microanalytic approach.

A second important influence was that of information theory and cybernetics. Information theory was significant, in that it led to the view that any aspect of behaviour can be regarded as potentially informative. This would apply not only to intentional speech and gesture but also to seemingly unintended actions, whose function does not in any sense appear to be communicative. Of course, such behaviour had already begun to come under scrutiny, from a psychoanalytic perspective, for what it might reveal about unconscious motivations, but the application of an information theory perspective encouraged investigators to regard all aspects of behaviour as potential signals (Kendon, 1982).

Parallel with the influence of information theory, there were important developments in the analysis of self-regulating systems, or cybernetics, as it has come to be known. Cybernetics developed initially as a means of designing an anti-aircraft gun that could track its moving target automatically (Wiener, 1948). The essential element of this design was feedback: the process whereby the action of the controlling mechanism was directed by information about the consequences of its own actions. The importance of this concept was that it could also be applied to human behaviour. In *Communication: The Social Matrix of Psychiatry*, published in 1951, Jurgen Ruesch (a psychiatrist) and Geoffrey Bateson (an anthropologist) argued for a convergence between psychiatry and ideas derived from cybernetics and communication engineering. By focusing not upon the person or the group, but upon the message and the circuit as units of study, they claimed that a way was found to connect these apparently diverse disciplines.

Before these ideas became current, interaction was often conceptualized in terms of stimulus–response sequences, in which the action of one partner served as a stimulus for the other, which in turn served as a stimulus for the former. Thus, interaction was regarded as a sequential chain, with each action appearing strictly as a consequence of the other's previous action. The advantage of the cybernetic perspective was that it allowed interaction to be conceptualized in a different way. From this perspective, each participant could be seen as pursuing a line of action, but each must adjust their actions in the light of the feedback that the other's actions provide. Again, from this perspective, interaction could be considered as organized at several different levels. So, for example, in a conversation between two people, one can recognize not only that conversation is organized in terms of the moment-to-moment feedback, but also at a higher level; for example, one of the participants might be seeking to persuade the other, and most of this person's actions can be understood in terms of this higher-order intent.

A third important influence was that of structural linguistics (Kendon, 1982). Linguistics, as it developed in the United States, evolved in close relationship with anthropology, and was particularly concerned with the task of producing systematic descriptions of American Indian languages, languages that had never been written down and whose structure was unknown. One of the first problems faced by investigators was to discover which sounds made by speakers of these languages were meaningful, and which were not. Because these languages were so unfamiliar, the researchers had no means of knowing which sounds to exclude. As a consequence, it was felt necessary to start by making complete transcriptions of all a speaker's vocal sounds. This method dealt directly with the analysis of speech behaviour, in contrast to the way in which linguistics had developed (especially in Europe), where the focus was principally on written text (Kendon, 1982).

This approach to linguistics, with its emphasis on fieldwork and the associated problems of dealing with speech, led to an appreciation of the way in which speech is embedded in broader aspects of social behaviour. The techniques developed for the analysis of American Indian languages could also be applied to other aspects of communication. So, for example, the term 'paralanguage' was introduced to refer to changes in tone of voice, which could affect the meaning of what is said (Trager, 1958). 'Kinesics' was an attempt to apply the methodology of descriptive linguistics to body movement (Birdwhistell, 1971). The focus of 'proxemics' was the study of space (Hall, 1963), and that of 'tacesics', the study of touch (Kauffman, 1969).

In 1956, all these different influences came together at the Institute for Advanced Study at Palo Alto (Kendon, 1982). A research group was set up, comprising two psychiatrists (Brosin and Fromm-Reichman), two structural linguists (McQuown and Hockett) and two anthropologists (Bateson and Birdwhistell). Both the psychiatrists had been heavily influenced by Sullivan's interpersonal orientation. Birdwhistell was already known for his attempts to develop a structural linguistic approach to the study of body movement. Bateson, in collaboration with Margaret Mead, had pioneered the use of film and photography in the analysis of social behaviour in natural settings (Bateson & Mead, 1942), as well as the application of ideas from information theory and cybernetics to the study of social interaction discussed above (Ruesch & Bateson, 1951).

This collaboration is widely reckoned to have initiated a major shift in the way in which we think about communication. As such, it represented the first attempt to examine a single interactional event recorded on film, taking into account every possible aspect of the behaviour of the participants (Kendon, 1982). Traditionally, from the origins of rhetoric in classical Greece to the measurement of information in the twentieth century, communication had been studied mostly in terms of what it should be – in terms, for example, of its efficiency, clarity or persuasiveness

(Bavelas *et al.*, 1990). What made the approach at Palo Alto so distinctive was the analysis of communication as it actually occurs – the attempt to observe, record, examine and describe social interaction in the finest of detail (Weakland, 1967). This has become so central to the microanalytic approach that it is no longer regarded as remarkable, yet at the time it was both significant and novel.

No publication emerged from this 1956 collaboration at Palo Alto and the members of the group went their separate ways. But subsequently, film, and more especially videotape, have been used with ever-increasing frequency as a means of studying social interaction. A number of distinctive approaches to this research can be distinguished, associated with a number of different academic disciplines. These have contributed in a variety of ways to the development of microanalysis and are discussed below.

Approaches to the analysis of communication

The structural approach

One of the participants at Palo Alto, Ray Birdwhistell, joined a psychiatrist, Albert Scheflen, in Philadelphia, who was another early pioneer of this kind of research. Their subsequent collaboration was based on a number of common assumptions, which made it highly distinctive. As such, it has been referred to as the 'structural approach' to the study of interpersonal communication (Duncan, 1969). In particular, Birdwhistell and Scheflen seemed to regard communication as a tightly organized and self-contained social system like language, which operates according to a definite set of rules. The task of the investigator they saw was to identify and articulate those rules.

For example, Scheflen (e.g. 1964, 1973) studied psychotherapy sessions in great detail using a technique that he called 'context analysis'. The method he recommended was a natural history one: through repeated viewing of videotape, the researcher can identify which of the nonverbal cues are ordered in sequential arrangements (Scheflen, 1966). One of his most important insights concerned the significance of what was termed postural congruence – the way in which people imitate each other's postures. He observed that when people share similar views or social roles in a group, they often tend to express this by adopting similar postures (Scheflen, 1964). Conversely, dissimilar postures can indicate a marked divergence in attitude or status. Posture mirroring can also be used as a means of establishing rapport – a person might imitate another's postures to indicate friendliness and togetherness. Thus, posture mirroring can be indicative of the relationship between people. It is discussed further in Chapter 2 (pp. 39–40) and in Chapter 6 (p. 148).

One of Birdwhistell's principal concerns was with the study of nonverbal communication, in particular with body movement. He coined the term 'kinesics', arguing that body movement could be analysed in a way that parallelled structural linguistics. In particular, he proposed that body motion is a learned form of communication, that it is patterned within a culture and that it is structured according to rules comparable to those of spoken language. Those elements of body movement that are significant in communication, Birdwhistell called 'kinemes'. Of course, kinemes do not occur in isolation, they occur in patterns or combinations, referred to as 'kinemorphs' (by analogy with the linguistic term 'morpheme'). By the same token, kinemorphs can be organized into more complex patterns, referred to as 'kinemorphic constructions'.

Birdwhistell also devised a highly detailed system for categorizing body movement (Birdwhistell, 1971), although it has never been clear how successfully this system could be applied in practice. In a very real sense, his work was programmatic: he was putting forward a plan for research, rather than actually carrying it out. Nevertheless, Birdwhistell was a highly influential figure. In particular, he focused attention on the culturally shared meaning of certain forms of body movement. This meant that the significance of body movement could not be understood purely in terms of a narrow psychological approach focused exclusively on its role as a means of individual expression (Kendon, 1982).

The significance of the structural approach can be usefully appreciated when set against the so-called 'external variable' approach (Duncan, 1969). This referred to an alternative strategy of attempting to relate communication to features external to the social context. Thus, a researcher might seek to investigate whether particular nonverbal behaviours are associated with particular personality traits: for example, by correlating scores on a questionnaire measure of extraversion with duration or frequency of gaze. This approach at one time typified much psychological research on communication, and was rightly criticized for its failure to take account of the structural organization of social interaction (Duncan, 1969). Almost all contemporary communication researchers would now regard an awareness of the importance of structure and context as axiomatic.

The sociological approach

Closely related to the structural approach is that taken within sociology. In fact, there are two distinctive sociological strands of research of particular importance: conversation analysis and the work of Erving Goffman.

Goffman

Goffman's principal concern was the study of social interaction. Of course, in this he was not alone, but a number of features make his particular approach distinctive. One important innovation was that he regarded everyday social interaction as something worthy of study in its own right, rather than as a means of studying more traditional sociological concerns, such as primitive or sophisticated mentality, or the structure of kinship or power relationships (Burns, 1992). Another was his ability to take what might be regarded as commonplace observations and to recast them in terms of a novel conceptual framework. Although Goffman has had a profound influence, in no sense was his work based on the detailed analysis of either video or audio recordings. Rather, he worked from his own participant observations of social interaction and from material such as etiquette books and advertisements. His significance was much more as a theorist, as someone who put forward a conceptual framework within which social interaction could be studied.

Thus, Goffman developed a theory to explain the ways in which people present themselves in daily life, support or challenge the claims of others, and deal with challenges to their own identity (Goffman, 1959, 1961, 1971). A particularly good example of Goffman's influence can be seen in the impact of his first published article 'On face-work: an analysis of ritual elements in social interaction' (Goffman, 1955). In this paper, he formulated a number of ideas about the importance of face in social interaction. In particular, he described examples of what he called face-work, strategies both for avoiding threats to face and repairing damage to face when it has occurred. Goffman's ideas have proved remarkably enduring. According to one review, the intellectual roots of virtually all contemporary research on face can be traced to this 'seminal' essay (Tracy, 1990).

Most significant of this more contemporary research is the work of two linguists, Penelope Brown and Steve Levinson (1978, 1987), who proposed a comprehensive theory of face that has come to be known as politeness theory. Following Goffman, they defined face as the public image that every person wishes to claim. Face claims, they proposed, can be positive or negative. Positive face concerns the desire to be appreciated by others, negative face the desire for freedom of action. Brown and Levinson also attempted to show how strategies in conversation can be seen to reflect these two principal aspects of face. Although the current status of their theory is still highly equivocal (Tracy, 1990), nevertheless it has spawned an enormous literature. The concept of face is discussed further in Chapter 3 (pp. 70–73), Chapter 4 (pp. 96–98), Chapter 5 (pp. 121–128) and Chapter 6 (pp. 150–151).

Conversation analysis

The other major sociological contribution is what has become known as conversation analysis. This emerged out of a sociological approach known as ethnomethodology. Ethnomethodologists were highly critical of the way in which quantitative sociologists imposed what they perceived as arbitrary categories in their classification of sociological phenomena. Instead, ethnomethodologists believed in the importance of the participants' own formulations of their everyday interactions, and advocated that these should be a principal focus of study. It was to these formulations that the prefix 'ethno' referred.

Many of the basic assumptions of conversation analysis stem from a series of lectures given by Harvey Sacks in 1964 and 1965 (Sacks, 1992). The innovative and striking feature of these lectures was the recognition that talk can be studied as an activity in its own right, rather than as a means of studying other processes. Other important features were the proposals that ordinary talk is systematically, sequentially and socially organized, and that no detail of interaction (however trivial it may seem) can be dismissed as disorderly, accidental or irrelevant (Heritage, 1989).

The idea that ordinary talk is orderly contrasted sharply with prevailing models of language at that time (Lalljee & Widdicombe, 1989). In seeking to analyse people's capacity for language, Chomsky had argued for an important distinction between competence and performance. Competence represented an idealized model of people's linguistic ability, whereas performance (what people actually do in their talk) was assumed to be a degenerate version of competence. In sharp contrast, Sacks argued that ordinary talk could be described formally in terms of socially organized, culturally available rules and procedures. It should be studied not as a deviant version of people's competence, but as orderly in its own right.

Although Sacks' lectures were delivered in the mid-1960s, conversation analysis only began to have a wider impact in 1974, following the publication of a paper on how people take turns in conversation (Kendon, 1988). This paper (Sacks et al., 1974) identified a number of distinctive features considered to characterize turn-taking, and proposed a system of rules to account for the way in which it is organized. Turn-taking is discussed in much greater depth in Chapter 2 (pp. 49–50), Chapter 3 (pp. 55–59) and Chapter 5 (pp. 117–119).

In the paper by Sacks et al. (1974), details were also given concerning a novel procedure for transcribing conversation. The aim was to reproduce as far as possible both the sound and the structure of conversation. To do this, standard spelling was frequently ignored. For example, 'back in a minute' becomes 'back inna minnit', while 'lighting a fire in Perry's cellar' becomes 'lightin' a fiyuh in Perry's celluh'. A number of conventions were also devised to indicate the sequential structure of utterances in conversation. A double oblique sign (//) indicates the point at which a current speaker's talk is overlapped by the talk of another, while an equals sign (=) refers to what was called 'latching', where there is no interval between the end of one person's utterance and the start of another. Subsequently, Jefferson (1984) has even been concerned to devise highly detailed ways of representing different kinds of laughter. In one excerpt, a laugh is transcribed as 'ihh hh heh heh huh', while in another a different form of laughter is transcribed as 'hhhh HA HA HA HA'. Thus, in conversation analysis the transcription becomes an important part of the research. Such faithful attention to detail was claimed to give other analysts the opportunity to identify systematic regularities that might have eluded the initial investigators.

This method of transcription is highly distinctive, and constitutes one of the most characteristic features of the conversation analytic approach. It is also the point at which Schegloff's work diverged most clearly from Goffman's. Although Sacks was a student of Goffman's, and clearly learned a great deal from him (Schegloff, 1989), their approach was fundamentally different. Whereas Sacks analysed social interaction in the finest of detail, Goffman painted with a broad brush. Whereas Goffman's influence was essentially that of a theorist, Sacks pioneered a methodology whereby it was possible to test empirically his own theoretical presuppositions concerning the structure and organisation of conversation.

Both Goffman and Sacks have had an enormous influence on communication research. If Goffman is open to criticism it is because he failed to back-up his observations through the analysis of either video or audio recordings. His contribution was to supply the theoretical scaffolding; the nitty gritty of detailed microanalysis he left to others. With Sacks, it is entirely the reverse. Sacks *et al.* (1974) wrote that the aim of a conversation analysis transcript was 'to get as much of the actual sound as possible into our transcripts, while still making them accessible to linguistically unsophisticated readers'. The success of this procedure is seriously open to question. There are plenty of features of speech that such transcriptions omit, for example, tempo, pitch, loudness, vowel quality and voice quality. At the same time, there is also a problem that the attempt to reproduce the sound of speech can make the text quite impenetrable. So, for example, one of Sacks *et al.*'s (1974) extracts reads 'I'd a' cracked up 'f duh friggin (gla-i(h)f y'kno(h)w it) sm(h)a(h) heh heh'. How accessible this is to a linguistically sophisticated reader – let alone to an unsophisticated one – is seriously open to question.

In this author's view, a transcript is best used not as a substitute for the recording but as a form of assistance. Researchers who work from the transcript alone can miss important points of detail that were not annotated on the original transcript. Indeed, Sacks *et al.*'s analysis of turn-taking has been criticized for precisely this point (e.g. Power & dal Martello, 1986; Cowley, 1998). The best technique is to view or listen to the tape in conjunction with a transcript, ideally in the form of a video recording, so that researchers can not only hear what is said and how it is said, but can also see any associated nonverbal behaviour for themselves.

Speech Act Theory

A parallel development in linguistic philosophy was the development of Speech Act Theory. Initially, these ideas were elaborated by John Austin in 1955 in the William James lectures at Harvard University, subsequently to be published posthumously in 1962 under the title *How to do Things with Words*. To acquire a fuller understanding of Austin's ideas, they need to be set in the context of academic philosophy at that time (Potter & Wetherell, 1987). In particular, Austin was attacking the view of logical positivism: that if a sentence cannot be verified as either true or false, it should simply be regarded as meaningless. More broadly, Austin was attacking a whole spectrum of views that regarded the central function of language as describing a state of affairs, or stating some facts. In contrast, the main proposition of Speech Act Theory was that language can be regarded as a form of action.

So, for example, to say 'I'm sorry' is not to convey information about an apology, nor to describe an apology; it does in itself constitute the act of apologizing. But Speech Act Theory is not based on a distinction between some sentences that do things and other sentences that describe things. Instead, it presents this distinction in a different way. Its fundamental tenet is that all utterances both state things and do things, that is to say, they have both a meaning and a force. Indeed, there is also a third dimension: utterances can have an effect, consequent upon meaning and force.

Speech Act Theory represented a radical departure from views that were then current in the philosophy of language. Previous work had been concerned with the formal, abstract properties of language, to be dealt with in the same way as logic and mathematics. In contrast, Speech Act Theory focused on language as a tool, as a means of doing things. In spite of this, Speech Act Theory is still essentially a branch of philosophy. It was developed primarily in the context of debates within philosophy and little consideration was paid to the practical problems of applying the theory to everyday talk occurring in natural situations. Its enduring influence has come from other intellectual traditions, such as conversation analysis and discourse analysis, which have sought to investigate empirically how social actions (such as ordering and requesting, persuading and accusing) are accomplished in language.

Discourse analysis

Discourse analysis is an approach that has a number of features in common with conversation analysis and speech act theory. The term 'discourse' is used in a broad sense to cover all forms of spoken interaction, formal and informal, as well as written texts of all kinds. So discourse analysis can refer to any of these forms of communication (Potter & Wetherell, 1987).

There are many forms of discourse analysis, associated with several different academic disciplines, indeed, 'discourse analyses' might be a more appropriate term. Discourse analysis originated in branches of philosophy, sociology, linguistics and literary theory. It is currently being developed in a variety of other disciplines as well, including anthropology, communication, education and psychology (Wood & Kroger, 2000).

At least three main approaches can be distinguished (van Dijk, 1997). First, there are those that focus on discourse 'itself', that is, on structures of text or talk. Such analyses are concerned with abstract properties such as the narrative structure of a story, the use of rhetorical devices in speeches or the placing of headlines in news reports. Second, discourse can be analysed in terms of the social actions accomplished by language users. One of the themes strongly stressed in both Speech Act Theory and conversation analysis is that people use language to do things. This focus on language function or action is a major component of discourse analysis. Finally, analyses of discourse presuppose that language users have knowledge. To understand a sentence or to interpret the topic of a text presupposes that language users share a vast repertoire of sociocultural beliefs on which their interpretations are based. Hence, the analysis of cognition has been a third substantive area of research.

One well-known example of discourse analysis is the work of Jonathan Potter, Margaret Wetherell and Derek Edwards. Their principal concern has been with language as a form of action, a means of accomplishing a variety of social functions. According to Potter and Wetherell (1987), a person's use of language will vary according to its function, that is to say, it will vary according to the purpose of the talk. For example, in describing a person to a close friend on one occasion and to a parent on another, a narrator may emphasize very different personal characteristics. Neither of these accounts is seen as the 'true' or 'correct' one, they simply serve different functions.

In cases such as these, it is proposed that people are using language to construct versions of the social world: 'The principal tenet of discourse analysis is that function involves construction of versions, and is demonstrated by language variation' (Potter & Wetherell, 1987, p. 33). The proposal is not that some forms of talk are merely descriptive, while others are deliberately constructed: all language, even language that passes as simple description, is regarded as constructive. However, the term 'construction' is not meant to imply that the process is necessarily deliberate or intentional. The person who produces the account does not necessarily do this in a calculating or conscious way. Nevertheless, a version emerges as people try to make sense of something that has happened to them or engage in such activities as justifying their own actions or blaming others.

Two further features are stressed in what has been called the Discursive Action Model (Edwards & Potter, 1993). One of these is the problem of 'stake' or 'interest'. An interested or motivated account runs the risk of being discounted on precisely that basis (for example, with the remark 'Well, he would say that, wouldn't he?'). Thus, speakers endeavour to construct their account in such a way that it will be understood as factual, and not dismissed as partisan or simply biased. Discourse analysis seeks to understand how such an account is constructed to achieve that particular effect.

The other feature is 'accountability' (Edwards & Potter, 1993). In reporting events, speakers routinely deal with the accountability of the people they are describing for their actions. At the same time, speakers are also accountable for their own actions – including the accuracy and interactional consequences of the narratives they produce. Thus, speakers might seek either to claim credit for or to distance themselves from the events that they report, depending upon the function of the talk. The ways in which both these aspects of accountability are constructed in narratives is the focus of a discourse analytic approach.

Within the framework of the Discursive Action Model, an analysis was conducted of eyewitness accounts of two atrocities in Northern Ireland (Beattie & Doherty, 1995). In one account of an attempted murder, a witness described how, when a car drove right in front of her, she initially thought it was a taxi driver pulling up alongside to say hello, then that it was simply a bad driver. These mundane interpretations of events serve to establish the storyteller as a credible witness, as an ordinary, everyday woman who had to 'put two and two together' before she realized that the driver was trying to kill her. Her vivid recall of events further reinforces her credibility. Through her narrative, the witness thus establishes herself as an ordinary person, who simply happened to be in the wrong place at the wrong time, not as someone who is partisan and who might have some vested interest in reporting these events. This is what is meant by the problem of stake or interest.

A second atrocity, the assassination of an innocent victim, is described by a witness in such a way as to suggest that this was a professional, sustained and deliberate attempt to kill: the gunman 'kicked' the door open, 'rattled off' and 'pumped' the bullets into his target at point-blank range. The victim, William, is presented as a young, hard-working individual, inter-ested in building a decent life for himself in the Belfast community. Given the widespread assumption in Belfast that paramilitaries do not have to work (Beattie & Doherty, 1995), this establishes that the victim was not a paramilitary but an innocent victim – without the observer ever having to explicitly say so. But if the killer was so professional, how did he settle on an innocent victim? The witness portrays the assassin as someone who is indiscriminate in his pattern of violence: he will rob Catholics (his 'own side') as well as Protestants, if he thinks there is a possibility for gain. In this way, the credibility of the witness's account is not compromised by the combination of a professional killer and a blameless victim. The respon-sibility for the assassination is thus attributed entirely to the gunman. This is what is meant by the issue of accountability.

This analysis of eyewitness accounts provides a good illustration of how issues of stake and accountability can be understood within a discursive framework. However, it should be noted that the discursive psychology of Potter, Wetherell and Edwards is only one formulation of discourse analysis; there are many others. Furthermore, there are also significant differences of opinion between different analysts. For example, van Dijk (1997) regards the analysis of cognition as one of three substantive areas of research in discourse analysis. Conversely, discursive psychology is presented as a radical alternative to cognitive social psychology, a means whereby cognitive concepts such as memory, attitudes and attributions can be reconceptualized in terms of discursive actions (Edwards & Potter, 1992). Thus, Potter and Wetherell (1987) regard language not as a means of representing inner thoughts, ideas or attitudes, but rather as a means of accomplishing a variety of social functions.

Another controversial feature of discursive psychology is that it seems to embody a position of philosophical relativism. According to Potter and Wetherell (1987), a person's use of language varies according to its function: it is not possible to say whether an account is a 'true' or 'false' one, accounts simply serve different functions. But if this is the case, it would appear that all accounts are as good as one another, and there would seem to be no way to choose between them. Again, if no thoughts, ideas or attitudes can be inferred from discourse, then it might appear that there is nothing beyond discourse, and discourse analysis can be used only to make inferences about discourse. Taken to this extreme, discursive psychology seems to lead to a dead-end. However, relativism is not intrinsic to all discourse analysis; indeed, discursive psychology has been criticized by other discourse analysts precisely because of its relativist stance (e.g. Parker, 1992).

Ethology

A characteristic feature of both conversation analysis and discourse analysis is that they are based on the analysis of naturally occurring situations. This is also true of another approach that stems from an entirely different intellectual tradition. Ethology developed initially as a branch of zoology, concerned with the study of animal behaviour in its natural habitat, but its techniques have subsequently been extended to the analysis of human behaviour. In ethology, special emphasis is laid on observing behaviour in its natural environment. The typical research methods are naturalistic observation and field experiment. Where films or tapes are made, ethologists have developed a number of techniques for concealed filming in order not to upset the natural flow of behaviour. Thus, a movie camera with an angle lens was used by the ethologist Iraneus Eibl-Eibesfeldt (1972) to make his recordings. This enabled him to make recordings at a different direction from that in which the camera was pointed, and was intended to minimize self-consciousness in the people he observed.

Ethologists work on the assumption that behaviour is to a considerable extent inherited, and they seek to interpret behaviour in terms of its evolutionary functions. One of the forerunners of ethology was Charles Darwin, who realized that if his theory of natural selection were to explain the evolution of animal species, then it also had to be able to account for behaviour. In fact, Darwin's work contains much material that would now be described as ethological, although it would be anachronistic to describe Darwin either as an ethologist or as the founder of ethology.

The first person to use the term 'ethology' in its modern sense was Oscar Heinroth, in a paper published in 1911 (Thorpe, 1979). The title, 'The father of modern ethology', was also applied to Konrad Lorenz (Huxley, 1963), who became most famous for his writings on aggression. However, Lorenz acknowledged Heinroth as the source of his inspiration and in one place defined ethology as 'the subject which Heinroth invented' (Thorpe, 1979).

Heinroth studied ducks and geese. He found that greylag geese would vocalize in one way when they were about to walk or fly as a family, and in another way just before merely walking rapidly. These distinctive vocalizations he called 'intention movements', because they typically occurred just prior to performing the actual behaviour. Julian Huxley (1914) studied the great crested grebe (a diving bird). He used the term 'display' to describe the complex postures and water 'dances' he observed. Subsequently, Tinbergen proposed that behaviour itself could evolve specifically for its signalling value, and that it did so by exhibiting the twin qualities of conspicuousness and simplicity (Tinbergen, 1953).

Lorenz and Tinbergen referred to these signalling behaviours as 'fixed action patterns', preprogrammed innate responses that would occur in response to appropriate 'releasers' in the environment. However, modern ethologists regard this analysis as mechanistic and outdated (Fridlund, 1994). They now regard culture as formative in its own right, and view both nonhumans and humans as more than reflexive automata. Thus, nonhuman postures, squawks and grunts have been observed to be dependent upon context in both their perception and production (e.g. Smith, 1969, 1977). Furthermore, if signalling evolves through natural selection, it could also evolve through learning: there appear, for example, to be regional dialects in birdsong (Smith, 1977).

A good example of ethological research comes from the study of social hierarchy in both man and animals. Ethologists have observed that conflicts between members of the same species often take place within specific rules; this has the advantage of reducing the risk of serious injury or death. Such conflicts can take the form of what are called 'threat displays', which signal one individual's likelihood of attacking another. The conflict can be resolved when one contestant performs 'appeasement gestures' as a sign of submission (Eibl-Eibesfeldt, 1973).

Appeasement gestures can certainly be seen in human conflicts. In one study, researchers observed fights between boys (Ginsburg *et al.*, 1977) and found that, just before the fighting ceased, the boy under attack would typically make himself smaller in some way. He would bow his head, slump his shoulders, lie motionless on the ground, kneel, tie his shoes or allow the aggressor to manipulate his body without offering muscular resistance (termed 'waxy flexibility'). All this seemed to support an observation by Charles Darwin that 'making oneself smaller' appeases and inhibits human aggression; in ethological terms, it acts as an appeasement signal. In this context, it is interesting that making oneself smaller is formalized in some human social hierarchies. Thus, an inferior might greet a superior by bowing or kneeling. In imperial China, the inferior would 'kowtow' by actually touching the ground with his forehead in absolute submission.

Threat displays also find a counterpart in human behaviour. Expressions of anger, such as staring, lowering the eyebrows, thrusting the face forward, wrinkling the nose and pressing the lips together with tightened mouth corners can all be seen as threat displays. Observations were made of such expressions in a study of conflicts between children over a toy (Camras, 1977). Children who won conflicts with a display of facial anger were more likely to defend the toy if another child subsequently attempted to take it away. However, such expressions did not precede a physical attack, no attacks occurred even following a child's aggressive expression and subsequent loss of toy.

In ethological terms, threat displays and appeasement gestures are seen as ways of resolving conflict; they can also lead to the establishment of social hierarchies through which future conflict can be regulated. An important clue to the nature of a social hierarchy is who looks at whom, known as the 'structure of attention' (Chance, 1967). According to this view, the most important animal, or the most important person in the group is the focus of the subordinates' attention. In fact, not only does the pattern of gaze provide clues to the social structure of the group, it also constitutes a means whereby influence is exerted: as the recipient of gaze, the dominant individual is more easily able to exert influence over others.

Ethological concepts have been highly influential on the microanalytic approach. Indeed, the parallels between ethology and other microanalytic approaches have been noted by a number of investigators. For example, Goffman, when he came to write *Relations in Public* (1971), adopted the title of 'human ethologist'. The continuing vitality of ethological concepts can be illustrated from the current debate concerning the role of the face in communication. In a recent chapter entitled 'The new ethology of facial expressions', Fridlund (1997) attacked the whole notion that the face somehow 'expresses' emotion. Instead, he proposed that facial displays can be understood simply as messages that influence the behaviour of others, because the reception of these signals evolved at the same time as the signals themselves. This debate concerning the facial communication of emotion is discussed in Chapter 2 (pp. 29–37).

Communication as skill: a social psychological approach

One of the most significant influences on the microanalytic approach has been the proposal that communication can be regarded as a form of skill. In 1967, an important paper appeared entitled 'The experimental analysis of social performance'. In this article, Michael Argyle and Adam Kendon argued that social behaviour involves processes comparable to those involved in motor skills, such as driving a car or playing a game of tennis. Given that we already know a great deal about motor skill processes, they proposed that this knowledge could be applied to advance our understanding of social interaction.

The social skills model – as it has become known – was subsequently elaborated in Argyle's books on social interaction (Argyle *et al.*, 1972; Argyle, 1978). In the original social skills model, six processes were considered to be common to motor skills and social performance: distinctive goals, selective perception of cues, central translation processes, motor responses, feedback and corrective action, and the timing of responses. Each of these processes is discussed in turn below:

1. Distinctive goals can be seen, for example, in the process of driving a car. The superordinate goal of reaching one's destination can also involve subordinate goals, such as overtaking a slow-moving vehicle, crossing a difficult junction or joining a main road in heavy traffic. So, too, social performance can be seen as having distinctive goals. In a job interview, the superordinate goal of the interviewer – to select the right person for the job – necessitates a number of subordinate goals, such as obtaining information from the interviewee and establishing satisfactory rapport in order to achieve those ends.

2. The selective perception of cues is a key process in the performance of any skill. Not all information is of equal value: that is to say, the skilled performer can pay particular attention to certain types of information relevant to achieving their objective, while ignoring irrelevant information. Indeed, one mark of skilled performance might be to learn what input can be ignored. Skilled public speakers learn to sense the interest and attention of their audience and to adjust their performance appropriately, whereas conversational bores completely fail to read the response of their listeners. Argyle also argued that psychiatric patients might be particularly poor at perceiving social cues. How well psychiatric patients perceive nonverbal cues is discussed further in Chapter 2 (pp. 43–45).

3. Central translation processes prescribe what to do about any particular piece of information. The term 'translation' refers to the rule by which a particular signal is interpreted as regarding a particular action. An important feature of skills acquisition consists in the development of such translations, which, once learned, can be readily and immediately

acted upon. It is in the development of new translations that a great deal of hesitancy and halting can often be observed.

4. Motor responses refer to behaviours that are performed as a consequence of central translation processes. The learner driver might initially find it extremely difficult to change gear but, with practice, the movements become quite automatic. So too with social behaviour. Initial learning might be quite awkward but, with extensive practice, large chunks of behaviour can become fluent and habitual. Indeed, social behaviour can become too automatic. The monotone of museum guides who have repeated their guided tour too often is one well-known example of automatized behaviour. Similarly, there was the unfortunate case of a lecturer who reported that 'he had reached a stage where he could arise before his audience, turn his mouth loose, and go to sleep' (Lashley, 1951, p. 184).

5. Feedback and corrective action refer to the ways in which individuals can modify their behaviour in the light of feedback from others. The term 'feedback' was derived from cybernetics (discussed on p. 3). Just as in a central heating system the information from a thermostat regulates the heating output, so too feedback is important in the context of social interaction. For example, teachers who see that their pupils have not understood a point might repeat that point slowly in another way; again, sales representatives who realize that they are failing to make an impact might change their style of behaviour. Argyle proposed that feedback is obtained principally from nonverbal cues. So, in conversation, a speaker will typically scan the other's face intermittently to check whether the listener understands, agrees or disagrees, and whether he or she is willing for the speaker to continue talking.

6. Good timing and rhythm are also important features of social skills. Without correct anticipation as to when a response will be required, interaction can be jerky and ineffective. Taking turns is the characteristic way in which conversation is structured, and the way in which turns are organized and managed is discussed in greater detail in Chapter 2 (pp. 49–50), Chapter 3 (pp. 55–59) and Chapter 5 (p. 117). Turn-taking in larger groups can sometimes be problematic because opportunities to speak can be quite restricted. Choosing the right moment to make a point in a group discussion is a useful example of the social skill of good timing.

In his most recent formulations, Argyle has argued for the central importance of social skills. He believes that social coping skills play a major part in determining the quality of interpersonal relationships, which are of prime importance to an individual's personal happiness (Argyle, 1999). Whereas the support of others is an important way of coping with stress (Argyle, 1999), rejection and isolation can in themselves be major sources of stress and can occur as a consequence of poor social skills (Argyle, 1994).

The concept of social skill has not been without its critics. Although there are significant similarities between motor and social skills, there are also important differences (Hargie & Marshall, 1986). For example, because social interaction by definition involves other people, it is necessary to consider the goals not only of one individual but of all those involved, as well as their actions and reactions towards one another. In this sense, social behaviour is often much more complex than motor performance.

The role of feelings and emotions is another feature neglected by the original social skills model. The importance of mood and emotional state in communication is widely recognized (e.g. Parkinson, 1995) and can have an important bearing on responses, goals and perceptions in social interaction. Furthermore, whereas we often take into account the feelings of other people with whom we interact, this is clearly not the case in learning to perform a motor skill. The communication of emotion is a central theme in social interaction; this is discussed more fully in Chapter 2 (pp. 29–37).

The perception of persons differs in a number of ways from the perception of objects. We perceive the responses of the other person with whom we communicate. We might also perceive our own responses, in that we hear what we say and can be aware of our own nonverbal behaviour. Furthermore, we can be aware of the process of perception itself, referred to as metaperception. We make judgements about how other people are perceiving us and we can also attempt to ascertain how they think we are perceiving them. Such judgements can also influence our own behaviour during social interaction (Hargie & Marshall, 1986).

The social situation in which interaction occurs is important for an understanding of social skills. Significant features that can affect social interaction are the roles that people play, the rules governing the situation, the nature of the task and the physical environment. In addition, personal factors, such as age, gender and physical appearance, will be important in the way in which people behave towards one another (Hargie & Marshall, 1986).

In the light of these criticisms, a revised version of the social skills model was proposed (Hargie & Marshall, 1986). The original model was extended to take account of two people interacting with one another: thus, feedback comes from our own as well as from other people's responses. The term 'central translation processes' was replaced with the term 'mediating factors' to allow for the influence of emotions as well as cognitions on behaviour. The original model was also further revised to take account of what was termed the person–situation context (Hargie, 1997a). Person factors can include personality, gender, age and appearance, while situation factors refer to features such as social roles, social rules and the cultural context within which interaction takes place.

Despite these criticisms, the social skills model continues to be highly influential. One of the most important proposals of the original model was that if communication can be regarded as a skill then it should be possible for people to learn to communicate more effectively, just as it is possible to improve performance on any other skill (Argyle & Kendon, 1967). This proposal was formalized in what was termed 'social skills training'. More recently, it has become known as 'communication skills training', and is used extensively in a wide variety of social contexts. These training procedures are discussed much more fully in Chapter 6 (pp. 130–144).

A comparison of different approaches to communication analysis

Thus, what has been termed the microanalytic approach can be seen to be derived from a wide variety of intellectual traditions. Between these traditions there are a number of important differences, differences of emphasis and also outright disagreements, as well as some fundamental similarities in approach. It is intended to consider first some of the more salient points of disagreement, before moving on to what might be regarded as the key features of microanalysis.

Points of disagreement

Some of the most important arguments have been concerned with methodology – on how to actually conduct research. Traditionally, one of the main planks of academic psychology has been a belief in the value of the experimental method and for many years, this approach typified social psychological research on interpersonal communication. Intrinsic to the experimental method is a belief in the importance of quantification and the use of inferential statistics. An important consequence of a quantitative approach is the need for categorization. The advantage of this procedure is that it allows the researcher to reduce observed behaviour to frequencies or rates of occurrence, rather than attempting a detailed description of each event. These data can then be subjected to some sort of analysis using inferential statistics. Hence, a salient feature of communication research in experimental social psychology has been a preoccupation with the development of coding systems.

This approach has been subject to intensive criticism by those who favour naturalistic observation and a qualitative approach. One target of criticism has been the artificiality of the data obtained in laboratories, where the participants either knew or suspected that they were being recorded for the purpose of an experiment. Although these problems are not insurmountable, the use of naturalistic observation has increasingly become the preferred method of making observations in communication research.

The use of coding systems has also been criticized, on the grounds that such procedures are typically arbitrary, reductionist and distort the data to fit it into preconceived categories (Psathas, 1995). Furthermore, it is claimed that context and meaning are dealt with only in so far as they are specified in the category system (Psathas, 1995). Researchers in both conversation analysis and discourse analysis have also become increasingly concerned not to 'impose' preconceived categories on the data but to make use of the ways in which people categorize themselves, as manifested in their own discourse (van Dijk, 1997).

However, this critique of categorization ignores a number of positive features. While it is certainly interesting to examine the ways in which people categorize themselves, this is not the only way of analysing interpersonal communication. Coding systems devised by outside observers can also be highly informative. Coding systems can also change over time. That is to say, they can be improved to make a better representation of the phenomena. A good coding system can also act as a valuable aid to perception, not necessarily as a hindrance. It can enable the researcher to identify phenomena that might not be immediately obvious to the untrained observer.

An excellent example is the Facial Action Coding System (FACS), developed by Ekman and Friesen (1978). This provides a detailed description of all the movements possible with the facial musculature. Facial movements are highly varied, often subtle and intricate, hence they can be difficult to describe. By concentrating on the anatomical basis of facial movement, Ekman and Friesen produced a system that is comprehensive. It can also serve as an invaluable guide to perception, by helping the observer to identify complex facial movements and providing a language with which to describe them. Indeed, FACS has become widely accepted as the main technique available for analysing facial expressions and there is now an extensive body of research using this procedure (see Ekman & Rosenberg, 1997).

Disputes over categorization are one instance of an ongoing disagreement within communication research. This can be illustrated through the current debate concerning a form of content analysis known as the Linguistic Category Model (Semin & Fiedler, 1988, 1991). The choice of one word rather than another to describe a person or an action might in itself, have considerable social significance, and forms the central concern of this model. However, Edwards and Potter (1999) have cited the model as an example of what they call 'coding-and-counting methods', and criticized it accordingly (Edwards & Potter, 1993, 1999). Their criticisms, the model itself and responses to those criticisms (Fiedler & Schmid,1999; Schmid & Fiedler, 1999) are discussed in Chapter 3 (pp. 73–76).

Central features of the microanalytic approach

It is important to be aware that communication scholars do have these significant disagreements. But it is also important to be aware that they do share a number of common assumptions. These similarities of approach tend to have been neglected in the literature but they form the basis of the central argument in this book. That is, it is possible and useful to discern certain basic themes that represent a novel and distinctive way of thinking about communication, which has been termed the microanalytic approach. These themes are listed below:

- *Communication is studied as it actually occurs.* A key feature is a concern with the analysis of communication as it actually occurs through the detailed analysis of film, videotape or audiotape. This marks a radical shift from the traditional concern with the study of communication in terms of what it should be – in terms of, for example, its efficiency, clarity or persuasiveness. The focus on communication as it actually occurs can be seen to characterize all the different approaches to the study of communication that have been described above, and can be regarded as one principal underlying theme of microanalytic research.

- *Communication can be studied as an activity in its own right.* Another feature is the proposal that communication can be studied as an activity in its own right. Just as Goffman made social interaction itself the focus of his investigations, so too an important and innovative feature of conversation analysis was the recognition that talk can be studied as talk, rather than as a means of studying other social processes. Similarly, the focus of discourse analysis is exclusively on discourse itself: how it is constructed, its functions and the consequences that arise from different ways in which discourse is organized.

- *All features of interaction are potentially significant.* A further distinguishing feature of the microanalytic approach has been the expansion of what behaviour can be regarded as communicative. In recent decades, the remarkable development of interest in nonverbal communication can be regarded as one such manifestation (see Chapter 2). So too is the extraordinary detail in which conversation analysts seek in their transcripts to represent as exactly as possible the way in which conversation sounds. The underlying assumption is that all features of interaction are potentially significant and therefore should not be dismissed out of hand as unworthy of investigation.

- *Communication has a structure.* A related proposal is that communication has a structure. Although interaction might at first sight seem to be disorderly or even random, it cannot be assumed to be so and one of the tasks of the investigator is to analyse whether an underlying structure can be discerned. Structure can take a variety of forms. Interaction can be organized sequentially, that is to say certain behaviours or features of conversation can occur in a regular order. Or it might be organized hierarchically, that is to say behaviour or conversation might be organized into higher-order units. It could also be organized in terms of social rules, although interactants might not be able to articulate those rules explicitly.

- *Conversation can be regarded as a form of action.* According to Speech Act Theory, language does not simply describe some state of affairs or state some facts: it is in itself a form of action. This proposal has been profoundly influential and underlies a great deal of research on the analysis of conversation. A principal concern has been the study of function. To a substantial extent, this represents the influence of Speech Act Theory: once it is accepted that speech is not only concerned with the transmission of information but constitutes a form of activity in its own right, it is logical to conduct analyses on the nature of that activity. This kind of research is dealt with in much greater depth in Chapter 3 (pp. 63–68).

- *Communication can be understood in an evolutionary context.* The proposal that communication can be understood in an evolutionary context is central to the ethological approach. Outside that tradition it has had comparatively little influence, this is not a concern of approaches such as conversation analysis, discourse analysis or Speech Act Theory. However, it has been of importance for social psychologists who study the nonverbal communication of emotion. It was, in fact, Charles Darwin who, in 1872, argued that the human facial expressions of emotion evolved as part of the actions necessary for life. This proposal is still highly influential, and is discussed much more fully in Chapter 2 (pp. 29–37).

- *Communication is best studied in naturally occurring contexts.* Common to almost all the approaches discussed above is the proposal that communication is best studied in naturally occurring contexts. The one exception to this has been experimental social psychology, whose proponents have traditionally made extensive use of laboratory-based experimentation as a means of studying communication. However, the trend in social psychology in recent years has also been towards naturalistic analysis.

- *Communication can be regarded as a form of skill.* The proposal that communication can be regarded as a form of skill represents one of the main contributions of the social psychological approach to communication. Indeed, it has been so influential that the term 'communication skills' has passed into the wider culture. However, social skills analysis has had no real influence on other approaches such as conversation analysis or discourse analysis. But the concept of communicative skill is by no means logically incompatible with these approaches. Because the focus of such techniques is on the analysis of conversational action, they might also be used to enhance our understanding of what constitutes skilful and unskilful communication.

In this context, it is interesting that conversation analysis is now being applied in clinical settings, particularly to patients whose speech has been impaired as a result of brain damage. Conversation analysis has been advocated as a way of advancing our understanding of these impairments (e.g. Perkins *et al.*, 1998). It is now also utilized as a means of giving practical advice to carers and speech therapists in improving interaction with patients (e.g. Booth & Perkins, 1999). This detailed advice on conversational strategies can arguably be understood as, in effect, instruction in appropriate communication skills. These clinical applications of conversation analysis are discussed further in Chapter 6 (p. 147).

- *Communication can be taught like any other skill.* A related proposal is that communication can be taught like any other skill. This again has been highly influential in the wider culture; social or communication skills training has been widely used in a variety of personal and occupational contexts. A much fuller description is given in Chapter 6 (pp. 130–144).
- *Macro issues can be studied through microanalysis.* Also of particular importance for the wider culture is the assumption that major – macro – social issues such as racism, politics or feminism can be analysed through microanalysis. Examples of this are given in both Chapter 4 on gender and in Chapter 5 on political communication.

Conclusions

The purpose of this chapter has been to show in the first instance how changing modes of thought led to the extensive use of recording technology in communication analysis. In the second section, an account and evaluation was given of the different intellectual traditions that have contributed to what has been termed the microanalytic approach to the analysis of communication. In the final section, a comparison was made of these different approaches. Points of disagreement were discussed, while the central features of what is regarded as microanalysis were also identified. On the basis of this analysis, it is proposed that microanalysis can be regarded as a distinctive and novel way of thinking about communication.

2 Nonverbal communication

The focus of this chapter is on nonverbal communication; the focus of Chapter 3 is on speech. These are the basic elements of face-to-face communication, hence detailed consideration is given to microanalytic research on both these topics.

This chapter is divided into two main sections. The first section deals with conceptual and methodological issues, the second with the principal functions of nonverbal communication in social interaction. These are summarized below:

Section 1. Conceptual and methodological issues:
      historical background
      methodology
      definition of nonverbal communication.

Section 2. The role of nonverbal communication in social interaction:
      emotion:
            evidence for the innateness of the facial expressions of
               emotion
            the neurocultural model of emotional expression
            emotional expression and recognition within particular
               cultures
            criticisms of the neurocultural model
      interpersonal relationships
      individual differences:
            encoding
            decoding
      nonverbal communication and speech.

Conceptual and methodological issues

Historical background

There is nothing new in the belief in the importance of nonverbal communication. Alfred Adler, the neo-Freudian analyst, liked to quote an aphorism from the sixteenth century Protestant reformer Martin Luther 'not to watch a person's mouth but his fists'. Indeed, the study of manual gesture can be traced back to ancient Rome, to Cicero and Quintilian. They both wrote treatises on rhetoric, which included a number of observations on the use of the hands in oratory. However, it was only during the seventeenth century, with the publication of works such as Bonifacio's *L'Arte dei Cenni* (1616) and Bulwer's *Chirologia; or the Naturell Language of the Hand, Whereunto is added Chironomia: or the Art of Manual Rhetoricke* (1644) that gesture acquired the status of a subject in its own right. Bulwer's work was exclusively concerned with what he called 'the naturell language of the Hand, as it had the happiness to escape the curse of the Confusion of Babel'. As the title indicates, there are two sections in the book: chirologia and chironomia. Chirologia comprises a descriptive glossary of sixty-four gestures of the hand and twenty-five gestures of the fingers. Chironomia is a prescriptive guide to the proper use of an additional eighty-one gestures during well-delivered discourse, as well as cautions against the improper use of 'manual rhetoricke'.

Methodology

The scientific study of nonverbal communication has only become possible with the development of sophisticated recording apparatus; most contemporary studies have used either film or videotape as the main technique of observation. In this respect, research on nonverbal communication provides an excellent illustrative example of the microanalytic approach. The great advantage of working with recorded material as compared with 'live' observation is that it allows for repeated viewing; this is particularly important for complex sequences of movement that are inaccessible to the naked eye but which can be replayed time and time again, if necessary in slow motion. There are now computer programs available such as THEME (e.g. Magnusson, 1996), whereby an observer can code the onset and offset of selected behavioural categories from a digitized video recording directly into a computer. THEME can then perform statistical analyses to identify sequential relationships between different behavioural categories or combinations of categories. These patterns might be hidden from the naked eye or simply too complex to uncover without this kind of technical assistance (Magnusson, 1996).

Nevertheless, even a procedure as sophisticated as THEME is still dependent on a human observer to transcribe and, if necessary, to code the behaviour into appropriate categories. When using manual methods of transcription, it is customary to conduct what is called a reliability study, in which the researcher's codings are correlated with those of an independent observer. Even so, transcription by hand is inevitably limited in its accuracy, and also extremely time-consuming and fatiguing.

As an alternative, researchers are seeking to develop fully automated systems of measurement. One technique involves attaching a data glove to the participant, which enables the investigator to track the persons's finger movements. The output from the data glove can then be subjected to computer analysis with the aim of developing techniques for the automatic recognition of different movements of the fingers. Using this approach a number of studies have been carried out for the automatic recognition of sign language (e.g. Harling & Edwards, 1997). One major practical outcome of such research is that it would provide a means whereby a deaf and dumb person could interact directly with a computer.

Another such system is known as polarized-light goniometry (e.g. Hadar *et al.*, 1983, 1984). This operates by projecting strong light from a single source through a plane polarizer material and a rapidly rotating disk on to a photosensor (or photosensors) attached to the participant. The reflected light is automatically processed by the goniometer to provide immediate information on properties of movement such as its rate, duration, range and speed. A major advantage of this system is its sensitivity to small movements, which a human observer working from videotape might miss or find very difficult to classify. Another advantage is its precision – by taking direct readings of speech amplitude, it is possible to make fine measurements of the relationship between head movements and speech. A disadvantage is that it does not allow a detailed description to be given of the visual appearance of particular movements.

However, both these automated systems suffer from the necessity of attaching recording apparatus to the body; participants are thus made aware of the focus of the investigation, which might make them self-conscious. But breakthroughs in computer image analysis now hold the promise of fully automated coding without the need for any such attachments (Bartlett, 2001). One study demonstrated that six facial actions could be coded from video image analysis with 91 per cent accuracy, which is as good as expert human coders and significantly better than non-experts (Bartlett *et al.*, 1999). Completely automated systems should not only dramatically increase the speed of coding, they should also improve reliability and precision. As such, facial expression measurement would become much more widely accessible as a research tool in behavioural science, medicine and psychophysiology (Bartlett *et al.*, 1999).

Definition of nonverbal communication

For an area of research that has become so popular, the definition of the term 'nonverbal communication' has been surprisingly vague. If the term 'verbal' is taken as meaning only the actual words used, then nonverbal communication can refer to vocal features such as intonation, stress, speech rate, accent and loudness. It can also refer to facial movement, gaze, pupil size, body movement and interpersonal distance. It can refer as well to communication through touch or smell, through various kinds of artefacts such as masks and clothes, or through formalized communication systems such as semaphore. Because the term 'nonverbal' is a definition only by exclusion, the number of features of human communication that can be included within this rubric are virtually limitless.

This chapter will focused on only one aspect of human nonverbal communication – bodily movement. The reasons for this are both practical and conceptual. The sheer range of phenomena embraced by the term 'nonverbal communication' is so vast that to do justice to the subject some degree of selection is necessary. At the same time, the features that can be included under the term 'body movement' do constitute a separate and distinctive form of communication. The term refers, in effect, to communication through visible forms of body movement – through movements of the facial muscles, the eyes, the pupils and the limbs, and movements of the body in relation to other people.

The definition of the term 'communication' presents even more problems, particularly with respect to what behaviours can be properly regarded as communicative. Some theorists have argued that all nonverbal behaviour should be regarded as communicative (Watzlawick *et al.*, 1968). Others have argued that only behaviours intended to be communicative should be regarded as such (Ekman & Friesen, 1969a). Both these viewpoints were criticized in an important theoretical paper by Wiener *et al.* (1972), who argued that for nonverbal behaviour to be regarded as communicative, it needs to be shown that it is used both to transmit and receive information: in their terminology, there is both systematic encoding and appropriate decoding. Thus, not all nonverbal behaviour is necessarily communicative.

Intention to communicate is not regarded as relevant to this definition. This is because (according to Wiener *et al.*) it is often difficult to establish exactly what a person does intend to communicate. Indeed, nonverbal communication might take place even against the express intentions of the encoder. For example, the author carried out a number of studies of the way in which listener attitudes and emotions are encoded in posture (Bull, 1987). Characteristic postures of boredom include leaning back, dropping the head, supporting the head on one hand and stretching out the legs. A member of an audience can show these behaviours without any conscious intent to communicate boredom; nevertheless, this might well be the message that the speaker receives. A member of an audience could even try to suppress these tell-tale signs by trying hard to appear attentive, but yet be incapable of suppressing the occasional yawn. To the speaker, the listener might still communicate that he or she is bored by the talk, despite the best intentions not to do so.

Communication can also take place without conscious awareness, in the sense that neither encoder nor decoder need to be able to identify the specific nonverbal cues through which a particular message is transmitted. People can be left with the feeling that someone was upset or angry without being able to specify exactly what cues were responsible for creating that impression. It can be argued that a great deal of nonverbal communication takes this form, and that one task of the researcher is to try and identify more precisely the cues that are responsible for creating such impressions.

This view of communication can be nicely demonstrated from studies of pupil dilation. In one study, it was observed that on viewing pictures of particular interest, the pupils of the participants tended to dilate (Hess & Polt, 1960). Women's pupils seemed to dilate when seeing a picture of a nude male and a picture of a mother and baby, while men's pupils dilated when seeing a picture of a nude female. In a subsequent study, a series of pictures were shown to twenty young men, including two photographs of an attractive young woman (Hess, 1965). The photos were touched up such that in one case the pupils of the young woman were extra large, and in the other case, extra small. The pupils of the young men tended to dilate more on seeing the woman with the dilated pupils, although most of the men said the pictures were identical. The findings were interpreted as showing that the men found the woman with dilated pupils more attractive, presumably because they felt she was more attracted to them. It was also found that when asked to describe the two photos, they said that the woman with large pupils was 'soft', 'more feminine' or 'pretty', while the same woman with constricted pupils was described as being 'hard', 'selfish' or 'cold' (Hess, 1975).

An interesting feature of these studies is that none of the students seemed to be aware of the pupils, although their perceptions of the woman were significantly affected by the differences in pupil size. Another important feature of pupil dilation is that, as a response of the autonomic nervous system, it is not under direct voluntary control; in this sense, it cannot be said to be an intentional form of communication.

If people communicate unintended messages without awareness through pupil dilation, what is being communicated? Hess proposed that the pupils dilate in response to stimuli we find attractive, and actually constrict in response to stimuli we find unattractive (the aversion–constriction hypothesis). In fact, this claim proved to be extremely controversial. Other studies suggest that the pupils simply dilate in arousal, whether that arousal is positive or negative. In one experiment, the pupil sizes of students were measured while they were listening to passages read from a novel (White & Maltzman, 1978). One passage was intended to be erotic, another to be neutral and a third passage was an unpleasant description of a lynching mutilation. The authors found an immediate dilation at the beginning of each passage, with the erotic and mutilation passages maintaining pupil dilation for about 60 seconds. Thus, it seems, that in arousal the pupil dilates, irrespective of whether that arousal is pleasant or unpleasant; furthermore, there is no intention to communicate, nor are people necessarily aware of pupil dilation.

The role of nonverbal communication in social interaction

Research has been focused on the role of nonverbal communication with regard to emotion, interpersonal relationships, individual differences, and speech (Bull, 1983).

Emotion

Particular importance is commonly ascribed to nonverbal cues in the communication of emotion. It was Charles Darwin (1872) who argued that the facial expressions of emotion are universal and constitute part of an innate, adaptive, physiological response. The idea that the facial expressions of emotion are universal was not novel; in fact, it can be found in Greek and Roman writers of antiquity (Evans, 1969). What made Darwin's approach so distinctive was the attempt to provide an evolutionary rather than a creationist account of the origins of facial expressions (Russell, 1994).

Darwin's theory proved to be extremely controversial – and still is. It has been hotly disputed by those who regard the influence of culture as paramount in the facial expression of emotion. Its most explicit rejection came from Birdwhistell (1971), who described how he was initially influenced by Darwin's views, but came to recognize that both the incidence and meaning of, say, smiling might vary between different social groups, that 'charts of smile frequency were not going to be very reliable as maps for the location of happy Americans' (Birdwhistell, 1971, p. 31). He rejected the view that smiles directly express underlying physiological states, arguing instead that meaning can be understood only within a particular social context.

These rival positions were reconciled in what has been termed the neurocultural model (Ekman, 1972), according to which the facial expressions of emotion are both innate and learned. In this section, a description and a critique is given of the neurocultural model of facial expression, preceded by a review of the evidence relevant to Darwin's theory.

Evidence for the innateness of the facial expressions of emotion

Recent research has provided support for Darwin's observations, although none of the evidence is conclusive. Thus, cross-cultural studies show that facial expressions associated with six emotions (happiness, sadness, anger, fear, disgust and surprise) are decoded in the same way by members of both literate and preliterate cultures (Ekman *et al.*, 1972). More recently, a seventh universal facial expression – that of contempt – has been postulated (Ekman & Friesen, 1986). However, even if one accepts the existence of universals in decoding, this only suggests that whatever is responsible for common facial expressions is constant for all mankind: inheritance is one such factor but learning experiences common to all mankind could equally well be another.

A second source of evidence comes from the study of children born deaf and blind. Such children were filmed by Eibl-Eibesfeldt (1973), who argued that they show the same kinds of basic facial expressions in appropriate situational contexts as children whose sight and hearing is unaffected. All the blind and deaf children were capable of smiling, usually during social play or when being patted or tickled. Raising the eyebrows in surprise for one child occurred when sniffing at an object, for another when tasting a piece of salted apple. One little girl would frown quite clearly when she was repeatedly offered a disliked object or when people persisted in unwelcome attempts at social contact. These children were severely disabled, yet still displayed these facial expressions of emotion; Eibl-Eibesfeldt regards this as strong evidence for the role of inheritance. However, it is still possible the expressions might be learned. For example, a child might be rewarded for smiling, if smiling prolongs the duration of social play. Similarly, it is quite easy to see how an anger expression might be reinforced, if the child finds that it inhibits others from unwelcome attempts at social contact or from persistently offering an unwanted object.

A third source of evidence comes from studies of the facial musculature. All but one of the discrete muscle actions visible in the adult can be identified in newborn infants, both full-term and premature (Oster & Ekman, 1977). Again, however, this does not prove that the association of particular facial expressions with particular emotions is innate. Smiling can be called a universal gesture in the sense that it is an expression that human beings are universally capable of producing, but this does not mean that it is innately associated with the emotion of happiness, nor that it has a universal meaning.

Thus, although the evidence supports the view that the capacity to produce facial expressions of emotion is inherited, it is by no means conclusive. The innate hypothesis does not automatically exclude the view that facial expressions are also learned and specific to individual cultures. The rival positions have been neatly reconciled in what is called the neurocultural model of emotional expression (Ekman, 1972). This is described below.

The neurocultural model of emotional expression

According to the neurocultural model, there are at least six fundamental emotions with innate expressions. These can be modified through the learning of what are called 'display rules', norms governing the expression of emotions in different contexts. Four ways in which an emotion can be modified are distinguished – through weakening its intensity (attenuation), through exaggerating its intensity (amplification), through hiding an emotion by adopting a neutral face (concealment) or through showing a different expression from the emotion that is being experienced (substitution).

The model can be clearly illustrated by a cross-cultural experiment in which groups of Americans and Japanese were shown a neutral and a stress-inducing film (Ekman *et al.*, 1970; cited in Ekman *et al.*, 1972). All the participants saw the films alone and their facial expressions were videotaped without awareness. Both groups differed in their response to the neutral and stress films, and showed highly similar facial expressions. After seeing the stress film, a member of their own culture entered the room to conduct an interview about their experiences. The Japanese appeared to engage in substitution by showing happy faces when inter-viewed by Japanese interviewers, whereas the Americans typically did not conceal signs of negative feelings when they talked with their American interviewer. This nicely supports informal accounts of Japanese culture where there is said to be a taboo governing the expression of negative emotions in public. It also suggests that the fundamental emotional expressions were shown when participants watched the films on their own, but that culturally learned display rules came into operation when inter-viewed by a member of their own culture.

An important feature of the neurocultural model is the distinction between two principal types of facial expression: those that are spon-taneous and those that are under voluntary control. A great deal of neuropsychological evidence is consistent with this. There are cases where a person has suffered paralysis of volitional facial movement, such that they are unable to retract the mouth corners on command, but can still smile spontaneously on the paralysed side if something strikes them as amusing (Rinn, 1991). There are also cases of paralysis of spontaneous facial expression, where the person still retains the ability to exercise voluntary control over facial movements (Rinn, 1991). A syndrome known as pseudobulbar palsy is characterized by frequent episodes of involuntary laughing or crying, occurring in the absence of the appropriate emotional experience. The patient is typically unable to inhibit the laughing or crying, and must simply endure it until it dies down of its own accord. This expressive display may be regarded as a fixed-action pattern, which can be triggered in its entirety by some internal signal (Rinn, 1991).

In general, it can be said that the cortical system mediates voluntary behaviour, whereas the subcortical system mediates nonvolitional behav-iour. Because of this, cortical behaviours vary widely from culture to culture (e.g. Ekman's display rules), whereas subcortical behaviours are universal across culture (e.g. emotional expressions). However, the cortical and subcortical circuits of the brain should not be regarded as taking it in turn to issue responses. In fact, they act simultaneously, each leaving its influence on the final pattern of muscle contraction. Thus, it is not really appropriate to speak of a given facial expression as being of cortical or subcortical origin, rather, both processes can affect it in various ways (Rinn, 1991).

Further evidence comes from studies of people born blind or blinded very early in life, who have been found not to have good cortical control of facial expression. When congenitally blind participants were asked to pose expressions of common emotions (fear, anger, surprise, disgust and humour), all the expressions were judged as significantly less adequate than those of sighted participants, with the exception only of humour, where there was no difference (Rinn, 1991). Conversely, in the study of spontaneous expressions by Eibl-Eibesfeldt (1973, referred to above), it was found that children born both deaf and blind showed the same basic repertoire of spontaneous facial expressions as non-affected children. People born blind could have difficulty posing emotional expressions for the same kind of reason that persons born deaf cannot easily learn to sing – that is to say, they lack the particular kind of feedback necessary to know how well they are doing (Rinn, 1991).

The neurocultural model has important implications for the significance we ascribe to the face. If facial expressions are innate, then they could be particularly important in communicating emotion. But if we also learn control of our facial expressions through display rules, how can we distinguish between expressions that are posed or spontaneous, between expressions that are faked or genuine? Studies of smiling have shown a number of differences between spontaneous and false expressions (Ekman & Friesen, 1982). In a spontaneous smile, three action units are involved: raising the corners of the lips, raising the cheeks (which might produce crows-feet wrinkles) and raising the lower eyelid. In a false or posed smile, the second and third action units may not be involved. The timing of the smile may also be important. A false smile may appear too early or too late. The apex of the smile might be too long – felt smiles seldom last more than 4 seconds. Onset could be too short, giving an abrupt appearance to the smile.

Another clue to an expression's genuineness is its symmetry: false smiles tend to be more asymmetrical than spontaneous smiles. This observation arose from a controversial proposal that emotions are expressed more intensely on the left than the right side of the face. In an experiment, photographs of facial expressions of emotion were constructed by first splitting them vertically down the middle and then rephotographing each half face together with its reflection in a mirror (Sackeim & Gur, 1978). The full composite left-side and right-side faces were then rated by judges together with the original photographs. It was found that for all the emotions (with the exception only of the facial expression of happiness) left-side photos were judged as significantly more intense with regard to the emotion portrayed.

These findings were criticized by Ekman on the grounds that most of the photos used were of deliberate facial movements. In the only case where the original photos were of spontaneous facial expressions (that of happiness), no significant effect for asymmetry was found. (All the photos in the experiment had been taken from Ekman and Friesen's (1975) book *Unmasking the Face*.) In another study, spontaneous smiles were compared with deliberate smiles; significantly more of the deliberate smiles were found to be asymmetrical (Ekman *et al.*, 1981).

Further data on this point comes from a meta-analysis of fourteen studies of asymmetry (Skinner & Mullen, 1991). Meta-analysis is a statistical technique whereby the data from a number of different studies are pooled. This procedure is employed because the spread of a set of scores can vary from one study to another, hence a direct comparison of data from different studies can be misleading. This problem can be corrected through the use of a measure of effect size (d), which standardizes mean differences between any two groups according to the amount of variation in the samples (Cohen, 1969). Effect sizes can be calculated for each of the studies collated in the meta-analysis, which are then directly comparable with one another. The results of Skinner and Mullen's (1991) meta-analysis showed that the effect of asymmetry was much more pronounced for posed emotional expressions than for posed neutral expressions. This suggests that asymmetry is another cue as to whether an expression is posed or spontaneous.

In this context, research on the nonverbal expression of pain is of interest. Motives for exaggerating or dissimulating pain can include financial incentives, release from unpleasant work or social responsibilities, and increased attention from others. Motives for concealing evidence of genuine pain might include the fear of loss of work, for example, by manual labourers or high performance athletes (Craig *et al.*, 1991). Both cultures and individuals can differ in display rules regarding the expression of pain, which can have important implications for medical diagnosis and treatment (Prkachin & Craig, 1995).

One study was conducted with a group of patients suffering from low back pain (Craig *et al.*, 1991). Their facial expressions were observed during a scheduled physical examination with a physiotherapist, in which they were asked to identify which of a range of leg movements was the most painful. Brow lowering and closing the eyes were the two movements most commonly observed in pain, as well as cheek raising, tightening of the eye lids, raising the upper lip and parting of the lips. When asked to repeat the movement but to conceal any signs of pain, the patients were strikingly successful in doing so. All that a trained observer could detect was a reduced incidence of blinking, and marginal evidence for tension around the eyes, produced by tightening of the eyelid.

The patients were also asked to repeat one of the movements that did not induce pain at all, with the instruction 'This time I want you to pretend as if the movement is really causing you a lot of pain. Let me know by looking at you that it is painful. Make a "pain face"'. There was considerable similarity between the genuine facial display of pain and the posed expression. To some extent, the faked expression represented a sort of caricature: relative to the spontaneous expression, the patients displayed more brow lowering, cheek raising and pulling of the corners of the lips.

Thus, the distinction between posed and spontaneous facial expressions of emotion is well supported by a range of evidence, which also provides further support for the neurocultural model of emotional expression.

Emotional expression and recognition within particular cultures

It should be noted that the neurocultural model provides a general theory of emotional expression across cultures. It does not seek to provide an explanation for why a particular pattern of emotional expression or recognition occurs within any one culture (Matsumoto, 1996). However, a series of studies within one specific culture, namely that of Japan, has been conducted, using the United States as the yardstick for comparison (Matsumoto, 1996). This research was based on two dimensions of cultural variability, referred to as 'power–distance' and 'individualism–collectivism', which were identified from an extensive set of cross-cultural studies by Hofstede (1980). It was proposed that these two dimensions affect not only how emotions are displayed, but also how they are interpreted (Matsumoto, 1996).

Power–distance refers to the extent to which a culture maintains differences in status and/or power between its members. Whereas Japan has been described as a 'vertical' society that emphasizes status and position differences between people, the United States is considered a 'horizontal' society that minimizes actual or perceived status (Nakane, 1970). In a high power–distance culture, it would be expected that people of lower status will display more positive emotions to higher-status others, to show respect and uphold their superior status. Similarly, people of higher status might be expected to show more negative emotions to lower-status others, thus serving to maintain their own superior position. In a low power–distance culture, the display of positive and negative emotions would not be expected to be so clearly differentiated according to status.

A second important dimension is individualism–collectivism – the degree to which a culture encourages individual needs, wishes, desires and values, as opposed to group or collective ones. Whereas a key aspect of Japanese culture is the emphasis on collective concerns and the surrender of individual aspirations for the wellbeing of the group as a whole, American society places much greater emphasis on individual rights and aspirations. Because collectivist cultures rely more heavily on preserving harmony within the ingroup, it is proposed that ingroup–outgroup distinctions will be keener. Consequently, members of collectivist cultures should display positive emotion more to members of ingroups, negative emotion more to members of outgroups. Conversely, in individualistic cultures, the display of positive and negative emotion should not be so clearly differentiated according to group membership.

To make comparisons of emotion recognition and expression between Japan and the United States, a new test was devised, based on a set of photographs called the Japanese and Caucasian Facial Expressions of Emotion (JACFEE) (Matsumoto & Ekman, 1989). A major problem with cross-cultural studies of emotion recognition is that they have typically used only Caucasian models to portray different emotional expressions, which could bias the results against non-Caucasian cultures. For this reason, the JACFEE comprehensively samples both Japanese and Caucasian models. The test is based on photos of fifty-six different people (twenty-eight Caucasian and twenty-eight Japanese). There are eight photos for each of seven emotions considered to be universal (anger, contempt, disgust, fear, happiness, sadness and surprise), with four photos each of Caucasians and Japanese (two males and two females for each culture).

In one study (Matsumoto, 1990), Americans and Japanese were shown photos from their own culture and asked to judge the appropriateness of displaying these emotions in a wide variety of different situations. In relation to outgroups (casual acquaintances and public situations), the Japanese rated anger and fear as less inappropriate than did the Americans. Conversely, in relation to ingroups (close friends and family members), the Americans rated disgust and sadness as less inappropriate than did the Japanese. This supported the hypothesis that, in collectivist cultures, negative emotions are displayed more readily to outgroups, whereas in individualistic cultures, the display of negative emotions to ingroup members is considered more acceptable. The Japanese also rated anger as less inappropriate to lower-status individuals than did the Americans, supporting the hypothesis that in high power–distance cultures, it is considered more acceptable to display negative emotions to low status individuals.

In another study, Japanese and American observers were asked to judge photos from the JACFEE (Matsumoto, 1992). No significant differences between them were found with relation to the emotions of happiness and surprise, but the Japanese were worse at identifying the photos of anger, disgust, fear and sadness. Moreover, this finding was obtained regardless of the race or gender of the model. The inferior performance of the Japanese on identifying negative emotions can be seen as highlighting the importance of group and collectivist issues in the vertical society of Japan (Matsumoto, 1992). In Japan, the display of negative emotions is discouraged, as they are potentially disruptive. The lower accuracy scores for the Japanese suggest that not only is the display of negative emotions discouraged, but so too is the perception of these emotions; such conventions governing the interpretation of emotional display have been referred to as 'decoding rules' (Buck, 1984). Thus, in Japan, conventions governing both the display and decoding of emotions can be seen to go hand in hand with maintaining the social order.

These results are of importance not only for their insights into Japanese society. Whereas research on the facial expressions of emotions has typically been concerned with similarities between cultures, these studies seek to explore cultural differences and the reasons for those differences. As such, they can be seen to extend the neurocultural model through an analysis of the way in which broad dimensions of cultural variability, such as power–distance and individualism–collectivism, are reflected in specific rules governing the display and decoding of emotional expressions.

Criticisms of the neurocultural model

The neurocultural model was widely accepted for about 20 years, but in the 1990s it was seriously called into question. A number of criticisms were made with regard to the evidence on which it is based. For example, the language used to describe emotion is by no means universal: neither the words for so-called basic emotions, such as anger and sadness, nor even the word for emotion itself is found in every culture (Russell, 1991). Furthermore, experiments such as Ekman's, which oblige people to identify facial expressions from a forced choice between a limited range of emotion categories could well overestimate universality by producing an artificially high level of agreement (Russell, 1991).

One way of answering criticisms of the forced-choice methodology is to give the raters an additional option to the effect that 'none of these terms are correct'. Even when participants were given this option, they were still found to select Ekman and Friesen's six emotion categories at a level significantly above chance (Frank & Stennett, 2001). Furthermore, when the raters were given additional emotion labels (alarmed, bored, contempt and excited), together with the option 'none of these terms are correct', they still tended to select the six emotion categories as predicted by Ekman and Friesen.

Other criticisms have been made of Ekman *et al.*'s (1972) experiment in which Americans and Japanese were monitored while watching stress-inducing films (Fridlund, 1994). In Ekman *et al.*'s (1972) book, it is stated that the Americans and Japanese showed similar expressions while watching the films alone and different expressions when interviewed by a member of their own culture afterwards. But from a re-examination of the original research report, Fridlund (1994) claimed that it was not the presence of an interviewer that produced a difference between the Americans and Japanese; it was only when being interviewed *while watching the films* that significant differences occurred. Fridlund (1994) went on to suggest an alternative explanation of the data. The Japanese smiled not to conceal their feelings but out of politeness to the interviewer (a graduate student) because it is the Japanese custom to smile when being addressed, especially by someone in authority. It would be far less rude for the American student to view the film while being addressed. Whereas the

Americans were responding to the film, the Japanese were simply showing politeness to the interviewer.

Fridlund (1994, 1997) has also proposed an alternative to the neurocultural model, in terms of what he calls Behavioural Ecology. According to this view, facial displays depend upon social context and are manifestations of social intent – that is to say, what we will do in the current situation, or what we would like the other to do. Thus, what Ekman might refer to as a facial expression of anger, Fridlund would term a readiness to attack. Similarly, what in the emotions view would be regarded as 'leaked' anger, in the Behavioural Ecology view would be regarded as conflict about anger: 'I want to attack and I don't want to attack'. Fridlund rejects the whole conceptual structure of the neuro-cultural model as an unnecessary encumbrance. In the Behavioural Ecology view, there are neither fundamental emotions nor fundamental expressions of them, there are simply behaviours, which are manifestations of social intent and dependent upon social context.

In a comparison of the two approaches, an experiment was conducted in which Canadian, Chinese and Japanese observers were shown photographs of Ekman and Friesen's seven universal emotions (Yik & Russell, 1999). Participants were asked to rate the facial expressions either in terms of Ekman's emotion categories or in terms of descriptions of social intent, based upon Fridlund's work. No significant difference was found in the amount of agreement between the social intent and emotion category conditions, both across the three cultures, or within each culture. Thus, faces convey social messages with as much consensus as they convey emotional ones.

Whichever view one takes – the neurocultural model or that of Behavioural Ecology – it is still the case that considerable importance is attached to the communicative significance of facial expression. In the neurocultural model, there are six or seven universal facial expressions, innately associated with different emotions, and there are certain key features in the expressions themselves that could help the observer discern their genuineness. According to the Behavioural Ecology view, behaviour itself has evolved for its signal value in terms of what ethologists have called intention movements (see Chapter 1, p. 14) – movements that signal a readiness or preparedness to perform a particular action – and thus constitute an important source of social information.

Interpersonal relationships

Because of the significant role played by nonverbal cues in the communication of emotion, they have also been regarded as of central importance in interpersonal relationships. In one study, participants were requested to give an account of their own intimate experiences, and often *defined* intimacy in terms of related nonverbal behaviours. For example, one individual wrote that: '. . . a touch of the hand . . . the meeting of our eyes, a kiss, conveyed our intimacy better than a thousand words' (Register & Henley, 1992).

Compared with speech, nonverbal cues appear to be particularly important in interpersonal relationships. In one study, video recordings were made of unacquainted pairs of American students: they had been asked to discuss a possible trip around the world and were seated at a table with a world map (Grahe & Bernieri, 1999). A short (30 second) video clip was taken from the video recording. Observers were asked to make judgements of interpersonal rapport from this clip under five different conditions: transcript only, audio only, video only, video + transcript and video + audio. These judgements were correlated with self-ratings of rapport made by the students. Correlations were highest in the video-only condition and lowest for the transcript. Interestingly, when the video combined with a transcript or with the sound, the correlations were actually lower than in the video-only condition, although not significantly so. Hence, nonverbal cues appear to be particularly important in judgements of rapport.

Other studies have shown that observers can guess the identity of an unseen conversational partner from the nonverbal behaviour of one participant alone. Even very young children can do this; they can accurately identify whether their mother is conversing with a friend or a stranger (Abramovitch, 1977). Adult observers can identify not only the gender of the unseen conversational partner, but also whether the person was a friend or a stranger and whether or not the person was of the same age as the other conversationalist (Benjamin & Creider, 1975). Observers could be using a number of cues. For example, when adults talked to children, their muscle tonus was low, the skin beneath the eyes and over the cheek bones was hanging loosely down except during broad smiles; when adults talked to other adults, their skin was bunched and raised. Facial activity also seems to vary between same-age and different-age conversations, conversations between people of the same age appearing much more animated (Benjamin & Creider, 1975).

Movement coordination is another important feature of interpersonal relationships. 'Interactional synchrony', identified from a frame-by-frame analysis of a conversation, refers to a process whereby speaker and listener appear to move in close harmony with one another (Condon & Ogston, 1966). It is believed to be a characteristic feature of everyday interaction (Condon & Ogston, 1971), as well as a fundamental, universal characteristic of human communication evident from the day of birth (Condon, 1975). It is also believed to provide constant feedback from the listener to the speaker concerning the listener's level of attention and interest, and hence could be seen as an indicator of rapport (Condon, 1975).

These far-reaching claims for the significance of interactional synchrony have been extensively criticized. People move so frequently in social interaction that some simultaneous movement could occur simply by chance, it is not in itself proof of synchrony (Cappella, 1981). One way of testing this alternative explanation is through the use of what have been called 'pseudo-interaction clips'. These appear to be taken from a genuine interaction but are in fact constructed through a split-screen special effects generator to combine the images of two people recorded at a different points of time in the same interaction. Observers, who are unaware of how the tapes have been constructed, then rate these pseudo-interaction clips together with true interaction clips of two people recorded at the same point in time. The pseudo-interaction clips should be perceived as synchronous if simultaneous movement is occurring by chance alone.

In one study of mothers and infants, pseudo-interaction clips were rated as significantly less synchronous than true interaction clips (Bernieri *et al.*, 1988). In another study of high school pupils taking on the roles of teacher and student, significantly less movement synchrony was also perceived in the pseudo-interaction clips. In addition, observer ratings showed a strong positive correlation with self-ratings of rapport by the participants (Bernieri, 1988). Given that pseudo-interaction clips are not perceived as synchronous, it would appear that interactional synchrony does not simply occur by chance; furthermore, it is also strongly related to feelings of rapport.

A similar concept to interactional synchrony is that of postural congruence, which refers to people adopting similar postures (Scheflen, 1964). It is taken to indicate similarity of views or roles in a group, while noncongruence might indicate marked divergence in attitude or status. Whereas interactional synchrony refers to simultaneous movement, postural congruence refers only to people maintaining the same postures at a given point in time, irrespective of how they came to take up those postures (LaFrance, 1979).

In a study of a psychotherapy session (Charny, 1966), postures were categorized as congruent or noncongruent. A further distinction was made between mirror-image-congruent postures, where one person's left side is equivalent to the other's right, and identical postures, where right matches right and left matches left. As the interview progressed, there was a significant trend towards spending more time in mirror-congruent postures. The associated speech was also more positive, suggesting that mirror-congruent postures could indicate rapport or relatedness. Identical postures rarely occurred during the session, so were not included in the final analysis. Another study was focused on the perception of postural congruence (Trout & Rosenfeld, 1980). Two male American graduate students role played therapist and client, and adopted either mirror-congruent or noncongruent postures; there was no sound-track and the faces were blocked out of the tape. Mirror-congruent postures were rated as indicating significantly more rapport than the noncongruent postures.

Postural congruence has been investigated in the context of American college seminars. In one study, a significant positive correlation was found between mirror-congruent postures and a questionnaire intended to measure rapport, a significant negative correlation between noncongruent postures and rapport, and no significant relationship between identical postures and rapport (LaFrance & Broadbent, 1986). In a second study, posture and rapport were measured on two separate occasions: during the first week (time 1) and the final week (time 2) of a 6-week seminar course. A method of statistical analysis (known as the cross-lag panel technique) was used to investigate causal relationships: whether it is mirror-congruent postures that lead to rapport or rapport that leads to mirror-congruent postures. According to the results of this analysis, it is postural congruence that leads to rapport (LaFrance, 1979).

A series of studies has been conducted on nonverbal communication in the context of marriage: skill in both encoding and decoding nonverbal cues correlates with the quality of the relationship. Thus, experiments have been conducted to assess the nonverbal communication skills of husbands and wives, based on a task that involves asking them to send messages to one another (Noller, 1984). For example, one message reads 'You and your husband are sitting alone in your living room on a winter evening. You feel cold'. The wife is then asked to communicate the statement 'I'm cold, aren't you' in such a way as to convey one of three possible messages: to enquire whether he is also cold, to request that he warm her with physical affection, or request that he turn up the heat. The husband is asked to select from these three options which message he thought his wife was trying to convey. Husbands and wives were both asked to convey twenty-seven such messages, a response being judged as accurate if the partner's intent was identified correctly. Given the predetermined verbal content of the message, their success in the task is entirely dependent upon their skills in nonverbal communication. Their performance on the task was also correlated with self-ratings of marital satisfaction.

Using this procedure, unhappy couples have been found to misunderstand one another's messages significantly more; this effect was especially pronounced for the husbands (Noller, 1980). Indeed, unhappy couples were actually significantly worse at decoding messages from their spouses than from strangers (Noller, 1981). Couples with lower marital satisfaction just before their wedding also became less accurate over the first 2 years of marriage at understanding each other's nonverbal messages (Noller & Feeney, 1994). It would seem that decoding nonverbal communication is not so much a general ability but can be impaired in unsatisfactory relationships.

A series of studies has been conducted on factors that predict divorce (Gottman, 1994). Interactions between marital partners have been video-recorded in a laboratory setting and the videotapes coded by trained observers, including measures of nonverbal communication. Facial displays of contempt and disgust in particular can indicate trouble for the relationship (Gottman, 1994). The husband's facial expressions of contempt are a powerful predictor of physical illness reported by the wife 4 years later. The wife's facial expressions of disgust are highly correlated with the number of months the couple will be separated in the next 4 years. Gottman likens the break-up of a marriage to a cascade, in which overt displays of contempt play a central role. In his 'cascade model', complaining and criticizing lead to contempt, which in turn leads to defensiveness, which leads to withdrawal from the interaction (stonewalling). He refers to these four corrosive marital behaviours as 'the four horsemen of the apocalypse'.

Individual differences

There are important individual differences in nonverbal communication. These are discussed below with regard to both encoding and decoding.

Encoding

The way in which we communicate social identity is of considerable social significance. Gender and race are two highly salient aspects of identity, but so too are culture, personality and social attitudes. Clues to other people's social identity are important, because they help us to decide how to behave towards them (Knapp & Hall, 1997). But direct, concrete evidence of social identity can sometimes be hard to come by, so it has been argued that people tend to rely on nonverbal cues as a source of social information (Argyle, 1988).

Accurate judgements of social identity can be made from quite brief sequences of behaviour. In one study, judgements of sexual orientation were investigated (Ambady *et al.*, 1999). The encoders were graduate students: gays and lesbians were recruited from graduate student gay and lesbian groups, heterosexuals from meetings of public service organizations. All the prospective models filled out a questionnaire, which included an item on sexual orientation. Those with an unambiguous sexual orientation were then asked to talk to a video camera on the topic of how they balanced extracurricular and academic activities. Video clips (of 1 and 10 seconds in length) were edited out from these video recordings. These were shown (without sound) to a group of judges, who also were shown a photograph of each of the models. Judges could rate sexual orientation at a level significantly above chance from the still photographs alone, but their performance was significantly better when they made the ratings from either the 1-second or 10-second video clips.

People also differ in the extent to which they transmit information through nonverbal cues; some are highly expressive, others less so. Two distinctive patterns of response have been identified, referred to respectively as internalizers and externalizers (Jones, 1960). Internalizers show high galvanic skin responsiveness (a change in the electrical resistance of the skin, related to sweating), but their outward behaviour is restrained, and they are judged to be calm and poised in their social relationships. Externalizers show little galvanic skin responsiveness, but tend to be talkative and animated, and display a great deal of motor activity.

Accordingly, it might be expected that the expressions of externalizers are easier to read than those of internalizers. Experiments have been conducted in which an encoder views a series of slides, while a decoder is asked to judge from the encoder's facial expression alone what sort of slide is being observed; the encoder's heart rate or skin conductance are monitored continuously during the slide presentation (Lanzetta & Kleck, 1970; Buck *et al.*, 1972). Decoders are typically found to be most accurate with the least physiologically aroused encoders and least accurate with the most physiologically aroused encoders – just as would be predicted from the concept of internalizers and externalizers. This negative correlation between physiological arousal and decoding accuracy is also consistent with the belief that overt expression reduces the strength of emotion, most famously proposed by Sigmund Freud. Freud maintained that verbal, bodily and physiological responses are alternative channels for releasing emotional energy: if one channel is blocked, the response through the others should increase in intensity (Freud, 1915/1925). From this perspective, the lower physiological arousal of more expressive people (externalizers) is exactly what might be expected – that is to say, they discharge their emotions through overt expression.

It should, however, be noted that the data do not support a simple dichotomy between internalizers or externalizers. Rather, the negative correlation between physiological arousal and decoding accuracy suggests a continuum of nonverbal expressiveness. There are those whose faces are an open book, there are also those whose poker faces give away absolutely nothing; behaviour can be seen as varying between these two extremes.

Decoding

Studies have been carried out to investigate whether groups differ in their decoding ability; whether, for example, women are superior to men in this respect or whether psychiatric patients are disadvantaged in comparison to the normal population. Individual differences in decoding are obviously important because if certain groups of people fail to decode nonverbal cues appropriately, then the significance of those cues as a form of communication might be limited to certain sectors of the population. Thus, subtle nonverbal cues of disapproval can be wasted on an insensitive individual who is relatively impervious to such communication, and a more explicitly verbal approach will be required. In this sense, the significance of nonverbal cues as a system of communication is dependent upon the decoding skills of the message receiver.

Such differences have been investigated through tests intended to measure nonverbal perceptiveness. One such test is the Profile of Non-verbal Sensitivity (PONS; Rosenthal *et al.*, 1979), in which a number of scenes were posed by a young American woman. The information available to the decoder includes both bodily cues (pictures of the face and body from the neck to the knees) and speech (especially processed by electronic filtering or randomized splicing to disguise the actual words spoken but to retain vocal information, such as pitch and amplitude). The decoders are given two alternate descriptions for each film clip (e.g. nagging a child/expressing jealous anger), and are asked to state which is correct. The criterion of accuracy is based on a combination of what message the encoder intended to send and what message the researchers, the encoder and a panel of judges decided the encoder had in fact sent (the items that achieved the highest level of agreement were included in the final test).

Results using the PONS show a number of significant effects due to age, gender, culture and psychopathology. When the PONS was administered to Americans of differing ages, accuracy was shown to increase in a linear fashion between the ages of eight and twenty-five. Cross-cultural studies show that non-American samples perform better than chance but worse than Americans. Psychiatric patients perform worse on the PONS than nonpsychiatric groups, and also seem unable to benefit from practice. Women perform better than men on the PONS, and this gender difference occurs even with children.

Research on gender differences in communication is discussed later in this book in Chapter 4. With regard to cross-cultural studies using the PONS, it is possible to propose at least three different interpretations of the role of culture in nonverbal communication (Rosenthal *et al.*, 1979). Given that it is an American test, if only Americans scored significantly above chance, this would support the view that nonverbal cues are specific to a particular culture. Conversely, if members of all cultures scored significantly above chance and did equally well on the test, this would support a universalist view that nonverbal cues can be accurately interpreted irrespective of culture. Again, if members of other cultures scored significantly above chance but their performance was still inferior to that of the Americans, this would support an interactionist position where some cues are universal and some specific to particular cultures. It was this interactionist position that the data supported. This position also forms the basis of the neurocultural model of emotional expression (discussed above, pp. 29–37). Furthermore, developmental findings with the PONS – that American samples significantly improve their performance with age – are consistent with the view that at least some nonverbal cues are learned and specific to particular cultures.

With regard to psychiatric patients, their impaired performance is consistent with Argyle's proposal (Chapter 1, p. 16) that psychiatric patients lack skill in person perception. However, the PONS is a test based exclusively on nonverbal cues that have been posed. Do psychiatric patients perform as poorly with spontaneous nonverbal cues? This was investigated in an experiment with a group of patients suffering from paranoid schizophrenia (LaRusso, 1978). This particular patient group (according to a number of clinicians) has a special sensitivity to nonverbal cues; the experiment was intended to test this observation through the use of an objective criterion for assessing skill in person perception.

Two videotapes were presented to a group of patients and to a control group of people with no history of psychiatric problems. The videotapes showed the facial expressions of encoders as they watched two lights (one red, one white) serving as signals. In one condition, encoders received a small electric shock after seeing a red light, but not after seeing a white light. In the second condition, encoders again saw the red and white lights, but were asked only to pose their reactions (as if they were receiving a shock after the red light, not after the white light). On a series of trials, the decoders were asked to judge from the facial expressions of the encoders which of the two light signals was being displayed. The great advantage of this task is the experimenter knows in each case which light signal was being displayed; hence, the criterion of accuracy is entirely objective, the decoders' responses can be scored right or wrong. Half the participants in each group saw the posed encodings, the other half spontaneous encodings. Results showed that the patients actually did significantly better than the controls when judging spontaneous encodings, but were significantly less accurate with posed expressions.

The association of heightened nonverbal perceptiveness with paranoid schizophrenia was also demonstrated in a study based on Ekman and Friesen's six universal emotions (Davis & Gibson, 2000). In this experiment, spontaneous emotions of happiness, sadness and anger were evoked by asking people to recall and re-experience particular emotions. The other three emotions were induced by the experimenter. Disgust was evoked by asking the participants to smell the contents of an airtight container that unexpectedly contained a rotten lamb chop! For surprise, a balloon was unexpectedly burst while the participants were free associating to it. For fear, electrodes were attached to the forearm and an expectation was created of a 'painful but non-tissue-damaging electric shock'. In addition, participants were also asked to pose all six emotions. These spontaneous and posed expressions were all recorded on video and the most convincing were used in the main part of the experiment.

In the decoding task, there were three groups of psychiatric patients (with diagnoses of paranoid schizophrenia, nonparanoid schizophrenia and depression) and a control group, with no history of psychiatric disorder. It was found that the paranoid schizophrenic group was significantly more accurate than the other three groups in decoding spontaneous facial expressions for surprise and for all the negative emotions (sadness, anger, fear and disgust). Conversely, with the posed expressions of these five emotions, it was the controls who were significantly more accurate than the other three groups.

Both these studies are of considerable interest. When judging spontaneous expressions, it was found that the paranoid schizophrenia group performed significantly better than the nonpsychiatric control group. Thus, Argyle's proposal that psychiatric patients simply lack the relevant social skills to decode nonverbal cues would seem to be at the very least a serious oversimplification. Furthermore, completely different results were obtained according to whether the encodings were spontaneous or posed. This provides further support for the importance of the distinction (discussed on pp. 31–34) between spontaneous expressions and those under voluntary control. Finally, it is important to note that in the experiment devised by LaRusso, the decoders were not asked to say which emotion the encoders were experiencing, but which light signal was visible – hence, in this case, the task was entirely objective.

These studies have important implications for how we measure accuracy in perceiving nonverbal cues. Tests such as the PONS, which rely solely on posed expressions, can be seen to be very one-sided. There is now ample evidence that posed and spontaneous expressions cannot be regarded as interchangeable. Furthermore, the LaRusso study shows that it is possible to devise objective criteria of accuracy in measuring person perception. In contrast, the criterion of accuracy in the PONS is based only on agreement with a panel of judges. Ultimately, this criterion is subjective, because we have no means of assessing objectively whether the original judges were accurate.

A test of person perception that does use objective criteria of accuracy is the Interpersonal Perception Task (IPT), devised by Costanzo and Archer (1989). This test is organized around five main types of social interaction: status, intimacy, kinship, competition and deception. There are six scenes for each of these areas and, for each of the thirty questions, there is an unambiguous criterion of accuracy. For example, in one scene, two men discuss a game of basketball that they have just played, and the viewer is asked to decide which man won the game; hence, it is possible to say whether the viewer's judgement is right or wrong. The IPT can be used in a full channel version (with both sound and vision) but, with the sound turned down, it can also be used as a test of nonverbal communication alone. A shortened version of the test has also been devised, based on only fifteen scenes (IPT-15; Costanzo & Archer, 1993).

A number of studies have been conducted with the IPT. In one, female students, who lived on the same floor of a university dormitory, all completed the IPT and also a rating scale for each of her peers. Those rated as more socially sensitive got significantly higher scores on the IPT (Costanzo & Archer, 1989). It has also been found that people who score high on a questionnaire measure of shyness are less likely to do well on the

IPT (Schroeder, 1995a, b) and on the IPT-15 (Schroeder & Ketrow, 1997). All these results suggest that the IPT is valid measure of social perception, in that it correlates significantly with other measures of social sensitivity and social confidence.

It has also been found that women perform significantly better than men on the IPT (Costanzo & Archer, 1989). In another study, the participants were asked to estimate the number of questions they had answered correctly on the IPT (Smith *et al.*, 1991). The men's estimates were significantly higher than the women's, although their performance on the test was actually significantly lower. This would suggest that not only are women better at decoding nonverbal cues but also that men overestimate their performance, or women underestimate their performance, or both.

Although the IPT has yet to be used as extensively as the PONS, there are enormous advantages in using scenes of spontaneous behaviour with an objective criterion of accuracy. In the author's view, this is a much more effective way of devising tests to measure nonverbal perceptiveness.

Nonverbal communication and speech

In the communication of emotion and interpersonal relationships, nonverbal cues have been considered as of particular importance. As a consequence, some writers have regarded body movement as an alternative system to speech, offering a more reliable indicator of people's true feelings. This hypothesis was investigated in a series of studies in which systematic comparisons were made concerning the relative importance of nonverbal cues and speech in the perception of interpersonal attitudes.

In one experiment, the perception of friendliness and hostility was investigated (Argyle *et al.*, 1972). Students were asked to rate videotapes of a female student reading friendly, neutral and hostile messages in a friendly, neutral or hostile nonverbal style. These messages and nonverbal styles had been previously rated by another group of students to match the relative strength of speech content and nonverbal style. To convey friendliness, the encoder used a warm, soft tone of voice, open smile and relaxed posture; to convey hostility, a harsh voice, frown with teeth showing and a tense posture; to convey a neutral attitude, an expressionless voice and a blank face. Both speech content and nonverbal styles were approximately equal in judged friendliness/hostility when rated independently of one another. When judged in combination, the nonverbal cues had a much more powerful effect on the judges' ratings, accounting for nearly six times as much shift on the rating scales as speech content.

In another study, inferior and superior attitudes were investigated (Argyle *et al.*, 1970). Students were asked to rate videotapes of a female encoder reading messages where the speech content was intended to convey an inferior, equal or superior attitude in an inferior, equal or superior nonverbal style. The nonverbal styles employed by the encoder for a superior attitude were an unsmiling facial expression, head raised and loud, dominating speech; for a neutral attitude, a slight smile with head level and neutral-to-pleasant speech; for an inferior attitude, a nervous, deferential smile, head lowered and nervous, eager-to-please speech. Both speech content and nonverbal styles were approximately equal in judged inferiority/superiority when rated independently of one another; when judged in combination, nonverbal cues were much more powerful, accounting for over four times as much shift on the rating scales as speech content.

Studies such as these consistently showed that nonverbal cues are certainly *perceived* as more important than speech (e.g. Walker, 1977). However, in each case, posed nonverbal cues were used and, as has been argued above (pp. 31–34), there are good reasons for suggesting that posed and spontaneous expressions are not necessarily interchangeable. An additional problem is that such studies are unrealistic, that is to say, they do not correspond to the ways in which people encounter conflicting cues in naturally occurring situations. Observers in these experiments are shown repeated sequences of conflicting cues, which could sensitize them to the purpose of the experiment; as a consequence, this skews the results.

To control for this problem, an experiment was devised in which inconsistent messages were suitably camouflaged amidst naturally occurring consistent messages (Trimboli & Walker, 1987). The inconsistent messages were portrayed by a highly trained actress, for example, in one extract she said 'What rotten luck!' in a happy nonverbal style (smiling with teeth showing, looking at the camera, some variations in pitch level and a slightly higher than normal pitch). Different levels of camouflage were employed, ranging from 0 per cent (where all thirty-six video clips were inconsistent messages) to 94 per cent camouflage (where only two of the thirty-six video clips were inconsistent messages). From ratings of these video clips, it was found that nonverbal cues were only dominant when the level of camouflage was low; the effect simply disappeared when the level of camouflage was high.

A further problem with studying discrepancies between nonverbal cues and speech is that it neglects the extent to which speech and body movement are coordinated with one another. Indeed, it might be the case that incidences in which nonverbal communication conflicts with speech are the exception rather than the rule. The relationship between body movement and speech has been the focus of a whole series of studies, which are reviewed below.

According to Condon and Ogston (1966), the body of the speaker moves closely in time with his speech; they called this 'self synchrony'. Self synchrony is not simply confined to hand gestures; movements of all parts of the body have been found to be closely synchronized with speech. However, this is not to say that *every* bodily movement is related to discourse. For example, in a study of psychotherapy sessions it was primarily noncontact hand movements (movements that do not involve touching the body or touching an object) that were judged as related to speech (Freedman & Hoffman, 1967). In a quite different context (that of political speech-making), it was again noncontact rather than contact hand movements that were principally related to speech (Bull, 1986).

One way in which body movement is related to speech is in terms of vocal stress. Spoken English is produced in groups of words, typically averaging about five in length, where there is one primary vocal stress, sometimes referred to as the 'tonic' (Halliday, 1970). This primary vocal stress is conveyed principally through changes in pitch, also through changes in loudness or rhythm. The group of words is referred to as a phonemic clause and is terminated by a juncture, in which the changes in pitch, rhythm and loudness level off before the beginning of the next phonemic clause (Trager & Smith, 1951). It has been observed that speakers of American English typically accompany their primary stresses with slight jerks of the head or hand (Pittenger *et al.*, 1960). It has also been found that it is not just movements of the head and hands that are related to vocal stress, but movements of all parts of the body (Bull & Connelly, 1985). In fact, most of the tonic stresses (over 90 per cent) in the study by Bull and Connelly were accompanied by some kind of body movement. Typically, these took the form of continuous movements, such as nodding the head or flexing and extending the forearm, where the apex of the movement was timed to occur at the same time as the tonic. So, for example, the downward movement of a head nod might begin before the tonic, the apex of the head nod coinciding with the tonic, the upward movement of the head occurring after the tonic.

Body movement has also been shown to be related to speech in terms of both syntax (Lindenfeld, 1971) and meaning (e.g. Scheflen, 1964). From an analysis of the speech of a patient in a psychotherapy session, movements were found to occur principally within the duration of a syntactic clause rather than across clause boundaries (Lindenfeld, 1971). It has also been observed that posture is related to structural units larger than a sentence (Scheflen, 1964, 1973). Changes in what is referred to as the 'position' – corresponding roughly to taking a certain point of view in an interaction – tend to be accompanied by a postural change involving at least half the body (Scheflen, 1964). Changes of topic are sometimes accompanied by changes in posture: in a study of television newsreaders it was found that the introduction of a different news item was frequently accompanied by a change in hand position (Bull, 1987).

Head movements are also closely patterned with speech and can signal not only yes or no but also a variety of other meanings (McClave, 2000). For example, vigorous head shakes may accompany emphatic words such as 'a lot', 'great', or 'really'. A wide sweep of the head can be used to indicate inclusiveness accompanying such words as 'everyone' or 'every-thing'. Again, when a person starts to quote directly from someone else's speech, a shift in head orientation can slightly precede or directly accompany the quotation (McClave, 2000).

If nonverbal behaviour is so clearly related to speech, what functions does it serve? Three types of function have been distinguished, referred to as emblems, regulators and illustrators (Ekman & Friesen, 1969a).

The term 'emblem' refers to those nonverbal acts that have a direct verbal translation. Their function is communicative and explicitly recognized as such. Emblems are generally assumed to be specific to particular cultures or occupations, but there do appear to be pan-cultural emblems such as the 'eyebrow flash', where a person raises the eyebrows for about a sixth of a second as a greeting; this has been observed this in a wide number of differing cultures (Eibl-Eibesfeldt, 1972). The geographical distribution of twenty different emblems has been mapped across western and southern Europe and the Mediterranean (Morris *et al.*, 1979). Some emblems are specific to one culture. In Italy, for example, pressing and rotating a straightened forefinger against the cheek (referred to as the 'cheek-screw') is a gesture of praise; it is, however, little known elsewhere in Europe. The meaning of other emblems varies between cultures. In the United Kingdom the gesture referred to as the 'ring', where the thumb and forefinger touch to form a circle, means something is good; in parts of France it means that something is worthless and in Sardinia it is an obscene sexual insult (Morris *et al.*, 1979).

Emblems have the particular advantage that they can be used when speech is difficult or impossible because of distance or noise; in such circumstances, emblems can function as an alternative system to speech (Ekman & Friesen, 1969a). So, for example, a policeman directing traffic on points duty can be said to be using emblems in a situation where speech is not possible. Some emblems are insults; if such emblems are used at a distance, this presumably has the advantage that it is more difficult for the insulted person to retaliate!

Regulators are movements that are assumed to guide and control the flow of conversation, for example, in the way in which people exchange speaking turns. Hand gesture clearly plays a role in turn-taking. Attempts by the listener to take over the turn can be essentially eliminated by the speaker continuing to gesture, referred to as an 'attempt-suppressing signal' (Duncan & Fiske, 1985). Conversely, when the speaker stops gesturing, this can function as a 'turn-yielding cue', a signal that offers a speaking turn to the other person. Four other turn-yielding cues have also been identified: the completion of a grammatical clause, a rise or fall in pitch at the end of a clause, a drawl on the final syllable and the use of stereotyped expressions such as 'you know'. The effect of all five cues has been shown to be additive; the more of these cues are displayed, the more likely there is to be smooth switch between the speakers (Duncan & Fiske, 1985).

All the observations of turn-taking referred to above were based on pairs of people in conversation (Duncan & Fiske, 1985). In groups of three, it has been shown that gaze is an important turn-taking signal, especially what is referred to as a 'prolonged gaze' (Kalma, 1992). One person might begin to look at another shortly before the end of the utterance and keeps on looking for at least 1 second after completing the utterance, during which time no-one else speaks. The person who displayed a 'prolonged gaze' typically yields the turn, while the gaze receiver is the one most likely to take over the turn (Kalma, 1992).

Illustrators are movements that are directly tied to speech, believed to amplify and elaborate the verbal content of the message. Under ordinary circumstances, adults can understand speech without the need for accompanying gestures. However, when the quality of speech is impoverished in some way, then gestures can facilitate comprehension (McNeil *et al.*, 2000). For example, improved comprehension by adult listeners has been shown when the spoken message is degraded (Rogers, 1978; Riseborough, 1981), ambiguous (Thompson & Massaro, 1986), highly complex (Graham & Heywood, 1976) or uttered in a soft voice (Berger & Popelka, 1971). It has also been shown that gesture can facilitate the comprehension of indirect requests. For example, if someone says 'It's getting hot in here', this is much more likely to be understood as a hint to open the window if the speaker is pointing towards it at the same time. In a series of experiments, it was shown that such indirect requests were significantly better understood when accompanied by gesture than when made either in the form of speech or gesture alone (Kelly *et al.*, 1999).

This threefold distinction into emblems, illustrators and regulators highlights some of the different functions of body movement in relation to speech. A major implication of this typology is that gesture is essentially secondary to speech, serving either as a substitute form of communication when speech is difficult or impossible, or to support the spoken message. An alternative view is that gestures do much more than merely 'illustrate' what is being said, they can instead be seen as an integral part of the message (Kendon, 1985, 1994; McNeill, 1992). Words and gestures can work together to create a sentence, a phenomenon sometimes referred to as 'mixed syntax' (Slama-Cazacu, 1976). Moreover, it is not just hand gestures that can function in this way, but also facial movements (Bavelas & Chovil, 1997).

As a silent, visual mode of expression, gesture has very different properties from those of speech and consequently is suitable for a different range of communication tasks (Kendon, 1985). It is often easier or quicker, for example, to point to an object than to describe it in words. Again, some gestures are like representative pictures in that they attempt to represent the visual appearance of an object, spatial relationship or bodily action, sometimes referred to as 'physiographic'. In one experiment (Graham & Argyle, 1975), English and Italian students were asked to communicate information about two-dimensional shapes to other students from their own culture, both with and without the use of hand gestures. The decoders drew what they thought the shapes were, the drawings were rated by

English and Italian judges for their similarity to the original shapes. When gesture was permitted, the drawings were judged as significantly more accurate. The Italians also did significantly better than the English when gesture was permitted. Gesture is of course widely believed to be of particular importance in Italian culture.

Because gesture is visual, it is a silent means of communication and can be employed when it is difficult or impossible to use speech. The speech channel might be blocked momentarily by noise but it might also be blocked because it is already in use. Thus, in multiparty conversations, gesture can be employed by people who are not actually talking as a means of commenting on an interaction, without interrupting the flow of speech. This can be done cooperatively or critically, so that the commentator does not have to take a speaking turn (Kendon, 1985).

An additional advantage is that gesture can be used without having to enter into the kind of mutual obligation or ritual conduct that seems to be required by conversation. Consequently, it can sometimes be quicker to make a passing comment through gesture rather than through words. It might also be used in situations where the speaker seeks to be less fully bound or committed to what he or she has to say. It can sometimes be adopted as a substitute for speech, where to actually formulate a thought in words might be regarded as too explicit or indelicate (Kendon, 1985).

Gesture, by its very nature, is a form of bodily action and this gives it certain advantages in communication. The appearance of an action can never be as adequately described in words as it can be represented through movement. Thus, gesture can be of particular importance in mimicry or in demonstrating how particular skills should be performed. Because gestures can be reminiscent of physical actions, they can acquire additional forcefulness as a consequence: a clenched fist can convey anger more effectively than a torrent of words. This might give gesture especial importance in the communication of emotions and interpersonal attitudes.

Not only is gesture a visual form of communication, it is also highly visible, especially in comparison to, say, facial expression or eye contact. In a study of a birthday party, it was observed how people used gesture as an initial salutation to capture one another's attention before entering into conversation (Kendon & Ferber, 1973). In a study of medical consultations, patients were found to use flamboyant gestures to attract the doctor's attention from their notes (Heath, 1986). In this context, gesture has the additional advantage of indirectness as well as visibility, because a direct request for attention from a higher status figure like a doctor might be seen as some sort of challenge to the doctor's authority.

Another situation characteristically associated with the flamboyant use of gesture is that of public speaking. For the orator, gesture has distinct advantages over other forms of nonverbal communication such as facial expression or gaze, which can be less discernible to a distant audience. A detailed analysis of the use of hand gesture in a political speech is discussed in Chapter 5 (pp. 110–112). The speech was delivered by Arthur Scargill, President of the British National Union of Mineworkers, who was found not only to make extensive use of hand gesture but also to accompany important parts of the speech with gestures involving both hands (Bull, 1986). This illustrates another communicative advantage of gesture. Not only is it a highly visible form of communication, there are also difference in visibility between different forms of body movement. More important aspects of speech can be indicated by larger movements (articulated from the shoulder, or indeed involving both arms) and/or by movements involving more than one part of the body.

Gesture is to some extent optional. Whereas features like vocalization, speech rate and amplitude are intrinsic to speech, that is to say, it is impossible to converse without them, it is perfectly possible to converse without the use of gesture. Consequently, the presence or absence of gesture can in itself be seen as a form of communication. In the analysis of turn-taking discussed above (Duncan & Fiske, 1977), it was described how gesture can be used as an attempt-suppressing signal to prevent someone else taking a turn, while ceasing to gesture acts as a turn-yielding cue. The role played by gesture in conversational turn-taking suggests that the use of gesture itself can be taken as indicating a wish to communicate. This proposition has a number of intriguing implications. Gesture can be used when people are interested in the topic they are talking about, or to accompany certain parts of speech that a person regards as more important. Similarly, it has been found that people attempting to be persuasive used significantly more gesture than when asked to present a message in a neutral fashion (Mehrabian & Williams, 1969). Conversely, an absence of gesture can indicate a lack of desire to communicate. People suffering from depression were found to use significantly fewer illustrative gestures on admission to hospital than on discharge (Kiritz, 1971; cited in Ekman & Friesen, 1974).

By emphasizing the distinctive properties of gesture, it is possible to acquire a fuller understanding of its distinctive role in communication. Gesture is arguably as fundamental as speech for the representation of meaning; they are joined together only because gesture is used simultaneously for the same purpose (Kendon, 1985). In the organization of an utterance, speech and gesture are planned at the outset; the encoding of the utterance can occur simultaneously through both speech and gesture. There is considerable evidence consistent with this view (McNeill, 1985). Not only do gestures occur primarily during speech, they are also synchronized with linguistic units; indeed, they have semantic and pragmatic functions that parallel those of speech. In addition, gesture develops simultaneously with speech in children, and dissolves together with speech in aphasia (any disorder of speech resulting from brain damage). Speech and gesture can be seen to interact with one another in creating meaning: not only does gesture clarify the meaning of the speech, speech can also clarify the meaning of the gesture (Kelly *et al.*, 1999). In short, gesture can be seen not just as an alternative to speech, but as an additional resource, as part of a multichannel system of communication, which allows the skilled speaker further options through which to convey meaning.

Conclusions

The detailed analyses that have led to improvements in our understanding of nonverbal communication over the past few decades can be seen to exemplify the microanalytic approach, especially the belief that all aspects of behaviour are potentially significant and worthy of enquiry. It has been argued that nonverbal cues are of particular importance in communicating emotions, interpersonal relationships and aspects of personal identity. It has also been shown that there are significant individual differences in the extent to which people send and receive messages through nonverbal cues.

But there is an alternative viewpoint. Research on nonverbal cues and speech has also demonstrated their close interrelatedness. From this perspective, the distinction between nonverbal communication and speech would appear to be a highly artificial one (Bavelas & Chovil, 2000). Hand and facial gestures in particular can be seen as visible acts of meaning, hence, it has been argued that they should be treated as part of natural language. Bavelas and Chovil (2000) have referred to this as 'face-to-face dialogue', and argue for what they term an integrated message model in which audible and visible communicative acts are treated as a unified whole.

This more recent perspective of language and gesture as a single integrated system differs markedly from the notion of a 'body language' – a communication process utilizing signals made up of body movements, which is regarded by its adherents as separate from and beyond speech (McNeill, 1992). If in the more distant past there was a tendency to neglect the nonverbal aspect of communication, there has perhaps also been a more recent trend to overemphasize its importance in contrast to language. In the next chapter, detailed consideration is given to the role of speech in interpersonal communication.

3 Speech

The analysis of speech has been a central concern of much microanalytic research. One principal theme has been the organization of conversation, its focus on the analysis of turn-taking and interruptions. Another principal concern has been the analysis of speech style, for example, the circumstances under which speakers either accommodate towards, or diverge from, one another. There is also a substantial literature concerned with the analysis of speech content, especially the ways in which particular types of linguistic action are accomplished, such as questioning and disagreement.

This chapter is divided into three main sections, focusing on each of these principal themes: organization, style and content. Each section is summarized below:

Section 1. Organization of speech:
   turn-taking
   interruptions and simultaneous speech.

Section 2. Speech style: Speech Accommodation Theory:
   convergence and divergence
   the optimal level of convergence
   other forms of convergence and divergence.

Section 3. The content of speech:
   analysis of function:
      the strategic implications of questions
      identifying replies and nonreplies to questions
   theory of equivocation
   the role of face
   the Linguistic Category Model.

The organization of speech

Turn-taking

One characteristic way in which conversation (or at least American and English conversation) is organized is in terms of an orderly exchange of turns, following the basic rule of one speaker at a time. A speaking turn is defined as the uninterrupted talk of one person; it can range from a single word to a lengthy monologue. The way in which turns are managed varies according to the social situation; these can be arranged on a continuum according to the turn-taking procedures on which they are based (Sacks *et al.*, 1974). At one extreme, there is informal conversation in which the order, length and content of turns are not fixed in advance but are managed by the participants. At the other extreme, there are ceremonies and rituals where virtually all the speaking turns (including the content of what is said) are prearranged. In between, there are situations where turn-taking is prespecified but only to a certain extent. Thus, in job interviews it is the interviewer who is expected to ask the questions and the interviewee to provide the answers, while in courtroom examinations, questions and answers are preallocated to the counsel and witness respectively (Atkinson & Drew, 1979). However, in both these situations, other factors such as the length and content of turns might be left free to vary.

Considerable attention has been paid to how speakers manage an orderly exchange of turns in conversations where turn-taking is not pre-arranged. The time between the end of one turn and the start of another is often remarkably brief; in a relatively smooth conversation, the majority of transition pauses may be less than 200 milliseconds in duration (Walker, 1982). This would support the view that the completion of a turn is to some extent projectable, the next speaker anticipating when the previous speaker has finished (Sacks *et al.*, 1974). The new speaker might be able to anticipate possible turn completions through so-called 'turn-yielding cues'. These were detailed in the previous chapter (p. 49): specifically, a rise or fall in pitch at the end of a clause, a drawl on the final syllable, the termination of hand gestures, stereotyped expressions such as 'but uh' and 'you know', and the completion of a grammatical clause. The more these cues are displayed, the more likely there is to be a smooth speaker switch between two conversationalists (Duncan & Fiske, 1977, 1985).

Exchanging turns in an orderly fashion (following the basic rule of one speaker at a time) is not the only way in which conversation may be organized. A second form of organization has been identified, termed the 'collaborative floor' (Edelsky, 1981). 'Floor' in this context refers to the conversational space available to the speakers (in the sense that a speaker can be described as 'holding the floor'). Whereas the main characteristic of the 'single floor' is that only one person speaks at a time, the 'collaborative floor' is open to all participants simultaneously. In an analysis of discussions at five university committee meetings, speech was observed to fluctuate between these two forms of organization (Edelsky, 1981). Talk that was more firmly oriented towards the meeting's agenda was characterized by a single floor, talk that strayed from the agenda by a collaborative floor. Collaborative floors typically involved shorter turns than single floors, much more overlapping speech, more repetition, more joking and more teasing.

Another analysis of the collaborative floor was based on informal conversations between women (Coates, 1989, 1996). In these conversations, nobody ever complained about overlapping talk or about being interrupted by any of the others. Indeed, the term 'interruption' did not even seem particularly appropriate. Thus, in a collaborative floor, the idea of trying to 'take the floor' becomes redundant, because the floor is already occupied by all the speakers. 'Crucially, there is no sense of competition, or of vying for turns. Speakers do not become aggrieved when others join in' (Coates, 1989, p. 112). 'The goal is not to take the floor from the other speaker, but to participate in conversation with other speakers' (Coates, 1989, p. 113).

The single and collaborative floors can be distinguished in a number of other ways. In a single floor, interruptions are characteristically corrected by what are called 'repair mechanisms'. These can take the form of interruption markers (e.g. 'Excuse me'), repeats or recycles of parts of a turn overlapped by others and premature stopping (i.e. before possible completion) by one or both parties to the simultaneous talk (Sacks *et al.*, 1974). In the collaborative floor there are no repair devices because there is simply nothing to repair.

Again, the single and collaborative floors seem to vary according to the relationship between the conversationalists. In a study of four-person groups, groups of friends were compared with groups of strangers (Dunne & Ng, 1994). Conversations between friends were more likely to be characterized by a collaborative floor, those between strangers by a single floor. The content of the two types of simultaneous speech was also shown to vary. Speech that broke up the regular flow of conversation (for example, by introducing contrary information or by asking for new information) was found to be associated with interruptions. Conversely, speech that was supportive of the other speaker (either through agreement or by building on what the other speaker says) was associated with non-interruptive simultaneous speech (Dunne & Ng, 1994).

Thus, conversation is not only organized in terms of an orderly exchange of turns, following the rule of one speaker at a time. In less formal settings, or where the content of conversation is less formal, or where people are well acquainted, interruptions and simultaneous speech can be much more the norm. This may or may not be problematic for the participants, depending on the nature of the interaction. According to Schegloff (2000), the set of practices whereby overlapping talk is resolved by the conversationalists can be seen as part of the turn-taking process. Hence, in seeking to understand the organization of talk, interruptions and simultaneous speech are of considerable importance. They are discussed in further detail below.

Interruptions and simultaneous speech

Typically, an interruption involves simultaneous speech, with two or more people talking at the same time. However, this is not always the case; there sometimes occur what are called 'silent interruptions' (Ferguson, 1977). Thus, a skilled interruptor might seize the opportunity to talk as the first speaker pauses to draw breath, leaving him or her so breathless that no simultaneous speech occurs. Conversely, not all simultaneous speech is necessarily interruptive. Phrases such as 'yeah', 'right', 'uh-huh', 'that's fine' and a number of nonverbal cues (such as head nods and smiles) can occur at the same time as the other speaker is talking; they signal continued listening attention and interest, rather than disruption of the other's speech (Brunner 1979; Duncan & Fiske, 1977). These vocal verbal and non-verbal signals have been referred to variously as listener responses (Dittman & Llewellyn, 1967), accompaniment signals (Kendon, 1967) or backchannels (Yngve, 1970).

Listener responses are readily identifiable and do not in themselves constitute an attempt to take a speaking turn. But if one of the conversationalists does wish to take over the speaking turn, quite different behaviours will be used. Thus, a new speaker might start to gesticulate, or make an audible inhalation of breath or speak more loudly (Duncan & Niederehe,1974). The new speaker might also turn the head away from the other conversationalist (Duncan & Niederehe, 1974), especially when answering a question (Thomas & Bull, 1981). None of these cues are associated with listener responses.

Whereas simultaneous speech refers just to two or more people talking at the same time, interruptions have the intent and/or effect of disrupting another person's speech. For example, a person might interrupt another speaker because he believes he knows what that person is about to say. Again, the listener might mistakenly start speaking because he believes another speaker has finished talking; in this case the effect is interruptive, although it was not intended to be so. Interruptions typically occur because someone wants to take over the speaking turn, but not always. The second speaker might interrupt with a brief interjection to divert the first speaker onto a different line of thought without actually wishing to take over the turn.

Interruptions might at first sight seem quite simple but detailed microanalysis shows that they can be extremely complicated (Roger *et al.*, 1988). A basic distinction can be made between single and complex interruptions, where complex interruptions involve two or more consecutive attempts to interrupt the speaker. Complex interruptions occur particularly in arguments where one person is determined to interrupt while the other speaker is equally determined not to give way. They might also take the form of interrupted interruptions, where one person's interruption is in turn interrupted by the other speaker. Another basic distinction can be made between successful and unsuccessful interruptions. In a successful interruption, the interruptor both prevents the speaker from completing an utterance and makes a complete utterance of his or her own. In an unsuccessful interruption, the interruptor may fail to prevent the speaker completing an utterance and/or fail to make a complete utterance of his or her own.

Hence, interruptions can be both successful or unsuccessful, and single or complex (Roger *et al.*, 1988). Within this framework, it is possible to make further finer distinctions. One type of successful single interruption has been dubbed the 'snatchback'. The first speaker offers the second speaker a turn (for example, by asking a question) and then starts to speak again before the other's response is complete, thereby literally 'snatching' back the turn. Another type of successful single interruption is the 'interjection', whereby the second speaker interrupts the first speaker with a brief but complete utterance (such as 'like what?' or 'so?'). Leaving the previous utterance incomplete, the first speaker now responds to the second speaker's interjection. Interjections are interesting because their function seems to be not to take over the speaking turn but in some way to influence the content of what the first speaker is saying. Thus, to be successful, interruptions do not necessarily have to result in an exchange of speaking turns (Roger *et al.*, 1988).

Excessive interruptions can be seen as a breakdown in conversational turn-taking. An interesting example comes from an analysis of an interview with Margaret Thatcher, the former British Prime Minister (1979–90). According to this analysis, Thatcher was frequently interrupted because of her misleading use of turn-yielding cues (Beattie, 1982a). When she used turn-yielding cues, the interviewer would start to speak, believing that she had completed her utterance. In the meantime, Margaret Thatcher would simply continue talking, thereby giving the appearance that she had been interrupted. Not surprisingly, this analysis of Margaret Thatcher's interview style proved extremely controversial; it is discussed in much greater depth in Chapter 5 (pp. 117–119), together with a critique of the evidence on which the original analysis was based (Bull & Mayer, 1988).

A tendency to interrupt can also be seen as a way of attempting to dominate conversation, so a number of studies have investigated the relationship between interruption rate and the personality trait of dominance. In one experiment, students preselected on the basis of a personality questionnaire conversed in pairs where the members of each pair were either high or low on dominance. When the students in a pair were both high on dominance, they tended to interrupt one another significantly more as the conversation progressed, suggesting that a tendency to interrupt is indeed related to personality (Roger & Schumacher, 1983).

Research has also been conducted on gender differences in interruptions. It has been claimed that men tend to interrupt women significantly more than women interrupt men. 'Just as male dominance is exhibited through male control of macro-institutions in society, it is also exhibited through control of at least a part of one micro-institution' (Zimmerman & West, 1975). Not surprisingly, this claim has proved extremely contentious. This claim and the relevant evidence will be discussed in Chapter 4 (pp. 93–96).

Although excessive interruptions can be seen as a breakdown in conversational turn taking, interruptions should not always be regarded as problematic. Conversation characterized by a completely orderly exchange of turns can seem stilted and boring; speakers might interrupt one another to convey their interest and enthusiasm in the topic. Indeed, in some cultures, interruptions appear to be the norm. For example, according to Umberto Eco:

> Italians interrupt one another. Everybody gets all excited and tries to make his views prevail by preventing the other from speaking and by trying to prove that he is a fascist or communist. Americans speak in turns. (It is no accident that the pragmatic theory of 'conversation turns' originated in the United States. Italian researchers who write articles about this matter treat it as an excavation from Mars).
>
> (Eco, 1986; translated by O'Connell *et al.*, 1990)

Similarly, there appear to be significant subcultural differences in patterns of turn-taking. For example, from an analysis of a conversation at a Thanksgiving party in Berkeley, California, it was observed that the New Yorkers present at the party tended to expect shorter pauses between speakers' turns at talk, so that the non-New Yorkers present had a harder time saying something before a faster talker had begun to talk (Tannen, 1984). Thus, turn-taking can be seen to reflect substantive differences in speaking style; this is discussed in the next section.

Speech style: Speech Accommodation Theory

One of the most influential theories of speech style is Speech Accommodation Theory. The theory is particularly concerned with what are termed 'speech convergence' and 'divergence'. Convergence refers to a strategy whereby individuals adapt to each others' speech through a wide range of linguistic features, such as accent, pronunciation, speech rate, pauses and utterance length. Divergence refers to the way in which speakers accentuate linguistic differences between themselves and others (Giles, 1973). Given that such linguistic features could vary in their social prestige, both convergence and divergence can be upward or downward (Giles *et al.*, 1987). For example, a speaker might show 'upward accent convergence' to gain the approval of another perceived as having a more prestigious accent or 'downward accent convergence' to reduce social embarrassment if the listener's accent is perceived as one of lower social prestige (Giles, 1973).

Convergence and divergence

In one of the first studies of speech convergence, a bilingual French–Canadian was asked to address a group of bilingual English–Canadians (Giles *et al.*, 1973). Given that the French–Canadian had the option of speaking in English, the extent to which he did so could be seen as showing convergence. In the experiment, the French–Canadian was asked to describe a picture, which the English–Canadians were required to sketch while listening. The English–Canadians were fully aware that the speaker had a choice of language available to him; he used four versions: French, mixed French and English, fluent English and non-fluent English. The more the speaker converged to the speech of his listeners (by speaking in English), the more favourably they evaluated him.

In another study of convergence, the accent of a girl working in a travel agency was observed (Coupland, 1984). As she spoke to different clients, the researcher simply counted the number of times which she sounded her h's. The percentage varied from 3.7 per cent to 29.3 per cent, and correlated highly with the percentage of h's sounded by the clients.

Speech convergence, according to Speech Accommodation Theory (Giles, 1977), can be understood in terms of three particular social psychological theories: similarity–attraction (Byrne, 1969), social exchange (Homans, 1961) and causal attribution (Heider, 1958). According to similarity–attraction theory, the more similar our attitudes and beliefs are to others, the more likely it is that we will be attracted to them (Byrne, 1969). Thus, interpersonal convergence through speech is one of many strategies a person can adopt in order for others to make more favourable evaluations. According to social exchange theory, behaviour is determined by rewards and costs (Homans, 1961). If social rewards (such as liking or approval) come from accommodating towards another's speech style, then accommodation is more likely to occur. According to attribution theory, we understand other people's behaviour, and evaluate the people themselves, in terms of the motives and intentions we attribute to them (Heider, 1958). Thus, if we perceive speech accommodation as motivated by a genuine desire for good fellowship, we might evaluate it very favourably; if we perceived it simply as expedient or ingratiating, that evaluation might be more unfavourable.

Speech divergence was demonstrated in a celebrated experiment with Welsh students attending a Welsh language course (Bourhis & Giles,

1977). During a language laboratory session, the participants were asked to take part in a survey concerned with second language learning techniques. They listened to questions on an audiotape posed in English by a very English-sounding speaker, who at one point challenged their reasons for studying what he called '. . . a dying language with a dismal future'. In making their replies following this attack, the participants tended to broaden their Welsh accents. Three of the participants introduced Welsh words and phrases, while one Welsh woman did not reply for a while, and was then heard to conjugate a less than polite Welsh verb into the microphone! This switch to the Welsh language could certainly be regarded as a stronger form of speech divergence than simply broadening one's accent.

Speech divergence has been linked to Social Identity Theory (e.g. Tajfel, 1972; Turner, 1975), according to which self-esteem and self-image are partly dependent on group identification. Group members make comparisons with other groups on dimensions that are important to them, such as personal attributes, abilities or material possessions. Intergroup comparisons can lead individuals to search for or even create dimensions on which they can make themselves positively distinct from other groups. In effect, people experience satisfaction from the knowledge that they belong to groups that enjoy some superiority over others. Given that speech style is for many groups a salient and valued dimension of their social identity, it may well be that accent divergence is an important strategy for achieving such positive distinctiveness (Giles, 1977). Thus, in the study of the Welsh language learning class, the students who broadened their accents in response to a critical English person could be seen as affirming their own distinctive social identity. In Accommodation Theory, accent and language are one of the principal ways of indicating and maintaining group identity, while speech style is an important symbol of group pride (Giles & Coupland, 1991).

The optimal level of convergence

Although failure to accommodate can be seen as impolite, rude or even downright hostile, convergence is not necessarily always the best strategy for all social contexts. It is possible to be overaccommodating, and consequently to be perceived as ingratiating or patronising. Thus, there may be optimal levels of convergence (Giles & Smith, 1979).

To test this hypothesis, an experiment was conducted on the effects of three different modes of convergence: content, pronunciation and speech rate (Giles & Smith, 1979). A Canadian male prepared a series of tapes describing the educational system in Ontario. The speaker accommodated by explaining the use of Canadian terms such as 'course credits' and 'grade 6' (message content), by using a more English accent (pronunciation) and by speaking more slowly (speech rate). Each of these three factors was systematically varied with each another and the tapes were rated by a group of teachers in England. The speaker was evaluated most favourably when he converged on speech rate and *either* content *or* pronunciation, but was actually evaluated *less* favourably when he converged on all three dimensions. Thus, the results supported the notion of an optimal level of speech convergence: too much convergence may be counterproductive.

The concept of overaccommodation has been used extensively in studies of communication with the elderly. In this context, overaccommodation refers to features such as slower speech rate, exaggerated intonation, use of high pitch, increased loudness, more repetitions, tag questions, altered pronoun use and simplification of vocabulary and grammar (Ryan & Cole, 1990). Sometimes the high pitch and exaggerated intonation can sound like a form of baby talk; consequently, it has been dubbed 'secondary baby talk' (Caporael *et al.*, 1983).

Overaccommodation is believed to occur as a result of stereotyped expectations of an older person's communication needs – referred to as the 'communication predicament of aging' (Ryan *et al.*, 1986). In principle, such stereotype-based speech strategies cannot be universally successful because of the great diversity in communication needs and preferences amongst people sharing the social category of elderly (Ryan & Cole, 1990). As a consequence, it might seriously underestimate the interpretative abilities of many elderly people. It could also undermine the older person's sense of competence and interfere with effective interpersonal communication. Indeed, such talk might not only induce momentary feelings of worthlessness in elderly people but could also lead to reduced life satisfaction and mental and physical decline (Ryan *et al.*, 1986).

The problem, however, is that under certain circumstances over-accommodation can actually facilitate communication. In a study of the recall of medical instructions, a videotape was made of an actor presenting such instructions in either an overaccommodative or a neutral speaking style (Gould & Dixon, 1997). The video recording was shown to a group of older women (mean age 71 years) and younger women (mean age 21 years). The older women were further subdivided into two groups according to the quality of their memories. Elderly women with better memories actually showed significantly better recall of the instructions when presented in overaccommodative speech. Furthermore, both young and elderly women rated the overaccommodative speech as significantly clearer, simpler and slower. But when asked which person they would prefer as their physician, both groups significantly preferred the one who used neutral speech.

The 'communication predicament of aging' is said to occur because people assume (in some cases incorrectly) that elderly people have lowered cognitive abilities (Ryan *et al.*, 1986). The results of this study suggest a further predicament: overaccommodative speech that enhances comprehension and recall can, at the same time, create a negative experience for the elderly person (Gould & Dixon, 1997). This would suggest that, if anything, the 'communication predicament of aging' is even more of a predicament than was originally supposed.

Other forms of convergence and divergence

Although convergence and divergence were initially studied in terms of their effects on language, Speech Accommodation Theory has subsequently been broadened to include nonverbal behaviour; as such, it has been renamed Communication Accommodation Theory (Giles *et al.*, 1987). In Chapter 2 (pp. 39–40), the phenomenon of postural congruence was described, which seems to provide an exact parallel in the nonverbal domain with convergence and divergence in speech. Whereas postural congruence might indicate similarity of views or roles in a group, noncongruence could indicate marked divergence in attitude or status (Scheflen, 1964).

Although Speech Accommodation Theory developed originally as a theory of speech style, convergence and divergence can also occur in terms of the content of what is being said (Giles & Smith, 1979). For example, people tend to use less technical language and jargon with those who do not share their expertise of a topic being discussed (Moscovici, 1967). Failure to accommodate appropriately can lead to a lack of comprehension, as in the case of doctors who use medical jargon that their patients do not understand. Further attention is given to the detailed analysis of content below.

The content of speech

Analysis of function

The principal concern in the analysis of speech content has been the study of function. To a substantial extent this represents the influence of Speech Act Theory (pp. 9–10), according to which speech is not only concerned with the transmission of information but constitutes a form of activity in its own right.

However, deciding the nature of that activity is far from straightforward. This is because the grammar of speech does not provide a clear guide to its function. For example, the question 'What are you laughing at?' is not necessarily a request for information; it could be an order to stop laughing, in a school classroom almost certainly so (Sinclair & Coulthard, 1975). In fact, the term 'question' is ambiguous. It might refer to the grammar of an utterance, whether it ends in a question mark and takes the interrogative form; it might also refer to the function of an utterance, namely, a request for information. The analysis of questions is considered in much greater detail below, as an example of the kinds of problems involved in the analysis of speech content.

If a question is considered (according to its function) as a request for information, then it does not necessarily require interrogative syntax. There are what have been termed 'declarative questions' (Quirk *et al.*, 1985); these are identical in form to a declarative statement, except for the final rising question intonation (e.g. 'You realize what the risks are?'; 'They've spoken to the ambassador, of course?'). Indeed, some declarative questions might not even be accompanied by rising intonation, although the function of the utterance is still clearly to request information.

Three principal question types that do take interrogative syntax can be distinguished in terms of the type of reply expected (Quirk *et al.*, 1985). Those that expect affirmation or negation (e.g. 'Have you finished the book?') are called yes–no questions. Those questions that expect as the reply one of two or more options presented in the question (e.g. 'Would you like to go for a walk or stay at home?') are referred to as alternative questions (sometimes also as disjunctive questions). Those that typically expect a reply from an open range of replies (e.g. 'What is your name?' or 'When are you going out?') are referred to as 'wh-questions', because they begin with the words 'what', 'when', 'why', 'who' and 'which' (Quirk *et al.*, 1985). In a study of political interviews it was also found necessary to include 'where' as an additional question word (Bull, 1994). The word 'how', which of course does not begin with 'wh-', is also a question word (Quirk *et al.*, 1985). Thus, because the term 'wh-question' is somewhat confusing, the term 'interrogative word question' is preferred in the subsequent discussion.

In addition to the four types of question discussed above, it is possible to identify two further types, neither of which take interrogative syntax, namely 'moodless' and indirect questions. Indirect questions make use of reported speech as a means of posing a question. Moodless questions are those that do not have a finite verb (Jucker, 1986). If, for example, one person interrupted another's reading with the utterance 'A good book?', this could be regarded as a moodless question.

Thus, it is possible to distinguish six principal types of question in spoken English. In a study of eighteen televised political interviews during the 1992 British general election, it was found that all the questions observed in the sample could be subsumed within these six question categories (Bull, 1994). Classifying different types of question is important in that it can assist in identifying what utterances should be regarded as questions; this, as has been argued above, is by no means unproblematic.

There are at least two other reasons why classifying different types of question can be of value. First, the use of different types of question can have strategic implications for social interaction, most noticeably in the way in which questioner seeks to impose control on the respondent. Second, the analysis of question types has implications for what responses should be regarded as replies. Thus, just as in deciding what constitutes a question, identifying replies is by no means unproblematic. These two concerns are discussed further below.

The strategic implications of questions

The implications of what has been termed the 'strategic' use of different question types were examined in a study of legal discourse in an American courtroom (Woodbury, 1984). One way of thinking of a trial is as a story-telling contest, in which contrasting interpretations of events are presented as facts. Each lawyer seeks to convince the jury that his or her side's version of the story is the correct, or at least is the more plausible version. But the lawyers cannot tell the story; indeed, if they do, that talk will be struck from the written record. Hence, one task of lawyers is to elicit the story from the witnesses without seeming to suggest it to them, because there is a rule prohibiting 'leading' questions addressed to friendly witnesses. Lawyers should also not seem to testify personally, because there is also a rule against 'presupposing facts that are not in evidence'. Not only do lawyers have to elicit the story version from the witnesses but they also have to challenge the opponent's version by eliciting testimony that will contradict or otherwise weaken it. To achieve these tasks, lawyers must find ways of controlling the evidence that is presented in court. The formal properties of questions can be used 'strategically' to achieve these ends.

A detailed analysis was thus carried out of courtroom questions (Woodbury, 1984). Of the three major interrogative question types, the 'either/or' type hardly occurred at all, and those that did were included in the yes–no questions. Yes–no questions were by far the most frequent type, accounting for 66.8 per cent of all the questions analyzed; interrogative-word questions accounted for the remaining 33.2 per cent. Yes–no questions were used so frequently because, arguably, they give the lawyer a much greater degree of control than interrogative-word questions. Not only do yes–no questions limit the witness to a choice between two possible answers, they also enable the lawyer to word the evidence. In fact, it is not really the utterances of witnesses that become evidence when yes–no questions receive a reply, but the utterances of lawyers. Effectively, it is the witnesses' affirmations or denials of what the lawyer has said that enter into evidence. Such questions allow the lawyers to speak to the jury directly through the witness.

In the context of a lawcourt, yes–no questions have clear strategic advantages for both prosecuting and defending counsel, but they are not necessarily optimal in other social situations. In counselling and psycho-therapy, clinicians have often praised the value of the open question because it enables people to talk more freely about their feelings. Yes–no questions are closed by definition, because they invite either the answer 'yes' or the answer 'no'. Interrogative-word questions can be either open or closed, depending on the nature of the utterance. If the question requests a specific item of information then it can be regarded as closed (e.g. 'When did you first meet your husband?'). If the question can be answered in a variety of ways (e.g. 'How do you feel about your husband?'), then it can be regarded as open.

The value of open or closed questions depends very much on circumstance. In the context of a medical consultation, a doctor might ask open questions to encourage a patient to talk more freely. A series of closed questions will be more appropriate if specific information is required in order to make a particular diagnosis, by checking whether the patient is experiencing certain symptoms characteristic of a particular disease or medical syndrome. Nevertheless, if the doctor only asks closed questions there is the possible risk of failing to elicit information that might not fit in with a preconceived hypothesis, or of failing to identify important problems that the patient might find difficulty in talking about.

One particular reason for this is that patients themselves often find it difficult to ask questions, because the right to ask questions can be seen as a prerogative of status. Although question–answer sequences are the principal means of exchanging information in doctor–patient consultations, it is the doctor who typically asks the questions and the patient who typically gives the answers. In one study, it was found that, of 773 questions in twenty-one medical consultations, the overwhelming majority (91 per cent) were initiated by doctors (West, 1984). Furthermore, whereas patients answered virtually all the questions posed to them by their doctors (98 per cent), doctors replied to a smaller proportion (87 per cent) of the very few questions that they did receive. Most interestingly, nearly half of the patients' questions (46 per cent) were characterized by marked speech disturbances, such as stuttering or reformulations, suggesting that even the simple act of asking a question caused the patients some anxiety. The doctor, it seems, stands in near godlike status to a patient, that is, as an entity not to be questioned (West, 1984).

Identifying replies and nonreplies to questions

The formal structure of questions has implications for identifying what utterances should be regarded as replies. At first sight, what constitutes a reply might seem quite unproblematic: thus, in the case of yes–no questions, an appropriate reply would obviously be either yes or no! In fact, a reply to such a question does not always have to be in the form of yes or no. For example, if someone is asked 'Do you like Honolulu?' and he replies 'Only a little', this would seem to constitute a perfectly acceptable reply, even though neither the words yes or no can accompany 'Only a little' (Bolinger, 1978).

Conversely, simply because somebody responds with a yes or no, does not always mean they are giving a reply. The word 'yes' can be used simply to acknowledge a question rather than reply to it, as in the following example from a televised British political interview:

INTERVIEWER: What about your attitude to trade unions? You've said you're going to give a massive return of power to trade unions if Labour comes back. Isn't that something again that people are fearful of, that is going to lose you votes?

POLITICIAN: Yes, I haven't said by the way that we're going to give massive return of power, I've never used such a phrase in my life.

(1987 British general election: Neil Kinnock (Leader of the Labour Party, 1983–92) interviewed by David Dimbleby)

In saying yes, the politician is not replying to the question but simply acknowledging it; in fact, he goes on to attack the question by claiming that he has been misquoted ('. . . I've never used such a phrase in my life').

Similarly, the word 'no' can precede an attack on the question, rather than signalling a negative reply, as in the following extract from another televised British political interview:

INTERVIEWER: . . . you would rather have stayed pure and lost?

POLITICIAN: No no, it isn't a question of purity, it's a question of perception . . .

(1987 British general election: Neil Kinnock interviewed by Sir David Frost)

In saying no, the politician is not replying to the question but attacking it, objecting to the use of the word 'purity'.

There are also questions that are couched in a yes–no format but for which neither yes nor no may be a sufficient reply:

INTERVIEWER: Were you to be returned tomorrow and come back as Prime Minister, is there anything you've learnt during this campaign, any lessons you've learnt during this campaign that you would apply in a next period of . . . government?

POLITICIAN: Perhaps you've taught me one – that it's not enough actually to do things which result in caring, you also have to talk about it . . .

(1987 British general election: Margaret Thatcher interviewed by David Dimbleby)

If the politician answered no to this question, then this would be a sufficient reply. But if the politician answered yes, then there is also an expectation that what has been learned during the election campaign should also be stated. In this sense, an affirmative answer can be seen as posing an implied interrogative-word question, and it is to this implied question that the politician's reply is addressed.

Of course, people do not always reply to questions. Politicians are notoriously evasive and the whole issue of political equivocation is further discussed in Chapter 5 (pp. 119–121). But politicians are not the only people who avoid answering questions. A general theory of equivocation (not just by politicians) has been developed by Bavelas *et al.* (1990); this is discussed below as an example of another form of content analysis.

Theory of equivocation

Equivocation has been defined as '. . . nonstraightforward communication; it appears ambiguous, contradictory, tangential, obscure or even evasive' (Bavelas *et al.*, 1990, p. 28) and, more recently, as the 'intentional use of imprecise language' (Hamilton & Mineo, 1998). Research on this topic has been heavily influenced by the pioneering studies of Janet Bavelas and colleagues (Bavelas *et al.*, 1990). According to their theory, people typically equivocate when placed in what is termed an 'avoidance–avoidance' conflict, where all of the possible replies to a question have potentially negative consequences but nevertheless a reply is still expected. Their underlying argument is that equivocation does not occur without a situational precedent; although it is individuals who equivocate, this has to be understood within the context of the individual's communicative situation.

Many everyday situations can be seen to create this kind of 'avoidance–avoidance' conflict. Perhaps the most common involves a choice between saying something false but kind and something true but hurtful. For example, people who are asked to comment on an unsuitable gift from a well-liked friend have two negative choices: saying, falsely, that they like the gift or saying, hurtfully, that they do not. According to equivocation theory, people will, if possible, avoid both of these negative alternatives – especially when a hurtful truth serves no purpose. What they do instead is equivocate; for example, someone might say 'I appreciate your thoughtfulness' with no mention of what they thought of the actual gift. A series of experiments has been conducted in which a number of these conflict situations are described (Bavelas *et al.*, 1990). In one such experiment, students were asked to respond to the following situation: 'Another student in a small class, which meets three times for the entire year, has just given a class presentation. It was very badly done – poorly prepared and poorly delivered. After he sits down again, he passes you a note, "How did I do?". You have to jot something down and pass it back to him. What would you write as an answer?'

Three kinds of equivocal responses were distinguished. First, there were equivocal responses that made the slight but distinct change from replying 'You did' to 'It was'. For example, 'It was OK, but there were things that could have been improved'. This subtly changed the answer from the person to the presentation. A second group of responses simply postponed the unpleasant reply. The respondent gives an oblique response, then changes the topic by suggesting a meeting later to talk more about it, rather than answering the question fully. For example, 'I wasn't quite sure what it was you were driving at sometimes. But the idea behind it was good. Why don't we have coffee after class so we can talk more easily?' The third kind of equivocal response is one that hints at an answer without answering the question directly. For example, 'You should have spent a little more time preparing for the presentation. All it needed is just a little more work and it would have been a really good presentation'.

The responses to these scenarios are then rated by observers along four dimensions: sender, clarity, receiver and context. Bavelas *et al.* (1990, p. 34) state that 'All messages that would (intuitively or otherwise) be called equivocal are ambiguous in at least one of these four elements'. The sender dimension refers to the extent to which the response is the speaker's own opinion; a statement is considered more equivocal if the speaker fails to acknowledge it as his own opinion, or attributes it to another person. Clarity refers to comprehensibility, an unclear statement being considered more equivocal. The receiver dimension refers to the extent to which the message is addressed to the other person in the situation, the less so the more equivocal the message. Context refers to the extent to which the response is a direct answer to the question – the less the relevance, the more equivocal the message. The results of these ratings clearly showed that responses associated with 'avoidance–avoidance' conflicts were judged as significantly more equivocal.

In the context of equivocation theory, the author conducted an analysis of the celebrated television interview between Martin Bashir and the late Diana, Princess of Wales (Bull, 1997). The interview was broadcast on 20 November 1995 and was widely considered to have accelerated the rift between Diana and Prince Charles, which led to the announcement of their divorce the following year (12 July 1996).

The focus of the analysis was on what Bavelas *et al.* would term the context dimension, the extent to which Diana gave direct replies to Martin Bashir's questions. Of particular interest were 'answers by implication', responses in which Diana did not make her views explicit but where, nevertheless, the response carried a strong implicative reply. It was noted that all Diana's answers by implication took the form of critical comments. Further analysis of critical comments throughout the interview as a whole showed that whereas criticisms of Prince Charles, the Royal Family and Mrs Parker Bowles (with whom Charles had publicly admitted having an affair) were typically implicit, criticisms of the Royal Household were typically explicit.

Such implicative responses would certainly be regarded as a form of equivocation in the theory discussed above, and could be readily under-stood in this context as reflecting an 'avoidance–avoidance' conflict. If on the one hand, Diana had been too outspokenly critical in this interview, she might have alienated public opinion, exacerbated and embittered an already difficult situation with her husband and with the Royal Family, she might even have been frightened of some form of retaliation. Conversely, if she avoided comment on her husband and the Royal Family, or even denied there were any problems between them, she would not be able to give her side of the story and would look foolish for having agreed to give the interview in the first place. This second difficulty can be seen as underlying not so much individual questions but the interview as a whole, in the sense that once having agreed to it, she put herself under considerable pressure to make at least some comment about her family relationships. However, whereas in equivocation theory no particular distinction is made between not replying to a question and answering by implication, in the context of the Diana interview, answers by implication had distinct interactional advantages. Although existing theory has greatly enhanced our understanding of the circumstances under which equivocation occurs, further consideration needs to be given to the interactional consequences of different forms of equivocation.

The role of face

Equivocation, according to the theory described above, is motivated by an 'avoidance–avoidance' conflict. However, this theory does not specify exactly what it is that people are trying to avoid, beyond certain kinds of negative consequences. In one particular context, that of political interviews, it has been proposed that it is the danger of losing face that is a prime source of 'avoidance–avoidance' conflicts (Bull *et al.*, 1996). That is to say, politicians seek to avoid making certain kinds of responses that might put them in a bad light. This emphasis on losing face is not presented as an alternative to the concept of the 'avoidance–avoidance' conflict, rather as an explanation as to why politicians find particular responses aversive (Bull, 1998a). Nor is it proposed as an explanation for every type of avoidance–avoidance conflict. For example, the conflict incurred by receiving an unwelcome gift (described on p. 68) does not seem to be readily explained in terms of threats to face (Bavelas, 1998). In this case, the dichotomy seems to be one of saying something that is true but hurtful or dishonest but avoids causing distress. However, in the context of political interviews, threats to face do seem to be of particular importance, and are discussed in much greater detail in Chapter 5 (pp. 121–128).

The importance of face management is not confined to political interviews. There are good reasons for believing that concerns with face are salient in virtually all social encounters (Goffman, 1955/1967). Not only do people defend their own face in social interaction, there is also an obligation to defend the face of others. In many relationships, the members come to share a face, so that in the presence of third parties an improper act on the part of one member becomes a source of acute embarrassment to other members (Goffman, 1955/1967). According to the theory of politeness devised by Brown and Levinson (1978, 1987), face preservation is a primary constraint on the achievement of goals in social interaction. Face is important in all cultures, it can be lost, maintained or enhanced. 'Some acts are intrinsically threatening to face and thus require "softening"' (Brown & Levinson, 1978, p. 24). Linguistic actions such as commands or complaints can be performed in such a way as to minimize the threat to what are termed positive and negative face, where positive face is the desire to be approved of by others and negative face the desire to have autonomy of action. So, for example, a request to do something could threaten someone's negative face (by restricting their freedom of action), whereas disagreements can threaten positive face (by showing a lack of approval).

Social interaction thus presents people with a dilemma. On the one hand, they wish to maintain each other's face, but on the other hand they often need to perform acts that threaten face. This dilemma can be resolved by engaging in what is variously termed 'face-work' (Goffman (1955/1967) or politeness (Brown & Levinson, 1978, 1987). The essence of politeness is the performance of a face-threatening act in such a way as to minimize potential threats to face (Brown & Levinson, 1978, 1987). For example, people often perform acts indirectly (e.g. 'Could you open the door?'), rather than directly (e.g. 'Open the door'), thereby seeking to minimize the threat to negative face through lessening the imposition on another's behaviour (Holtgraves, 1998).

People will also seek to soften the force of utterances, such as disagreements, which threaten the positive face of others. A number of ways of doing this were identified from a study of conversations between students asked to discuss topics on which they were known (from a previously administered attitude questionnaire) to have divergent opinions (Holtgraves, 1997). Three main strategies were identified: seek agreement, avoid disagreement and assert common ground.

'Seeking agreement' and 'asserting common ground' are one means of softening overall disagreement. For example, in a discussion between two people who disagreed about capital punishment, one person was able to develop the argument that state-sponsored executions involve hypocrisy, a point with which the other person could agree. Again, two people who disagreed about abortion found that they could agree over the subtopic of the point at which life actually begins. 'Asserting common ground' was often signalled by the use of the phrase 'you know', whereby the speaker seeks alignment with the other conversationalist by claiming that the other is familiar with the general idea of what is being asserted. Agreement might also be expressed through simply repeating a portion of the prior speaker's remarks, thereby demonstrating attentiveness to what he or she is saying.

'Avoiding disagreement' was the other main strategy identified. In fact, on closer inspection, this often appears to be not so much a means of avoiding disagreement but of reducing its force. For example, there are degrees to which a speaker can commit him or herself to the strength of the proposition being expressed. Rather than simply asserting one's beliefs baldly (e.g. 'Abortion is wrong'), a more polite way is to 'hedge' the opinion in some way (e.g. 'I think abortion is wrong'). In Holtgraves' sample, this was by far the most common strategy. Similarly, the disagreement might be started with the preface 'Well', or might be preceded with agreement with part of what the other speaker has just said.

The speaker might also soften the force of the disagreement by downgrading him or herself personally. A relatively frequent strategy was to personalize one's opinion, that is to say, a speaker would sometimes state that this was only his or her opinion, and hence not to be taken as some absolute truth. Again, the speaker might use some other form of self-deprecation as a way of downplaying the disagreement, for example, by negatively evaluating their own ideas. Similarly, the speaker might express distaste with some aspect of the position they are advocating. Thus, one speaker says in relation to abortion, 'I think that it should be allowed because *not that I'd ever want to have one* but it's just that it's the woman's choice regarding her body'.

Conversation analysts have also studied disagreements, but their analysis does not make use of the concept of face. Instead, they regard discourse as having what is termed a 'preferred structure'. So, for example, the preferred responses to assessments and offers are agreements and acceptances; the dispreferred responses are disagreements and refusals respectively. A disagreement is a dispreferred move and, when such moves occur, they are marked (in the linguistic sense) in some way. For example, disagreements can be characterized by different forms of delay (Pomerantz, 1984). One form of delay is silence: in the course of disagreeing, a person might initially simply not respond. Another type of delay is requesting clarification, for example by 'what?', 'hm?' or by simply repeating what has been said. Disagreements can also be delayed within a speaking turn. A speaker could preface the disagreement with 'uh' or 'well' (thus displaying reluctance or discomfort), or by agreeing with part of the speaker's utterance, thereby softening the force of dissent.

However, there might be certain circumstances under which disagreements are preferred to agreements. If one person makes a self-deprecating remark, then if the second speaker agrees it is tantamount to making a criticism. In such circumstances, disagreements commonly take the form of partial repeats, negations or complements. One speaker might say, 'I'm trying to get slim' to which the other speaker replies 'Slim? You don't need to get any slimmer'; here, a partial repeat is followed by a stated disagreement. Disagreements can also include negations. One speaker might say 'You're not bored?' to which the other speaker replies 'Bored? No, we're fascinated'. Disagreements with self-deprecations also frequently include complements.

In contrast, agreements as a preferred conversational move do not show the kind of linguistic masking characteristic of dispreferred actions. Different types of agreement have been distinguished, referred to as upgrades, downgrades and same evaluation (Pomerantz, 1984). The upgrade is the strongest form of agreement in which one speaker emphatically endorses the opinion of another. This might be through use of a stronger evaluative term. One speaker might say 'Isn't he cute?' to which the second speaker replies 'Oh he's adorable'. Another form of upgrade occurs when the second speaker intensifies the evaluation. One speaker might say 'You must admit it was fun last night' to which the second speaker replies 'It was *great* fun'.

Same evaluation is another type of agreement in which the second speaker simply repeats the evaluation of the first speaker. One speaker might say 'She was a nice lady – I liked her' to which the second speaker replies 'I liked her too'. Same evaluations constitute a form of agreement but they can also preface disagreements and, for this reason, can be considered a rather weak form of agreement. This trend is even more pronounced with downgraded agreements where one person agrees with another but in a weakened form. So, for example, one speaker might say 'Oh it was just beautiful' to which the second speaker replies 'Well, thank you, I thought it was quite nice'. Downgraded agreements frequently precede disagreements.

These analyses of disagreements by Holtgraves and Pomerantz are similar in many ways. But whereas Holtgraves makes explicit use of the concept of face, Pomerantz (working within the framework of conversation analysis) talks only of dispreferred and preferred actions. However, just as the concept of face can be used to provide an explanation for why in certain circumstances 'avoidance–avoidance' conflicts lead to equivocation, so too can it be used to provide an explanation for why certain forms of linguistic action are dispreferred and are consequently softened or masked in some way.

The Linguistic Category Model

Rather than focusing on conversational moves such as disagreements or equivocation, a different level of analysis is that of the individual words themselves. The choice of one word rather than another to describe a person or an action can, in itself, have considerable significance. It is a central concern of what is known as the Linguistic Category Model (Semin & Fiedler, 1988, 1991). According to this model, words used in connection with interpersonal events and persons can be divided into four main types: descriptive action verbs, interpretative action verbs, state action verbs and adjectives.

In a descriptive action verb there is no interpretation of the action, merely a description of it. Typically, it refers to one particular activity and at least one physically invariant feature shared by all the actions to which the term is applied, for example, kiss always involves the mouth, phone always involves the phone, kick always involves the foot. In contrast, interpretative action verbs not only classify and discriminate behaviours but also interpret them, for example, encourage, mislead, cheat, flatter. Furthermore, there is no physically invariant feature in the case of interpretative action verbs, which refer to a multitude of different actions that might have nothing in common (e.g. there is no single common feature shared by the different instances of helping, hurting or challenging). State verbs refer to mental and emotional states or changes therein, as opposed to overt behaviour (e.g. like, hate, notice, envy), whereas descriptive and interpretative action verbs normally have a clearly defined beginning and end. Adjectives (such as honest, impulsive, reliable or helpful) are highly abstract, have no object or situation reference and are detached from specific behaviours.

The point of these distinctions is that exactly the same behaviour can be described at different linguistic levels and that this freedom of choice allows the potential for different linguistic strategies. For example, an aggressive episode can be downplayed as merely 'pushing' or 'shouting' (descriptive action verbs) when referring to oneself or one's own group, but raised to the interpretative action level (e.g. 'hurting' or 'insulting') or adjective level (e.g. 'brutal' or 'mean') when the same behaviour is performed by someone who is a member of another group (Fiedler & Semin, 1996).

A study of lexical choice in the context of intergroup rivalry was conducted in the context of the *palio* (Maass *et al.*, 1989) – a kind of horse race held in various cities in Italy, most famously Siena. Members of the various sections or quarters of the city (so-called *contrada*) compete against one another. The *palio* is a public festival that takes place in the central square of the city, where members and supporters of each *contrada* cheer for their teams. Identification with each *contrada* is very strong, partly because they are in direct competition with one another but also because of the *palio*'s long historical tradition.

The *palio* of Ferrara dates back to 1279, it was only ever interrupted during the extremities of the Black Death in the fourteenth century. In an experiment conducted in modern Ferrara, people from two *contradas* were asked to describe a series of cartoons depicting either socially desirable behaviours (e.g. helping) or socially undesirable behaviours (e.g. dropping litter); these behaviours were attributed either to a member of their own *contrada* or to a rival *contrada*. Exactly as predicted, socially desirable behaviours were described at a higher level of abstraction when attributed to a member of the person's own group, whereas socially undesirable behaviours were described at a higher level of abstraction when attributed to a member of the other group (Maass *et al.*, 1989).

Thus, the use of abstract language can be seen indirectly to reflect intergroup rivalries. In another study, a comparison was made between language abstraction and other more direct measures of discrimination. The experiment was conducted in the context of the rivalry between two Italian basketball teams (Franco & Maass, 1996). One of these teams

(Benetton) was known for its uninhibited expression of intergroup hostility, the other (Viola) for considering such aggressive behaviours unacceptable. In order to test overt discrimination, the fans were asked to say how they might distribute fictitious funds from the Italian Olympic Organization to the rival clubs, and to list three adjectives that best described their own team and the rival team. On these measures, Benetton fans were found to show significantly more bias than Viola fans in favour of their own club. But when asked to describe a series of cartoons (as in the Maass *et al.* (1989) study above), both groups showed a comparable level of linguistic bias by describing negative behaviours (such as unfair play) at a more abstract level when displayed by the outgroup as opposed to the ingroup. Thus, it would seem that Viola supporters showed less discrimination only when tested on overt, explicit measures of intergroup rivalry. When tested on more subtle measures based on language abstraction, both Viola and Benetton fans showed a significant bias against the rival team.

These findings have some interesting implications. In recent years there has been considerable interest in the development of unobtrusive measures of prejudice, given that, as a result of widespread social change, the overt expression of discriminatory attitudes has become far less socially acceptable. Level of abstraction might be one such unobtrusive measure of prejudice, in the sense that people might be either unaware of language abstraction or unable to exert intentional control over it.

Prejudiced attitudes can also be notoriously difficult to change, and these findings suggest one possible explanation for this. For example, a man is observed running into a burning house and returning a few seconds later carrying a small child in his arms. News reporters could relate this story at different levels of abstraction. They might provide an interpretation ('The man saved the child from the flames'), or they might attribute abstract dispositions to the man, describing him as courageous or heroic. Furthermore, they might communicate the story at a lower level of abstraction if the man is a member of a different group. If socially undesirable behaviours by members of outgroups are seen as reflecting enduring ethnic dispositions, then even positive behaviours by the outgroup might not modify prejudiced attitudes, they could simply be seen as no more than exceptions to the underlying rule. As abstract descriptions, stereotypes may be highly resistant to disproof through contrary information.

The Linguistic Category Model has been extensively criticized by Edwards and Potter (1993, 1999) from the perspective of discursive psychology (see Chapter 1, pp. 11–13). In particular, they object to the notion that some information exchanged in discourse can be treated as purely descriptive (descriptive action verbs). From the perspective of discursive psychology, no talk is purely descriptive, it always represents a construction of events (Edwards & Potter, 1993). More fundamentally, Edwards and Potter object to the abstraction of words from context, which, they argue, is a key feature of Linguistic Category Model methodology. They reject what they call 'coding-and-counting methods', which '. . . systematically, methodically, omit the kinds of sequential, contextualized, interaction-oriented nature of what conversation analysts call "talk-in-interaction"' (Edwards & Potter, 1999, p. 828).

Fiedler and Schmid (1999) strongly reject these claims. They point out that contextual information is intrinsic to their four main dimensions of analysis. Thus, descriptive action verbs are the most context-dependent and adjectives the least, which is one reason why adjectival trait descriptions are more resistant to change. They further point out that the Linguistic Category Model has been successfully applied to a number of examples of 'talk-in-interaction', such as verbatim protocols of the Nuremberg Trials (Schmid & Fiedler, 1996) and transcripts of speeches in simulated courtrooms (Schmid & Fiedler, 1998). They also rather wittily analysed the choice of words in Edwards' and Potter's (1993) own paper to illustrate how its rhetoric was biased to promote their own Discursive Action Model at the expense of the Speech Category Model (Schmid & Fiedler, 1999). Clearly, this is a debate that will continue!

Conclusions

Three principal ways in which speech can be analysed have been presented in this chapter: organization, style and content. There is, of course, considerable overlap between these three different dimensions of speech; possible interrelationships are discussed in this final section.

One way in which conversation (or at least American and British conversation) is characteristically organized is in terms of an orderly exchange of turns, following the basic rule of one speaker at a time (the single floor). A second, less formal pattern of conversation has also been identified, referred to as the collaborative floor. In this form of conversation, overlapping speech is commonplace but seems not to be regarded as interruptive. Such conversations seem to be essentially a collaborative, cooperative activity, which do not follow the basic rule of one speaker at a time. Through microanalytic research, interruptions have been distinguished from noninterruptive simultaneous speech in a variety of ways. Interruptions have also been related to personality, gender and speech style.

The analysis of communicative style has been the principal concern of Communication Accommodation Theory. Its focus has been on the circumstances under which both convergence and divergence can occur. Convergence refers to a strategy, whereby individuals adapt to each other's speech through a wide range of verbal and nonverbal features, such as accent, pronunciation, speech rate, pauses and utterance length. Divergence refers to the way in which speakers accentuate communicative differences between themselves and others. It is also possible to be either over- or underaccommodating in communicative style, hence it has been proposed that there are optimal levels of convergence.

A number of forms of content analysis were also discussed in this chapter. Particular attention was given to analysing the functions of speech, using questions, replies and nonreplies to questions as an example. The theory of equivocation was discussed, as was the Linguistic Category Model, the role of face and face management. In Communication Accommodation Theory, it is readily acknowledged that convergence and divergence can occur in terms of content as well as style (e.g. Giles & Smith, 1979), but in practice this possibility has been given relatively little consideration.

The theory of equivocation is of interest in this context, given that equivocation can arguably be regarded as an important form of speech accommodation. Thus, a person who equivocates to avoid commenting unfavourably on an unsuitable gift from a well-liked friend is in effect accommodating to avoid upsetting the friend. In fact, many of the 'avoidance–avoidance' conflicts presumed to underlie equivocation could be created in part by a wish to avoid speech divergence (speech that contradicts or upsets the opinions of others). Equivocation and speech accommodation can both be motivated by concerns about face management – the need to avoid making oneself or other people look bad – and the need to show approval of others (positive face). Theories of speech accommodation, equivocation and face management have developed largely in isolation from one another but their possible interrelationships might be worth further consideration.

One particular advantage of the concept of speech style is that it can be used in a nonevaluative sense. While recognizing that groups can differ in their style of communication, there is no necessary implication that one style of communication is better than another. However, differences in style can underlie difficulties in communication between members of different cultures or subcultures. Nowhere has the concept of style in intergroup communication been more influential than in the study of language and gender (Tannen, 1991). Although men and women within a given culture may speak the same language, it has been argued that they learn to use it in different ways. Hence, it has been proposed that communication between the sexes can be seen as a form of cross-cultural communication, plagued by mutual misunderstandings in the same way as other forms of intercultural communication. This proposal is considered in much greater depth in the following chapter as part of a wider discussion of gender and communication.

4   Gender and communication

This chapter is the first of two intended to present the results of micro-analytic research in particular contexts. Its topic – gender and communication – is an enormous one, which can be approached from a variety of perspectives. Contemporary feminism has been one major influence, in particular the belief that microanalysis can identify how male dominance is exerted and sustained in a predominantly patriarchal society. Again, there are researchers who have been inspired less by any particular political agenda, more by a concern simply to document and understand whether men and women differ in the way in which they communicate. Other perspectives have included a focus on sexual identity, for example, communication by gays, transsexuals or transvestites. In addition, there has been considerable interest in masculinity and femininity as dimensions of personality, which could be reflected in different patterns of communication.

All these are interesting perspectives in their own right but the aim of this chapter is not to provide a comprehensive review of gender. The intention is rather to address one particular issue as an illustrative example of microanalytic research, specifically, whether men and women differ in the way in which they communicate. The chapter is divided into two main sections, the first on nonverbal communication, the second on speech. Each section is summarized below:

Section 1. Nonverbal communication:
     touch
     other nonverbal gender differences:
          judgement accuracy
          expression accuracy
          channel differences:
               smiling
               gaze
               body movement
               interpersonal distance
     explanation of gender differences in nonverbal behaviour.

Section 2. Speech:
     gender, language and power
     powerless speech
     empirical studies of women's language:
         hedges and tag questions
         intonation
         interruptions
         politeness
     communication between cultures
     the work of Deborah Tannen
     evaluation of the two-cultures approach.

Nonverbal communication

Touch

The analysis of gender differences in touch provides a striking example of the explicit link between feminism and microanalytic research. In one study by Nancy Henley (1973), observations were made of intentional touch in various locations around the American city of Baltimore. The results showed a significant gender difference: men typically initiated touch, women were typically its recipients. Touch, it was argued, has traditionally been regarded as expressive of intimacy, but it can also be interpreted in terms of power. In effect, touch can be understood as the nonverbal equivalent of calling another person by their first name. If people feel free to reciprocate the use of first names, then it can express friendliness, affection or intimacy. But if someone is addressed by their first name and does not feel free to reciprocate, then it can indicate a difference in status or power. So too with touch. It can indicate closeness and togetherness when used reciprocally but status and power when used nonreciprocally. Thus, the intimacy and status interpretations of the meaning of touch are not incompatible (Henley, 1973).

According to this analysis, touch between men and women is often related to power rather than intimacy; in short, it is one of the chief means used by men to 'keep women in their place'. Gestures of power provide the micropolitical structure, the thousands of daily acts through which non-verbal influence takes place, which underlie and support the macropolitical structure. Nonverbal control is of particular importance to women, who are more sensitive to such cues. Researchers have overemphasized the expressive functions of nonverbal communication, while neglecting its significance as a means of maintaining social control (Henley, 1977).

This analysis is both forceful and provocative, it acquires much of its impact through the explicit link between microanalysis and feminism. But the conclusions are by no means self-evident: both the observations and their interpretation are open to dispute. For example, even if touch is typically initiated by men, this need not necessarily reflect male dominance. One possibility is that women have a preference for warm, intimate relations with others, that they simply like being touched; men in touching them recognize this fact (Hall, 1984). Alternatively, women in public places might well avoid touching men for fear of receiving unwelcome sexual advances; no information was given on the relationships between the participants, so we do not know whether these touches were between friends, intimates or strangers. Again, different kinds of touch have different meanings; women may well feel patronized and demeaned by a pat on the bottom, whereas a gentle touch on the hand might well communicate affection, intimacy and concern. Because the analysis was based simply on counting the number of touches between men and women, the observations are open to a variety of different interpretations.

The use of frequency counts presents a further problem; the results could simply reflect the fact that more males than females walk the streets of Baltimore. It would be more appropriate to calculate touches as a proportion of the total number of men and women observed in the study (Hall, 1984). And, of course, the pattern of touching in Baltimore might not be the same as touching in other locations, or even in Baltimore on another occasion.

In fact, whether Henley's results can be replicated has been the subject of intense debate. On the one hand, a significant gender difference was found in a study based on observations in two American cities (Major *et al.*, 1990). Men were significantly more likely to initiate touch than women in non-intimate public settings, although there was no gender difference when touch was observed in greetings or partings. On the other hand, a review of fourteen studies of touch showed, on average, little difference between men and women (Stier & Hall, 1984).

If the overall amount of touch does not differ, there might still be significant differences in particular types of touch. In one study, observations were made of 4,500 pairs of individuals in public places in the greater Boston area of Massachusetts (Hall & Veccia, 1990). Males were were significantly more likely to initiate an 'arm-around' gesture (in which the arm goes around the shoulders of the other person), whereas females showed a significant preference for an 'arms-linked' gesture (in which the arm is put through the other person's arm). However, the overall results for all observations of touch showed no difference between men and women.

In another study, touch was analysed in relation to both gender and status (Hall, 1996). Observations were made unobtrusively at three large academic meetings. The names of the observed individuals were subsequently retrieved from published sources in order to evaluate their relative personal and institutional status. There were no overall significant findings relating either to gender or status as to who initiated touch. However, when men and women were of equal status, then the man was significantly more likely to be the initiator. The type of touch was also significantly related to status. Whereas lower status individuals were more likely to initiate handshakes, higher status individuals were more likely to initiate what was termed a 'spot touch' (which was brief and very discrete).

Thus, the evidence does not seem to support broad generalizations about gender, status and touch. The problem is that there are many kinds of touch, which can serve many functions (e.g. Jones, 1994). So, for example, whereas a high status person might want to display status through touch, a low status person might use it to gain status, for example, by initiating a handshake with a more important person (Hall, 1996). Status might also be quite irrelevant to other forms of touch, which express affection, concern or intimacy. Henley (1995) stresses she never denied that nonverbal behaviour might express closeness and togetherness. Her point was rather that it does so only when used reciprocally, and that it expresses status and power when used nonreciprocally. But as she wryly observes, current debates over power and intimacy interpretations do seem rather like the proverbial argument as to whether a glass is half full or half empty. It would seem that much more detailed microanalytic research on the many different forms and meanings of touch is needed if its social significance is to be more effectively understood.

Other nonverbal gender differences

Despite these disagreements about whether it is men or women who initiate touch, there do appear to be consistent and reliable gender differences in nonverbal communication. In this respect, a particularly valuable contribution has been made by Judith Hall. The significance of Hall's work is that it is based on an extensive review of published studies on nonverbal communication. For example, in the study by Henley described above, how typical is the pattern of touch she observed? Have other researchers replicated the same pattern of touch in their own research? The only way to answer these questions is through an intensive review of the literature and this is what Hall (e.g. 1978, 1979, 1984) has done.

In summarizing this extensive literature, the material is organized under three main headings: judgement accuracy, expression accuracy and 'channels' of nonverbal behaviour (Hall, 1984). Studies of judgement accuracy are intended to test whether men and women differ in the accuracy with which they perceive (or decode) nonverbal cues. Studies of expression accuracy are concerned with whether men and women differ in the amount of information which they convey through nonverbal behaviour. Finally, studies of 'channels' focus on differences between men and women in their use of facial expression, gaze, interpersonal distance, touch and body movement.

Judgement accuracy

It has been shown consistently that women are better than men at decoding nonverbal cues. In one review, seventy-five studies of judgement accuracy were reported, based on both posed and spontaneous expressions (Hall, 1978). For posed expressions, the decoders' task was to guess, for example, which emotions the encoder intended to convey. For spontaneous expressions, encoders were asked to watch films or slides intended to arouse different emotions; the decoders' task was to guess from the encoders' nonverbal behaviour which films or slides they were watching. In all seventy-five studies, decoder judgements were made from the face, the body and from tone of voice, presented either alone or in combination on drawings, photographs, films or videotapes.

Tone of voice, it should be noted, presents special problems for the researcher, because it is hard for decoders to make judgements without being affected by the actual content of speech itself. For this reason, a number of special techniques have been devised, intended either to standardize or eliminate the effects of speech content. In standard-content speech, the encoder recites meaningless or emotionally ambiguous material, while varying the vocal expression to convey the intended emotion. Electronic filtering involves filtering all the speech frequencies above a certain level, so that the content becomes unintelligible; the result of this filtering process sounds like 'a kind of mumble as heard through a wall' (Starkweather, 1956). Randomized splicing involves cutting a stretch of recording tape into pieces and splicing them back together in random order, which makes the speech almost totally unintelligible (Scherer, 1971). Its major advantage over electronic filtering is that it preserves the full voice spectrum, but of course randomized splicing also destroys any paralinguistic information that is dependent upon the original speech sequence.

Of the seventy-five studies of decoding reviewed by Hall (1978), twenty-four showed a significant gender difference, twenty-three of which were in favour of women, a proportion that is statistically highly significant. The gender of the encoders does not make any difference: women are better decoders whether they are judging men or other women. Gender differences in decoding are also unaffected by the age of either the encoders or the decoders. Girls are better decoders than boys, just as women are better decoders than men, and it makes no difference whether the encoder is a child or an adult. Subsequently, a further fifty studies of gender differences in decoding have been reviewed (Hall, 1984). Eleven of these showed a significant gender difference, ten of which were in favour of women, providing further evidence in support of a significant female advantage in decoding nonverbal cues.

Expression accuracy

Women also typically encode more clearly than men, in the sense that they are more expressive and their nonverbal behaviour is easier to read (Hall, 1984). This has been referred to as expression accuracy. The term is intended to embrace not only skill in conveying meaning but also the transparency of the face, body or voice when emotion is experienced without conscious intent to communicate. Twenty-six studies of gender differences in expression accuracy were included in one review (Hall, 1979), a further twenty-three in a second review (Hall, 1984). In these studies, groups of judges (varying from two to 200 in number) were asked to make judgements from either posed or spontaneous nonverbal expressions. The criteria of accuracy for posed and spontaneous expressions were the same as in the decoding studies discussed above.

Both these reviews clearly show that the expressions of women are easier to judge than those of men. Of the twenty-six studies in the first review (Hall, 1979), nine showed a significant gender difference, eight of which were in favour of women. Of the seventeen studies in the second review (Hall, 1984), nine again showed a significant gender difference, seven of these were in favour of women. An analysis of all studies from both reviews showed that there was an important difference between visual and vocal cues. For visual cues there was a much larger gender difference; indeed, vocal cues on average showed no gender difference. Visual cues also correlated positively with age: the gender difference for visual cues is larger for adults than for children. However, most of this age effect was due to one study, which found that the spontaneous facial expressions of preschool boys could be more easily judged than those of preschool girls. But between the ages of 4 and 6 years, there is a dramatic decrease in the accuracy with which the spontaneous facial expressions of boys can be judged (Buck, 1977).

Channel differences

Women typically encode more clearly than men, in the sense that they are more expressive and their nonverbal behaviour is easier to read. A number of other studies have been focused on whether there are characteristic patterns of nonverbal behaviour associated with each gender:

SMILING

It is frequently reported that women smile much more than men. But this difference is much more pronounced for adults than for children or infants. Of eighteen studies of infants, only one showed a significant difference in smiling (Hall, 1984). Of twenty studies of children, only two showed a significant difference in favour of girls (Hall, 1984). However, of twenty-three studies of adults, over half showed that women smiled significantly more than men (Hall, 1984). A positive correlation of 0.45 between age and the magnitude of the gender difference (based on twenty studies) confirmed that this effect is much more pronounced for adults than for children (Hall, 1984).

A much more extensive review of gender and smiling was conducted, based on a total of 59,076 participants in 147 research reports (LaFrance & Hecht, 2000). The results of this meta-analysis showed a highly significant gender difference (mean weighted effect size: $d = 0.40$). With regard to age, the effect was most pronounced for the 18–23-year-old group, least pronounced for the 24–64-year-old group and intermediate for the 13–17-year-old group. Cross-cultural comparisons showed that the gender difference was most pronounced for the Caucasian group, which was significantly greater than the African–American participants. The gender difference for Caucasians was also greater than that for Asian participants, although not significantly so.

GAZE

Another commonly reported finding is that women gaze at other people more than men. In one study, American students took part in discussion groups comprising three people of the same gender. Women spent significantly more time looking at one another both while speaking and while listening, and also exchanged significantly more mutual glances (Exline, 1963). In fact, Exline (1972) reported that in all his studies of gender differences in gaze, women looked at others significantly more than men. A comparable trend was reported by Hall (1984). She reviewed studies of gaze for infants (thirty-three studies), children (twenty-five studies) and adults (sixty-one studies). In every study that showed a significant gender difference, females were found to gaze at others significantly more than males. Given that even from the earliest age, females appear to look at others more than males, it is perhaps not surprising that they should also show such a consistent advantage on tests intended to measure skill in decoding nonverbal cues.

BODY MOVEMENT

Body movement, it has been proposed, can be regarded as a 'gender identification signal' (Birdwhistell, 1971). That is to say, not only does each gender use characteristic forms of body movement, but 'feminine' males and 'masculine' females will also move in distinctive and identifiable ways.

Is it possible to ascertain a person's gender attitudes and gender identification from their nonverbal behaviour alone? An experiment was conducted in which three groups of participants were selected from a questionnaire intended to measure sex-role attitudes (Lippa, 1978). One group had strongly masculine characteristics, another strongly feminine characteristics and the third was described as 'androgynous' (with characteristics of both genders). Each participant was then asked to role-play being a junior high school math teacher and each performance was videotaped. The videotapes were shown to observers, who were asked to rate the participants in terms of masculinity/femininity under five different conditions: from the vision alone (head and body), the head only, the body only, the voice and from a still photograph. The observers were able accurately to guess the sex-role attitudes of the encoders only in the vision alone and the body alone conditions. Physical appearance or clothing seemed to be unimportant, as the observers could not make accurate guesses when they saw only the still photographs. Thus, movements of the body do seem to be of especial significance in conveying information about sex-role identification.

Exactly what body movements can be seen as characteristically masculine or characteristically feminine has received little systematic research. One exception to this trend comes from observations of the way in which books are carried (Jenni & Jenni, 1976). Two methods were distinguished. In type 1, one or both arms are wrapped around the books, the forearm on the outside of the books supports them. In type 2, the books are held underneath the arm at the side of the body. In a study at the University of Montana, 92 per cent of the women observed used the type 1 method of carrying books, whereas 95 per cent of the men used type 2. This observation was confirmed at a number of locations in North and Central America (Ontario, New York, El Salvador and Costa Rica). However, observations of children at kindergarten and first grade school showed that both boys and girls carried books like mature males (Jenni & Jenni, 1976).

However, there are gender differences in gesture that occur as young as 4 or 5 years old. Children with sexual identity problems have been shown to make exaggerated use of gestures associated with the opposite gender (Rekers, 1977). Three such gestures have been termed the 'limp wrist', 'flutters' (rapidly moving the arms up and down), and 'walking with a flexed elbow' (where the angle between the upper arm and forearm is between 0 and 135 degrees). In a study of normal children (aged between four and five, and between eleven and twelve), these three gestures were used significantly more by girls than boys (Rekers *et al.*, 1977). In another study of normal children (aged between seven and eight, and between ten and eleven), girls made significantly greater use of gestures referred to as a 'hand clasp' (touching the hands together in front of the body) and 'palming' (a grooming movement that involves touching the palm to the back, front or sides of the head above the level of the ears) (Rekers & Rudy, 1978). All these five gestures were also used by gender-disturbed boys regarded as 'effeminate' (Rekers, 1977).

Body movement thus does seem to serve as a gender identification signal. It seems to operate as a sort of 'code', a means whereby people (possibly quite unconsciously) convey messages about their gender attitudes and gender identification.

INTERPERSONAL DISTANCE

Consistent gender differences have been observed in the interpersonal distances that men and women prefer. In one study, American students took part in small discussion groups. The members of each group were always of the same sex, although the leader could be either male or female. Women sat significantly closer to each other than did men, and students of both sexes sat significantly closer to a female than to a male group leader (Giesen & McClaren, 1976).

In another study, observations were made of pairs of people looking at animals in a zoo (Baxter, 1970). Comparisons were made in terms of both age and ethnicity. Opposite-sex pairs of black and white Americans stood significantly closer than female pairs, who in turn stood significantly closer than male pairs. With Mexican–Americans, it was the female pairs who stood closest, but it was still the male pairs who stood furthest apart. Results for children (estimated ages between five and ten years) were less consistent. Whereas pairs of Mexican–American girls stood closer than other pairs, black American girls actually stood further apart than other pairs; for white American children there appeared to be no gender differences in interpersonal distance.

Explanation of gender differences in nonverbal behaviour

There do appear to be a number of consistent gender differences in non-verbal behaviour. Women are better than men in decoding nonverbal cues, they also typically encode more clearly, in the sense that they are more expressive and their nonverbal behaviour is easier to read. In addition, they look more at other people, smile more, show a preference for closer interpersonal distances and use distinctive types of body movement.

Differences between men and women in nonverbal behaviour have typically been interpreted as a function of their roles in society. Some authors have stressed the importance of differences in social power (e.g. LaFrance & Henley, 1997). According to this perspective, women's superior decoding skills could be due to their inferior position in society. Because of their lower social power, women have to become more alert to the behaviour and moods of powerful others, consequently, they develop more subtle means of exercising social influence (e.g. Weitz, 1974). Women's greater nonverbal expressiveness could also be understood in terms of power. People with less power might be expected to be more disclosing, which makes them more vulnerable and accountable, whereas those with greater power might exercise control through greater com-posure and concealment (Henley & LaFrance, 1984; LaFrance & Henley, 1997). Again, women's greater use of smiling, gaze and closer interpersonal distances can be understood as conveying a more submissive attitude (Henley & LaFrance, 1984; LaFrance & Henley, 1997).

This analysis in terms of power has been heavily criticized on the grounds that there are many other ways of interpreting gender differences in nonverbal behaviour (e.g. Hall & Halberstadt, 1997). For example, one proposal is that women are socialized to be more accommodating towards others (Rosenthal & DePaulo, 1979). Accommodating people are seen as wanting to understand what others are trying to communicate, and to make their own messages easy to understand. This concept of accommodation can also be used to interpret most of the gender differences in nonverbal behaviour reviewed above. Thus, women's greater skill in decoding can be seen as reflecting a wish to understand others, their clearer encoding a wish to make their own messages understood. Women's greater use of gaze, smiling and closer interpersonal distances can also be seen as conveying a more receptive, affiliative attitude.

The concept of accommodation does not, however, necessarily exclude explanations in terms of power. Being more accommodating could be seen as adopting a more submissive role and hence adapting to an inferior position in society (Henley & LaFrance, 1984; LaFrance & Henley, 1997). However, it cannot even be assumed that gender differences in nonverbal behaviour can only be explained in terms of sex-role socialisation. Even with newborn infants, it has been found that girls looked significantly longer at an adult than boys (Hittelman & Dickes, 1979). Perhaps there are innate differences between the sexes in the interest that they have in other people.

Speech

Gender differences in nonverbal communication are numerous and well-substantiated. It has also been claimed that there are important gender differences in the use of language. Men and women are said to differ not only in the way their talk is organized but also in their pronunciation, syntax and even in the actual words they use.

Gender, language and power

The term 'women's language' was introduced by the linguist Robin Lakoff in an article published in 1973, which she followed with a book, *Language and Woman's Place*, published in 1975. Lakoff identified a set of features occurring more frequently in women's speech than men's, which gave the impression that speakers were polite, tactful, hesitant, lacking in authority and not to be taken very seriously. Girls are brought up learning women's speech to avoid being criticized as unfeminine, but afterwards it is used against them to claim that women are unable to think clearly, to speak forcefully or to take part in a serious discussion. Women's language, according to Lakoff, is reflected in vocabulary, syntax and intonation; a number of the features she observed are listed below:

- Describing colours. Women make far more precise discriminations: words like beige, ecru, aquamarine and lavender are unremarkable in a woman's vocabulary but typically absent from that of most men. Lakoff describes observing a man helpless with suppressed laughter at two women discussing whether a book jacket was to be described as lavender or mauve. Men are considered to find such discussions amusing because they consider the question trivial, irrelevant to the real world. This lexical disparity reflects a social inequity in the position of women. Because women are not expected to make decisions on important matters, they are relegated the non-crucial decisions as a 'sop' – such as deciding how to name colours.
- Adjectives expressing approval or admiration. Some adjectives are neutral as to the gender of the speaker, that is, either men or women may use them (e.g. great, terrific, cool, neat). Other adjectives seem largely confined to women's speech (e.g. adorable, charming, sweet, lovely, divine). For a man to use the female words is likely to be damaging to his reputation, but a woman's use of the female words in the wrong context is also likely to present risks. For example, if a female advertising executive at an advertising conference said 'What a terrific idea' this might be perfectly acceptable. However, if she said 'What a divine idea' this might cause raised eyebrows and the reaction 'That's what we get for putting a woman in charge of this company'.
- 'Hedges'. Women's speech seems in general to contain more instances of words such as 'well', 'y'know', 'kinda', and so forth: words that convey the sense that the speaker is uncertain about what he or she is saying, or cannot vouch for the accuracy of the statement. Women make greater use of hedges because they are brought up to believe that asserting themselves strongly is not nice or ladylike, or even feminine.
- Tag questions. Phrases like 'isn't it' or 'wasn't it' can be tagged to the end of a declarative statement, turning it into a question, such as 'It was a very interesting play, wasn't it?'. Tags are used by women when a speaker is stating a claim but lacks full confidence in the truth of that claim, hence tag questions express uncertainty.
- Intonation. An intonational pattern, involving a rising inflection associated with a declarative sentence, is used only by women. For example, in response to the question 'When will dinner be ready?', a woman might say 'Oh, around six o'clock?'. It is as though the second speaker is saying 'Six o'clock, if that's all right with you, if you agree'. It is as if the speaker is seeking confirmation, although she might be the only one who has the requisite information. But, as a consequence, women might be perceived as unsure about their own opinions and, hence, not to be trusted with any serious responsibility.

These linguistic features identified by Lakoff have been referred to as a language of 'powerlessness'. Just as touch is supposedly used to keep women 'in their place', so too, women's speech is considered to reflect and perpetuate their inferior position in society. But to what extent is this style of language especially associated with women?

Powerless speech

The term 'powerless speech' was initially prompted by descriptions of women's language (Erickson *et al.*, 1978). However, it has been extended to refer to a speech style that, if used in various contexts (e.g. in court-rooms or job interviews) can result in speakers receiving less favourable evaluations in terms of intelligence and credibility than 'powerful' speakers (Erickson *et al.*, 1978). A powerless speech style is characterized by frequent use of those features believed to characterize women's language, such as intensifiers, hedges, hesitation forms and questioning intonation. But these features are considered to be more closely linked to social power and status than to gender (Erickson *et al.*, 1978).

To test this hypothesis, an experiment was conducted on how witnesses present evidence (Erickson *et al.*, 1978). The same substantive evidence was presented by either a male or female witness in either a powerful or powerless style. A witness using a powerful style was perceived as more attractive, irrespective of the gender of the witness or the rater. A witness using a powerful style was also perceived as more credible, but this effect was stronger when the witness and the rater were of the same gender. But most important of all, ratings of masculinity/femininity were not affected by the manipulation of powerlessness. This latter finding is very much in line with the proposal that a powerless style is more closely linked to social power and status than to gender.

In another study, recordings were made of over 150 hours of trials in a North Carolina superior criminal court (O'Barr & Atkins, 1980). By no means all the female witnesses in the sample showed a high frequency of the features that Lakoff describes, and indeed, some of the male witnesses used this manner of speech. However, more women tended to be higher in these features, and more men lower in these same features. Of course, such differences could be due – at least in part – to a greater tendency for women to occupy relatively powerless social positions. Furthermore, not only could powerless speech be a reflection of a powerless social situations: it would also seem to reinforce such inferior status.

Empirical studies of women's language

An important feature of the results described above was that ratings of masculinity and femininity were not affected by the manipulation of powerlessness: in short, powerless speech was not perceived as distinctively feminine. This raises the more fundamental question as to whether such linguistic features are specifically associated with women's speech, indeed, to what extent is it possible to justify the use of the term 'women's language?' Most of Lakoff's analysis was based on her own personal observations, presumably as a member of her own white, middle-class North American community in the early 1970s. So the question naturally arises, to what extent are these observations supported by more systematic research? Relevant studies are discussed below, as part of a wider consideration of empirical studies of women's language.

Hedges and tag questions

According to Lakoff, women make greater use than men of hedges and tag questions, both of which convey uncertainty. These two linguistic features were analysed in an experiment based on student discussions. The students were paired either with a lecturer or with a student of the same or opposite sex; thus, it was possible to tease out whether powerless language was associated with gender, or status or both (McFadyen, 1996). For hedges, no significant gender differences were found. (Hedges were defined as fillers and qualifiers. Fillers are empty words, such as 'you know', which fill gaps in talk; qualifiers, such as 'maybe', weaken the force of other words.) However, there were two significant gender differences. Whereas women made greater use of tag questions, men made greater use of hesitations; both these findings were unaffected by the relative status of the participants. Thus, if hesitations as well as tag questions are understood to reflect uncertainty, these results do not support the characterization of women's language as powerless.

It was also noted that so-called powerless speech might be used alongside powerful actions (McFadyen, 1996). For example, a male lecturer used the qualifier 'perhaps' in what was in effect a directive: '*Perhaps* if you were to look at question 2'. In another example, so-called powerless speech was used to qualify a powerful action (in this case a criticism) when a male lecturer said 'In a way, that's *sort of* dodging the issue . . .'. In both these examples, a person in authority used hedges to soften the force of his actions; but those actions were not powerless, nor does the use of hedges seem to indicate powerlessness.

In fact, hedges can serve a variety of functions. A study of the term 'you know' (regarded by Lakoff (1973) as a hedge) was conducted on New Zealand English (Holmes, 1986). It was found that 'you know' can express two quite distinct and opposing functions. It can express certainty and conviction (e.g. '*You know* very often you have presidents who are men . . .'). But it can also express the opposite, conveying doubt and uncertainty (e.g. 'The money seems to be going for basics rather than for things like *you know* extra equipment . . .'). Whereas women used 'you know' significantly more to convey certainty, men used it significantly more to convey uncertainty (Holmes, 1986). This is completely the opposite of what might have been expected from Lakoff's observations. A variety of ways were distinguished in which 'you know' can convey uncertainty. The crucial subcategory for the concept of powerlessness was termed the 'appealing' function of 'you know', that is to say, instances that convey the speaker's lack of confidence and need for reassurance in a social situation. There were no significant gender differences in the use of this subcategory.

Another hedge is the term 'I think'. But just as 'you know' can serve more than one linguistic function, so too can 'I think'. In fact, two principal functions have been identified, referred to as 'deliberative' and 'tentative' (Holmes, 1985). In its deliberative form, 'I think' is used to express confidence and commitment to a proposition, for example, 'I think they're absolutely wonderful!'. In its tentative form, it may express doubt and uncertainty, for example, 'It would be about two o'clock, I think'. An analysis of these two functions was conducted on a 25,000-word sample of New Zealand English (Holmes, 1985). Although there was no difference in the overall frequency with which men and women used 'I think', women used it as a booster more frequently than as a hedge, while the reverse was true for men. Again, this is precisely the opposite of what would have been expected from Lakoff's observations.

Just as the hedges 'you know' and 'I think' can serve a variety of linguistic functions, so too can tag questions. An analysis of gender differences in the use of tags was conducted on a 60,000-word corpus from predominantly middle-class, well-educated native speakers of New Zealand English, ranging in age from school children to people in their sixties (Holmes, 1995). The corpus was carefully matched for the quantity of female and male speech produced, and for the number of female and male contributors. It included equal amounts of informal conversations (collected in relaxed situations in people's homes) and formal interactions from classrooms and broadcast interviews.

Four principal functions of tag questions were identified. One is to express uncertainty; the speaker is simply uncertain of the facts and seeks confirmation (e.g. husband searching in newspaper says 'Fay Weldon's lecture is at eight isn't it?'). Another function is to facilitate conversation by inviting people to participate (e.g. to a guest at a dinner party 'You've got a new job Tom haven't you?'). Tags can also be used either to intensify or soften the force of a criticism. Thus, tags can be used in a confrontational manner, to pressure someone into a reply, or to boost the force of a criticism or a reprimand (e.g. 'Your performance will really have to improve, won't it? Otherwise you will be out of a job.'). But, with a different intonation, they can also be used to soften the force of a criticism (e.g. older brother to a younger brother who has just spilled milk on the floor 'That was a really dumb thing to do wasn't it?').

The results of the analysis did show significant gender differences, but in the reverse direction from what might have been expected from the portrayal of women's language as 'powerless'. Whereas men made much greater use of tags expressing uncertainty, women made much greater use of facilitative tags. Facilitative tags are used more extensively by those who might be seen as having some sort of responsibility for the success of an interaction, such as teachers in the classroom, interviewers on TV or radio, or the hosts at a dinner party. Their use in such contexts was found to occur irrespective of gender, but in situations that did not involve any obvious power or status differences, it was actually women who made greater use of facilitative tags (Holmes, 1995).

Thus, the studies reported above failed to show that women make greater use of hedges and tags to convey uncertainty. In fact, when these linguistic forms do convey uncertainty, they are used more by men. But hedges and tags do not only convey uncertainty, they can be used for a number of other reasons. This is important, because it highlights a basic problem with Lakoff's analysis of women's language. This is the assumption that an utterance's function can be analysed purely in terms of its linguistic form. Given that hedges and tags serve a number of different functions, this assumption is clearly mistaken. In short, the function of an utterance cannot be understood from an analysis of its linguistic form alone.

Intonation

Distinctive intonation is another feature believed to characterize women's language. Lakoff describes a particular pattern of intonation, involving a rising inflection associated with a declarative sentence, which she believes is used only by women, and which conveys uncertainty.

Gender differences in intonation were investigated in a study conducted on an American university campus (Edelsky, 1979). On the grounds that they were doing a survey for a class, male and female interviewers asked university students one of two questions: either where the student was born or what was their favourite colour. The students' replies were recorded and the intonation patterns analysed. Rising intonation was hardly ever used by either sex, but both males and females made frequent use of falling intonation. The only pattern used more frequently by women was a 'rise–fall–rise' intonation in response to questions from a female interviewer.

This 'rise–fall–rise' pattern, it was proposed, might have been used not to signal lack of conviction but to convey a desire for a longer conversation. A similar interpretation was proposed from the results of a dialect survey of New Zealand English (Britain, 1992). Not only were New Zealand women found to use high rising intonation more than men, but younger people used it more than older people, and Maoris more than Pakehas (the Maori term for a New Zealander of European descent). All these groups, it was proposed, share the value of involvement in discourse and use this particular intonation pattern to create involvement. High rising intonation was also found to occur most often in sections of narrative rather than in sections expressing the speaker's personal opinions. This would again be consistent with the view not that it indicates uncertainty, rather that it invites the listener to acknowledge what is being said, and hence to participate in conversation.

Although a number of studies have shown gender differences in language, there is little evidence to support the characterization of women's language as powerless: they do not seem to make greater use of either rising intonation or hedges or tags to convey uncertainty. But this does not rule out all interpretations of gender language differences in terms of power. For example, even if women's language is not characterized by 'powerlessness', men's language might be characterized by 'powerfulness'. Much less attention has been given to the concept of a men's language than to that of women's language, but there is one exception: the extensive literature on gender and interruptions. According to some analysts, the use of interruptions is a characteristic feature of men's conversational style, a means whereby they seek to maintain social control and deny women equal rights as conversational partners (Zimmerman & West, 1975). The literature on gender differences in interruptions is discussed in further detail below.

Interruptions

In the most well-known study of gender and interruptions, surreptitious tape-recordings were made of conversations between opposite sex pairs, pairs of men and pairs of women (Zimmerman & West, 1975). Three-quarters of the conversations were recorded in coffee shops and other public places in a university community. Whenever possible, the conversationalists were subsequently informed of the recording and their consent was obtained, although in some cases the abrupt departure of the participants made this impossible. The remaining quarter of the conversations were recorded in private residences to which the authors had casual access. In every case, consent was obtained after the recording had been made, and no refusals or complaints were encountered.

The authors then inspected the transcripts of the conversations for instances of simultaneous speech, subdivided into overlaps and interruptions. In an overlap, the second speaker starts to speak just before the first speaker stops talking (i.e. during the final word), hence overlaps were not regarded as interruptive.

In conversations between members of the same sex, both interruptions and overlaps appeared to be symmetrically distributed between speakers. But in conversations between members of the opposite sex, almost all the interruptions and overlaps were initiated by men. The authors compared their results to adult–child conversations, where the child often has only restricted rights to speak and to be heard. They argued that men deny women equal status as conversational partners, in effect, they treat women like children. 'Just as male dominance is exhibited through male control of macro-institutions in society, it is also exhibited through control of at least a part of one micro-institution' (Zimmerman & West, 1975).

However, this study has been severely criticized. In the eleven conversations between members of the opposite sex, there were forty-eight interruptions, of which forty-six came from men. The problem with this is that you might have one very talkative man who contributed a large proportion of the interruptions; indeed, one man did contribute thirteen interruptions, over one-quarter of the total (Beattie, 1982b). Nor do we know for how long each participant spoke: if one conversational partner was doing the bulk of the talking, it might have been necessary for the other to interrupt. Why people interrupt is an extremely important issue, which raises a much more fundamental criticism of the whole study. The authors defined interruptions as 'violations of a speaker's right to complete a turn' (Zimmerman & West, 1975), which seems to assume that interruptions are never justified. In fact, interruptions can occur for a variety of different reasons, not just as a means of exercising conversational dominance. They can, for example, reflect speaker enthusiasm and interest, they might simply reflect an aspect of conversational style (Tannen, 1984). As there was no analysis of the content of the conversations in the study, it is impossible to ascertain whether or not the interruptions might be regarded as justified.

This point can be neatly illustrated from another study by the authors in which they reported the following conversation (West & Zimmerman, 1983):

FEMALE: So uh you really can't bitch when you've got all those on the same
    day but I uh asked my physics professor if I couldn't change that
MALE: **Don't touch that**
FEMALE: What?
    (pause)
MALE: I've got everything jus'how I want it in that notebook, you'll screw
    it up leafin' through it like that.

Because the man's 'Don't touch that' occurs in the middle of the woman's sentence, it is regarded as an interruption and hence presumably as a 'violation of the speaker's right to complete a turn'. But interrupting to ask the woman to stop leafing through the notebook does not in itself violate the woman's right to talk. It seems a perfectly understandable reaction to ask someone to stop meddling with one's personal property at the time they are doing it, rather than waiting for the appropriate conversational transition point to do so (Tannen, 1991). Interruptions might or might not be justified but it cannot be arbitrarily assumed that interruptions are invariably violations of another person's right to speak.

It should further be noted that the gender differences observed by Zimmerman and West (1975) have not always been replicated by other observers. In another study (Murray & Covelli, 1988) just the opposite results were found: women interrupted men twice as often as men interrupted women. This study is directly comparable to that by Zimmerman and West because the tapes were made in the same historical period (mid-1970s), so that differences in the results should not be due to the effects of social change. In addition, the same coding procedures were employed, but on a much wider sample of conversations with a much larger corpus of interruptions (400 as opposed to fifty-five). Furthermore, comparisons were also made of different speech settings, and this was found to be a much more significant factor, which overrode any differences due to gender.

Opposing conclusions on gender and interruptions have also been reached by the authors of several narrative reviews. Whereas Holmes (1995) argues that men do initiate interruptions more than women, other reviewers maintain that there are no consistent gender differences (James & Clarke, 1993; Aries, 1996). One way of tackling these competing claims is through the techniques of meta-analysis. Forty-three published studies of gender and interruptions were examined by Anderson and Leaper (1998). Their meta-analysis showed that although men were significantly more likely than women to initiate interruptions, the effect size ($d = 0.15$) was insubstantial. But when the analysis was restricted to what were termed 'intrusive interruptions' (attempts by one speaker to usurp the other's speaking turn), then the effect size was much larger ($d = 0.33$). However, the results were also affected by situational factors: the effect was more pronounced when the observations were made in naturalistic as opposed to laboratory settings, and in groups of three or more persons rather than pairs of conversationalists.

Hence, it is important not to consider gender in isolation from other factors that can affect interruptions. One interesting example comes from a study of gender and status, based on observations of female British recruitment consultants who worked in employment agencies (Mott & Petrie, 1995). During the course of a day's work, the consultants would speak to both men and women of higher and lower status to themselves; hence, this was an ideal setting for the study. A client – one to whom the personnel service was being supplied by the recruitment consultant – was regarded as being of higher status. An employee, or someone seeking to be employed or placed in work by the agency, was regarded as of a lower status. Telephone conversations between the consultants and both clients and prospective employees were tape-recorded. Women who were seeking employment were interrupted significantly more frequently and successfully than any of the other three groups (men seeking employment, male clients, female clients). Thus, there was a clear interaction between gender and status: lower status females were more likely to be interrupted by the higher status female recruitment consultants.

In summary, although Anderson and Leaper's meta-analysis does show that men are significantly more likely than women to initiate interruptions, it is also important to be aware that interruptions are highly sensitive to situational context, and to the relationship between the conversationalists.

Politeness

Powerfulness and powerlessness are not the only way in which gender differences in language can be understood. One alternative interpretation is in terms of politeness. Lakoff (1973, 1975) observed that women are expected to be more 'polite', and cited in support of this differences in pronunciation. In particular, women make use of more standard language forms than men. For example, in spoken English, the suffix 'ing' can be pronounced with the final 'g' (standard form) or without the final 'g' (non-standard form). The results of a study conducted in the English city of Norwich showed that the standard form was used more by women, the non-standard form more by men (Trudgill, 1983). A self-evaluation test of language use was also administered. Self-reported use of standard English was underestimated by men, but overestimated by women. Standard English, it was proposed, has connotations of femininity, non-standard of masculinity. Hence, not only do men and women differ in their actual use of these linguistic forms, they would also like to think that they use them more than they actually do. Even when allowing for other variables such as age, education and social class, it has been shown in a number of American studies that women consistently use more standard language forms, for example, in New York City (Labov, 1966), North Carolina (Levine & Crockett, 1966) and Detroit (Shuy *et al.*, 1967).

Politeness does not just underlie gender differences in pronunciation. In her book *Women, Men and Politeness*, Janet Holmes (1995) has argued that it is politeness, not powerlessness, which is the fundamental difference between men and women in the way in which they use language. This proposal is set in the context of politeness theory (Brown & Levinson, 1978, 1987), which was discussed in Chapter 3 (pp. 70–71). Holmes' argument is that women tend to be more polite than men, in particular they are likely to express more positive politeness or friendliness in the way in which they use language.

In addition, Holmes (1995) proposes that gender differences in politeness can be understood in the context of an important distinction between what are termed the 'referential' and 'affective' functions of language. The 'referential' is the function of conveying information, facts or content; the 'affective' is the function of conveying feelings and reflecting social relationships. Every utterance must express both functions, although one could be primary. According to Holmes, women tend to focus on the social, or affective, function of talk, men on its referential function.

For example, the term 'you know' can be used with either a referential or affective function. In its referential function, it can indicate doubt or uncertainty, signal linguistic imprecision, or mark a qualification; in this sense, it is used more by men (Holmes, 1986). In its affective function, it can signal that the speaker attributes understanding to the listener, it can appeal to the listener's sympathy or it can function as a booster to emphasise the mutual knowledge of the participants. In this latter sense, it conveys certainty and conviction, and is used more by women (Holmes, 1986). By expressing confidence that the listener knows or understands what is being talked about, it conveys a positive regard for the listener, and can be understood as a form of politeness.

Gender differences in the use of the term 'I think' can also be understood in terms of the referential/affective distinction. In its referential form, 'I think' can serve as a hedge, indicating uncertainty, whereas in its affective form it serves as a booster. However, its affective form can be either positive or negative. Where 'I think' is used to boost an agreeing statement, it can also be regarded as a form of positive politeness. So if the second speaker endorses what the first speaker has just said with 'I think that's absolutely right', this clearly expresses positive regard. But 'I think' can also be used to strengthen a disagreement, such as 'I think that's complete rubbish', which certainly is not at all polite! Women not only used 'I think' considerably more frequently than men as a booster, they also did so to boost agreeing statements; hence, it can also be understood as a form of positive politeness (Holmes, 1985).

A number of different functions of tag questions have been distinguished (Holmes, 1995). Tags can convey uncertainty and, in this referential form, are used more frequently by men. But tags can also be used as a means of facilitating conversation, and as such are used more frequently by women. In this sense, tags can be understood in terms of politeness, a means whereby women seek to involve others in conversation and express a positive regard for them. A similar function has been argued for high rising intonation, which is used by a number of social groups (including women) as a means of creating involvement (Britain, 1992).

Thus, a number of the linguistic forms that Lakoff unsuccessfully tried to interpret in terms of powerlessness can be much more readily understood in terms of politeness. It should be noted that Lakoff and Holmes differ significantly in the way in which they understand politeness. Lakoff regards politeness as one aspect of the powerlessness of 'women's language', as a kind of handicap that perpetuates their inferior position in society. Holmes seems to regard politeness rather as an aspect of communicative style, that is to say, women attach greater value to politeness in language. Holmes's view is consistent with an alternative perspective that has developed in recent years, according to which men and women can be seen as coming from two cultures, who communicate in different ways. Although these two cultures share a common language, they differ both in the way in which they interpret language and in the way in which their language is interpreted. They can also sometimes have trouble in communicating with one another, because, for example, they have different ways of interpreting and understanding politeness. The two-cultures approach is discussed below.

Communication between cultures

The origins of this two-cultures approach lie in the work of the linguist John Gumperz. Gumperz (1982, 1992) explored the idea that distinct groups of people developed their own styles of communication. Consequently, people who are socially distant from one another might experience frustration and misunderstanding through miscommunication. Conversation proceeds on the basis of shared assumptions, and miscommunication can take place when those common assumptions are not shared. Minor stylistic differences, such as whether a speaker uses a rising inflection with a question, can influence whether the speaker is perceived as hostile or polite and friendly. In Gumperz's work, the focus was on ethnic groups. In the situations he studied, inaccurate perceptions were not usually recognized as problems in communication. Instead, they were attributed either to personality problems or to negative racial stereotypes. Problems in interethnic communication were not assumed to be the result of bad faith or bad intention: miscommunication can occur even when well-intentioned people are trying their best to understand one another.

The two-cultures approach was first applied to gender differences in language by the anthropologists Daniel Maltz and Ruth Borker (1982), who took the view that men and women can be seen as belonging to two distinct subcultures and that failures in communication can be seen as comparable to the difficulties that arise when people from two different cultures converse. But it is not that men and women belong to two different cultures who speak different languages, rather, that it is their rules for interpreting language that differ. These different rules, it is proposed, are learned predominantly between the ages of five and fifteen, when boys and girls interact primarily with members of their own sex.

A good example is the interpretation of listener responses. Listener responses provide signals of continued interest and attention in what others are saying (see Chapter 3, p. 57) and it is well documented that they are used more frequently by women than by men (e.g. Roger & Schumacher, 1983; Roger & Nesshoever, 1987). But men and women also differ in the meaning they attach to listener responses, according to Maltz and Borker. They propose that for women a minimal response means 'I'm listening to you; please continue', whereas for men it has a stronger meaning, such as 'I agree with you' or at least 'I follow your argument so far'. Women's more frequent use of listener responses is in part simply that they are listening more often than men are agreeing. But this can also lead to misunderstandings. A man who receives frequent listener responses from a women might mistakenly believe that she is agreeing with every word that he says, whereas she is simply indicating that she is listening. Conversely, a women who receives only infrequent listener responses from a man might think that he is not listening, whereas he could believe that he is indicating only that he does not always agree. This explanation seems to account for two frequent complaints in male–female communication: women who get upset with men who never appear to be listening, and men who complain that because women always seem to agree, it is impossible to tell what they actually think.

In addition to listener responses, Maltz and Borker suggest five other areas where men and women probably have different conversational rules:

1. The meaning of questions. Women seem to see questions as part of the process of 'making conversation', whereas men seem to view them principally as requests for information.
2. Beginning an utterance and connecting it to what has been said before. Women's rules seem to require both an explicit acknowledgement and a link with the previous utterance. Men seem to have no such rule and in fact some male strategies call for ignoring the preceding comments.
3. Verbal aggression. Women seem to interpret this as personally directed, negative and disruptive. Men simply seem to see it as one way of conducting conversation.
4. Topic flow and topic shift. In particular, the literature on story telling seems to indicate that, for men, topic is fairly narrowly defined, it is adhered to until finished and shifts between topic can be abrupt; conversely, women have a system in which topic is developed progressively and shifts gradually.
5. Problem sharing and the giving of advice. Women tend to discuss problems with one another, sharing experiences and offering reassurances. In contrast, men view women and other men who present them with problems as making explicit requests for solutions. They respond by giving advice, by acting as experts, even by lecturing their audiences.

The idea that communication between men and women can be seen as communication between members of different cultures has been substantially developed and elaborated by Deborah Tannen (1991). This is discussed below.

The work of Deborah Tannen

Tannen has drawn a number of broad distinctions about the ways in which men and women approach the world, which have profound differences for the ways in which they communicate with one another. In particular, she sees men as approaching the world as an individual in a hierarchy, in which they are either one up or one down. Conversations are negotiations in which people try to achieve and maintain the upper hand if they can, and try to protect themselves from the attempts of others to push them around. Women, on the other hand, she regards as approaching the world as an individual in a network of connections. Conversations are a means of becoming close with other people, a means of achieving and preserving intimacy and avoiding isolation.

These different orientations have significant effects on the ways in which men and women communicate, in that they are trying to realize different aims in conversation:

- Joint plans. A man who checks with his wife before going out at the weekend might resent this, seeing it as a threat to his independence – as 'asking permission'. Conversely, the wife actually likes him doing this – it makes her feel involved with someone else and is evidence of connection and intimacy. Women can see evidence of connection as a virtue, whereas men might see it as reflecting incompetence or insecurity.
- Talking about troubles. Talking about troubles is another of the many conversational tasks that men and women do differently. Women expect others to match troubles talk with descriptions of their own troubles, whereas men adopt a more practical, problem solving approach. Women may find this practical approach distancing, and so resent it; conversely, men can become upset if their advice is not welcome or acted upon. Sympathy can be seen as potentially condescending, as putting the recipient in a one-down position, and men can dislike a woman's expression of sympathy for this reason. In refraining from expressing excessive sympathy with one another, men might, in fact, be seeking to avoid upsetting their mutual balance of power.
- Asking for information. Giving information can reinforce bonds between people, enhancing connection and intimacy; hence women are quite happy to ask for information. But in so far as information sets one up as the expert, the superior in knowledge, and the other as uninformed, inferior in knowledge, it can be seen as a move in the negotiation of status. Hence, many men dislike asking for information, because they feel it puts them in a one-down position.
- Public and private speech. Tannen proposes that men are more comfortable doing what she calls 'public speaking', whereas more women feel comfortable doing 'private speaking'. Another way of describing these differences is by using the terms report-talk and rapport-talk.

    For most women, the language of conversation is principally a language of rapport: a way of establishing connections and negotiating relationships. People feel their closest connections at home or in settings where they feel at home – with one or a few people with whom they feel close or comfortable. Emphasis is also placed on displaying similarities and matching experiences. From childhood, girls criticize peers who try to stand out or appear better than others. This makes it much harder for females to talk on public occasions, because of the fear of social disapproval.

For most men, talk is primarily a means to preserve independence, and to negotiate and maintain status in a hierarchical social order. This is done by exhibiting knowledge and skill, for example, by holding centre stage through activities such as story telling, joking or imparting information: this is what Tannen calls report-talk. From childhood, men learn to use talk as a way of getting and keeping attention, and receive approval for this. So they are more comfortable speaking in larger groups made up of people they know less well, hence with speaking in public.

Evaluation of the two-cultures approach

This two-cultures approach has become widely known in recent years, not least because of the immense popular success of Tannen's book *You Just Don't Understand*, which was published in 1991. One criticism of Tannen's work is that the evidence for her observations is essentially anecdotal. Nevertheless, the two-cultures approach does provide the basis for more systematic empirical investigations.

For example, participants in one study were asked to rate transcribed conversations to test whether men and women ascribe different meanings to listener responses and questions (Mulac *et al.*, 1998). In accordance with Maltz and Borker's (1982) observations, men rated listener responses and questions as significantly more controlling (in the sense of leading the conversation), whereas women rated listener responses as significantly more other-focused (in the sense of showing interest in the other person's opinion). Men also rated questions as significantly more sensitive, which seems much less consistent with Maltz and Borker's observations. Nevertheless, the results overall do support the proposal that men and women interpret language in different ways.

Another important criticism of the two-cultures approach is that although the analysis is essentially in terms of communicative style, the same gender differences can also be understood in terms of power. Thus, all the differences ascribed to culture by Maltz and Borker can equally be understood as reflecting cultural dominance (Henley & Kramarae, 1991):

● Listener responses. Men's sparing use of listener responses can be seen as not merely a cultural difference but also as a form of dominance. Given that there is ample evidence that people talk more when given this form of encouragement, the lack of such responses can discourage interaction and lead to the failure of topics initiated by women to become joint topics of the conversation (Fishman, 1983).

- The meaning of questions. Men's understanding of questions as requests for information rather than as conversational maintenance devices can alternatively be heard as taking to themselves the role of authority.
- Problem sharing and the giving of advice. The same interpretation can be offered of men's tendency to take the mention of a problem as an opportunity to act as experts and offer advice, rather than to sympathize or share their own problems.
- Topic flow and topic shift. Men supposedly tend to make abrupt topic shifts and either do not have or ignore a rule that demands that one's utterance links to the previous utterance. Controlling a situation and ignoring the other's rules (or the common rules) can also be understood as prerogatives of power.
- Verbal aggression. Men's overt use of verbal aggression can also be seen as a prerogative of power. In situations of inequality, the one of lesser power dare not show aggression to the other.

It should be noted that Tannen does not reject the proposal that cultural differences can also be understood in terms of power. In fact, she regards the opposition of culture and power as a false dichotomy (Tannen, 1994). To propose that women's and men's styles of communication can be understood in terms of cultural difference is not to deny that dominance also exists. Quite the contrary, in fact: the cultural framework provides a model for explaining how dominance can be created in face-to-face interaction. Stylistic differences can work very much to the disadvantage of groups that are stigmatized in society, and to the advantage of those who have the power to enforce their interpretations.

A further important criticism of the two-cultures approach is the serious danger of polarizing the behaviour of men and women (e.g. Aries, 1996, 1998). An extreme example is the popular best-seller on communication style in which men and women are portrayed metaphorically as coming from two different planets (*Men are from Mars, Women are from Venus,* Gray, 1995). The prevalence of this mode of thought can easily lead to an underestimate of the considerable overlap in behaviour between men and women. Furthermore, differences that have been found can be misrepresented as mutually exclusive.

This danger of polarization also applies more generally to all studies that have shown statistically significant differences between men and women. Such differences can be obtained even when there is considerable overlap between men and women and only a very small average difference between the groups (Aries, 1996). In an extensive critical review and re-evaluation of the research literature, Elizabeth Aries (1996) has described how originally she found the two cultures approach to be quite compelling (Aries, 1987) but subsequently came to realize its limitations. She goes on to argue that anyone is capable of displaying both masculine and feminine styles of interaction (Aries, 1996). Furthermore, the style employed will depend on other factors, such as the person's status, role, goals, conversational partners, and the characteristics of the situational context.

In the context of this debate, an interesting series of studies has been carried out by Anthony Mulac to assess whether untrained observers can identify gender just from transcripts of spontaneous speech. Typically, the speakers are asked to engage in a particular communication task (e.g. to describe a landscape photograph or solve a problem with a partner); their speech is recorded on audiotape and transcribed for later analysis. Mulac (1998) reviews five of his studies which consistently show that the observers cannot accurately identify the sex of the communicators with an accuracy that is any better than chance – in which case, the communicators must be displaying a high degree of linguistic similarity.

However, Mulac has also shown that the speech of men and women can be distinguished using a statistical procedure called stepwise discriminant analysis. This enables the investigator to look at variables in combination with one another, rather than taking one at a time. It is then possible to test whether weighted combinations of variables can be used to predict a criterion – in this case, the sex of the communicator. Mulac first used this procedure to analyse the public speeches of thirty university students (Mulac *et al.*, 1986). By using a weighted combination of twenty linguistic variables, it was found that the computer could reclassify the transcripts of these public speeches with 100 per cent accuracy. Mulac (1998) subsequently has reported a number of such studies, which show that weighted combinations of linguistic variables can accurately predict the sex of the communicator with a precision of between 70 and 100 per cent.

Mulac's findings have been criticized on the grounds that only a few linguistic markers of speech consistently discriminate between men and women (Aries, 1996). Out of thirty-five language variables studied, the majority were found either to predict gender differences in only a single study or to predict one sex in one study but the opposite sex in another study (Ragan, 1989). The most consistent features were a greater use of intensive adverbs and personal pronouns by women, and a greater use of directives by men (Aries, 1996).

Furthermore, it is possible that Mulac's results could be an artefact of the constrained experimental conditions under which the material for his transcripts is obtained. In another study (Martin, 1997), students were encouraged to record conversations at a time and a place of their own choosing; they could talk about anything they liked and were encouraged to record a conversation that was as naturalistic as possible. Raters read brief excerpts from transcripts of these conversations, from which all obvious gender identifiers had been removed. The overall accuracy of judging whether conversationalists were male friends, female friends or cross-sex friends was 63 per cent, which is statistically highly significant (the accuracy rate by chance alone would be 33 per cent). The topic of conversation was by far the most common feature that raters reported using in their judgements, followed by the language of the conversationalists (for example, use of slang or swear words). Hence, in this more naturalistic study, it was demonstrated that raters could accurately identify the gender of unseen conversationalists.

Mulac's results are thus still very much open to debate. Nevertheless, his findings for women's and men's language do present an interesting paradox: there is both similarity and difference. Linguistic differences do exist, but they are not so obvious that untrained observers in his studies can accurately identify the sex of an anonymous author from a transcript alone. However, this paradox does not lead Mulac to reject the two-cultures approach. Indeed, he argues that his results can best be understood within this framework. He concludes:

> Far from appearing as if they come from different planets, the women and men studied appear to have come from different states in the same country. It is obvious that they grew up in different groups – groups that have subtly different styles and therefore subtly different ways of accomplishing the same communication task.
>
> (Mulac, 1998, p. 146).

Conclusions

According to the evidence reviewed in this chapter, there are significant differences between men and women with respect both to verbal and nonverbal communication. But how those differences should be interpreted has been the focus of intense debate.

The characterization of women's language as powerless is inconsistent with the findings of a number of detailed empirical studies of language. So, for example, women do not seem to convey uncertainty through greater use of either rising intonation, hedges or tag questions. An alternative interpretation in terms of politeness has been discussed. A number of studies have shown that women do make use of more standard forms of English. Again, women's greater use of terms like 'you know' and 'I think' in certain contexts can be understood as conveying a positive regard for the listener. Similarly, women's greater use of tag questions and high rising intonation in certain contexts can be understood as a means of involving others in conversation, thereby expressing a positive regard for them. This interpretation dovetails well with the proposal that women are more accommodating in their nonverbal communication. Accommodating people want to understand what others are trying to communicate, and also want to make their own messages easy to understand (hence the female advantage in decoding and encoding nonverbal cues). Women's greater use of gaze, smiling and closer interpersonal distances can also be seen as conveying a more positive regard for others. In the sense that women attend more to positive face, their nonverbal communication, as well as their use of language, can be understood in terms of politeness.

In contrast, researchers such as Henley, Lakoff, Zimmerman and West have placed a much more explicit emphasis on differences in societal power. Although some of their observations have not stood up to close empirical scrutiny, research conducted in response to their claims has produced some surprising and interesting findings. Indeed, through their stimulating and often provocative ideas, these scholars have made an enormous contribution to research on gender and communication. Furthermore, it should certainly not be concluded that explanations in terms of power have been effectively ruled out. Certainly, over a whole range of studies, there does appear to be enough evidence to suggest that it is men who are more likely to initiate interruptions. Furthermore, it can still be argued that women are more polite and accommodating precisely *because* of a power imbalance in society, that it is incumbent on those with less power to be more polite. Clearly, the debate continues!

Power is, of course, a topic in its own right, not just an issue in communication between men and women. The study of power forms the main theme of the next chapter, which is specifically concerned with micro-analytic studies of political communication.

5 · Political communication

This chapter on political communication is the second of two intended to focus on microanalytic research in particular contexts. There is now a widespread international interest in the analysis of political language (e.g. De Landtsheer & Feldman, 2000; Feldman & De Landtsheer, 1998). Research topics have included political metaphors (e.g. De Landtsheer, 1998; Wilson, 1990, Lakoff & Johnson, 1980), how politicians refer to themselves and others (e.g. Wilson, 1990) and the use of pronouns (e.g. Wilson, 1990), All these are interesting topics in their own right, but the aim of this chapter is not to provide a comprehensive review of political language. The intention rather is to focus on two particular settings, namely speeches and interviews, as an illustrative example of microanalytic research on political communication.

The chapter is based on analyses of politics in the United Kingdom, and is divided into two main sections. The first section is on applause in political speeches, the second is on political interviews. Each section is summarized below:

Section 1. Applause in political speeches:
        Atkinson's theory of rhetoric
        validating Atkinson's theory of rhetoric
        invited and uninvited applause.

Section 2. Political interviews:
        turn-taking
        equivocation
        issues of face
        evaluating the interview performance of interviewers
        evaluating the interview performance of politicians:
            'no necessary threat' questions
            'avoidance–avoidance' questions.

Applause in political speeches

Atkinson's theory of rhetoric

Rhetorical techniques used by politicians to invite audience applause have been the focus of research by the sociologist Max Atkinson (e.g. Atkinson, 1983, 1984a, b). Atkinson pointed out that applause is not random, it occurs in response to a relatively narrow range of actions on the part of the speaker, such as advocating the speaker's own political position or attacking the opposition. The timing of applause is also characterized by a high degree of precision: typically it occurs either just before or immediately after a possible completion point by the speaker. Similarly, speakers usually wait until the applause has finished before starting or continuing to speak. In fact, just as conversationalists take it in turn to speak, so speaker and audience also take turns, although audience 'turns' are essentially limited to gross displays of approval or disapproval (such as cheering or heckling). As Atkinson points out, if the audience was not restricted in this way, it is hard to imagine how public meetings could ever take place in the ensuing verbal chaos!

The close synchronization between speech and applause suggests that audience members are not only paying close attention to the speaker but, in addition, must be able to predict possible completion points in advance of their occurrence. If this were not the case, one would expect to find frequent delays between speech and applause, more instances of applause starting in places other than possible completion points and more incidences of isolated or sporadic applause. The fact that audiences seem for the most part to applaud 'on cue' suggests that there must be some system of signals that enables them to recognize where and when applause is appropriate.

Atkinson's critical insight was to propose that features in the construction of talk itself indicate to the audience when applause is appropriate. One of the cues he identified is a list of three items. In conversation, the completion of a list can signal the completion of an utterance – a point at which another person can or should start talking. Such lists also typically consist of three items, so that once the listener recognizes that a list is under way, it is possible to anticipate the completion point and hence the end of the speaker's utterance (Jefferson, 1990). In political speeches, Atkinson proposed that the three-part list can serve a comparable function, but in this case signalling to the audience appropriate places to applaud. For example, Tony Blair (at that time Leader of the Opposition) was duly applauded in his speech to the British Labour Party Conference (1 October 1996) when he said that '. . . there is no future for Britain as a low wage, low skills, low technology economy'. He was also applauded for a more famous three-part list in the same speech: 'Ask me my three main priorities for government, and I tell you: education, education and education'.

Another comparable rhetorical device is the contrast. John Major (Conservative Prime Minister 1990–7) was duly applauded when he told the Conservative Party conference (11 October 1996) that '. . . we are in Europe to help shape it and **not** to be shaped by it'. Contrasts can be used to do a number of things, including boasting about one's own side, attacking the opposition or doing both things at the same time. To be effective, the second part of the contrast should closely resemble the first in the details of its construction and duration, so that the audience can the more easily anticipate the point of completion. If the contrast is too brief, people could have insufficient time to recognize that a completion point is about to be reached, let alone to produce an appropriate response. According to Atkinson, the contrast is by far the most frequently used device for obtaining applause. He also proposed that the skilled use of both contrasts and three-part lists is characteristic of 'charismatic' speakers (Atkinson, 1984a, pp. 86–123), and that such devices are often to be founds in those passages of political speeches that are selected for presentation in the news media (Atkinson, 1984a, pp. 124–163).

Given that Atkinson's research was based on the analysis of selected extracts, one possible criticism is that he might have focused on examples that support his argument but are not necessarily representative of political speech-making as a whole. The only effective answer to this criticism is comprehensive sampling. This was the intention of John Heritage and David Greatbatch (1986), who analysed all the 476 speeches that were televised from the British Conservative, Labour and Liberal Party conferences in 1981 – a truly heroic study! They found that contrasts were associated with no less than 33.2 per cent of the incidences of collective applause during speeches, lists with 12.6 per cent; hence, almost half the applause occurring during these 476 speeches was associated with the two rhetorical devices originally identified by Atkinson.

Five other rhetorical devices for obtaining applause were identified, referred to as puzzle–solution, headline–punchline, position taking, combination and pursuits (Heritage & Greatbatch, 1986).

In the puzzle–solution device, the speaker begins by establishing some kind of puzzle or problem and then, shortly afterwards, offers the solution; this is the important and applaudable part of the message. The puzzle invites the audience to anticipate or guess at its solution, while at the same time listening carefully to the speaker's own solution when it is delivered. As the delivery of the solution naturally coincides with the completion of the political message, the audience is normally able to anticipate the point at which applause should properly begin. For example, Paddy Ashdown (Leader of the Liberal Democrats, 1988–99), was applauded for the solution to the puzzle posed in this speech to the annual Liberal Democrat Party Conference (24 September 1996). 'And here's another Conservative solution to the problems of the health service. The Private Finance

Inititiative – PFI. But what the NHS really needs is **a different kind of PFI** [puzzle]. **Patients First Instead** ' [solution].

The headline–punchline device is structurally similar to the puzzle–solution format, although somewhat simpler. Here, the speaker proposes to make a declaration, pledge or announcement and then proceeds to make it. The applaudable part of the message is emphasized by the speaker's calling attention in advance to what he or she is about to say. Thus, the speaker might use headline phrases such as 'I'll tell you what makes it worthwhile . . .', 'And I'll say why . . .', 'And I repeat the promise that I made at the election that . . .', 'And our number one priority is . . .' or 'And I can announce to you that . . .'. For example, the following extract from a speech by Tony Blair to the Labour Party Conference (30 September 1997) **'And I tell you that** [headline] I will never countenance an NHS that departs from its fundamental principle of health care based on **need not wealth'** [punchline]. The punchline 'need not wealth' also contains a contrast, and is duly applauded.

In position taking, the speaker first describes a state of affairs towards which he or she could be expected to take a strongly evaluative stance. The description itself contains little or no evaluation. However, at the end of the description, the speaker overtly and unequivocally either praises or condemns the state of affairs described. Thus, John Major in his speech to the Conservative Party Conference (11 October 1996), is applauded for condemning the following state of affairs: 'I still hear too many stories of politically correct absurdities that prevent children being adopted by loving couples who would give them a good home [state of affairs]. If that is happening we should stop it' [evaluative stance].

All these devices can be combined with one another, with the result that the completion point of the message is further emphasized. The most common form of combination identified by Heritage and Greatbatch links a contrast with a three-part list. The following extract comes from Tony Blair's speech to the Labour Party Conference (1 October 1996) in which both a contrast and a three-part list are 'nested' in another contrast. The two parts of the first contrast are referred to as A1 and B1, those of the second as A2 and B2; the three items of the list are numbered 1, 2 and 3: '(A1) It is sometimes said you know that the Tories are (A2) cruel but they're (B2) efficient (B1) in fact they're the most (1) feckless, (2) irresponsible (3) incompetent managers of the British economy in this country's history'.

If an audience fails to respond to a particular message, speakers can actively pursue applause. A common method of doing so is to recomplete the previous point, as in the following speech by John Major to the Conservative Party Conference (11 October 1996) 'New Labour, no new services, in Glossop or elsewhere. In the most important part of a health service, the family doctor's surgery. **That's what new Labour would mean'.** John Major failed to receive applause after the contrast 'New Labour no new services in Glossop or elsewhere', consequently he reiterated the point in a slightly different way.

In the 476 speeches analysed by Heritage and Greatbatch (1986), more than two-thirds of the collective applause was associated with the seven rhetorical devices. Most effective were contrasts and lists, the two devices originally identified by Atkinson as significant in evoking applause. Thus, the results of this comprehensive survey of political speeches provided impressive support for Atkinson's original observations. In effect, it demonstrated what is in effect a strong positive correlation between rhetorical devices and collective applause.

An obvious objection to this whole analysis is that audiences do not simply applaud rhetoric, they also respond to the content of a political speech. This point is readily acknowledged by Atkinson, Heritage and Greatbatch, but they also propose that audiences are much more likely to applaud if content is expressed in an appropriate rhetorical format. For example, in an analysis of two debates at the Conservative and Labour Party conferences, Heritage and Greatbatch looked at one particular class of statement the audience might be expected to applaud, referred to as 'external attacks'. These are statements critical of outgroups such as other political parties, which should evoke unambiguous agreement amongst party conference participants. Whereas 71 per cent of external attacks expressed in one of the seven rhetorical formats were applauded, only 29 per cent of non-rhetorically formatted external attacks received applause.

Applause can also be affected by the speaker's intonation, timing and gesture. The manner in which a message is delivered can strongly complement and reinforce its rhetorical structure, providing further information to the audience that this is a point where applause would be appropriate (Atkinson, 1984a). A sample of speeches formulated in one of the seven basic rhetorical devices was coded in terms of the degree of 'stress' (Heritage & Greatbatch, 1986). Stress was evaluated in terms of whether the speaker was gazing at the audience at or near the completion point of the message, whether the message was delivered more loudly than surrounding speech passages, or with greater pitch or stress variation, or with some kind of rhythmic shift or accompanied by the use of gestures. In the absence of any of these features, the message was coded 'no stress'. One of these features was treated as sufficient for a coding of 'intermediate stress', while the presence of two or more features was categorized as 'full stress'. Over a half of the 'fully stressed' messages were applauded, only a quarter of the 'intermediate' messages attracted a similar response and this figure fell to less than 5 per cent in the case of the 'unstressed' messages. Thus, the manner in which a message is delivered would seem to play a substantial role in influencing audience applause.

A detailed case study of the way in which hand gesture can highlight rhetorical devices in a political speech was conducted by the author (Bull, 1986). The analysis was based on a speech delivered by Arthur Scargill

(President of the National Union of Mineworkers) to a Labour Party rally in St George's Hall, Bradford, during the general election campaign of 1983. Two-thirds of the incidences of collective applause in this speech were found to be associated with the seven rhetorical devices described above. The three most commonly occurring devices were contrasts, three-part lists and the headline–punchline device.

In the case of contrasts, Arthur Scargill made use of a particularly interesting device – that of ambidextrous gesturing. Typically, he illustrated one part of the contrast with one hand, the other part of the contrast with the other hand. However, this device was not simply confined to contrasts. Switching from one hand to the other seems to be a characteristic feature of Arthur Scargill's speaking style: in this speech, it occurred on no fewer than eighty occasions, invariably at some kind of syntactic boundary (e.g. at the end of a clause). Thus, the use of ambidextrous gesturing to illustrate contrasts would appear to be just one example of the way in which Arthur Scargill uses this form of gesture to mark out the syntactic structure of speech.

In the case of three-part lists, each of the three items in the list were marked out by carefully synchronized gestures. Where a three-part list comprised three words, each word was stressed vocally and accompanied with a single hand gesture. Where a three-part list included a phrase or a clause with more than one vocal stress, then a repeated hand movement was usually employed, picking out two or more vocal stresses and terminating at the end of the list item, a new gesture starting on the next item. Typically, Arthur Scargill used non-contact gestures to illustrate each item in the list but, on one occasion, he actually smacked one hand on the other to emphasize each of the stressed words in the list.

In the case of the headline–punchline device, on several occasions the final part of the punchline was presented with a gesture using both hands. Although bilateral gestures are another characteristic feature of Arthur Scargill's speaking style, this is the rhetorical device with which they are principally associated. In association with the headline–punchline device, they seem to have the effect of bringing the punchline to a climax, highlighting the fact that here is an appropriate point in the speech for the audience to applaud.

What Arthur Scargill's hand gestures appear to do is pick out the structure of rhetorical devices, singling-out pairs of statements in a contrast, identifying the items in three-part lists and highlighting climaxes. At the same time, his gestures also play an important role in controlling applause, for example, by holding up his hand, either with hand or index finger outstretched. Typically, these applause-suppressing gestures occur just before a point where applause might be considered more appropriate, when he was about to present a statement in one of the rhetorical devices discussed above. In effect, Arthur Scargill actually seemed to conduct his audience. His gestures not only accompanied rhetorical devices that invited applause but also curtailed applause once it had been aroused – even to the extent of indicating to the audience points at which they should or should not applaud.

Validating Atkinson's theory of rhetoric

Atkinson's demonstration of the ways in which political speakers use rhetorical structures to invite applause has provided some fascinating insights into the processes of political speech-making. Yet the theory itself has never been subjected to systematic critical analysis. In particular, the evidence put forward suffers from one serious and underlying weakness – a failure to examine negative examples that might be inconsistent with the theory. For example, Atkinson places great emphasis on the importance of the synchronization of speech and applause. But how often does applause occur that is not synchronized with speech? Another question relates to the role of rhetorical devices. How often does applause occur in the absence of rhetorical devices? If applause does occur in the absence of such devices, how do audiences succeed in coordinating their behaviour without clear completion points projected by the speaker? These are all important questions, the answers to which could have significant implications for Atkinson's theory of rhetoric.

To address these issues, two studies were conducted by the author. In one study, an analysis was conducted of non-rhetorically formatted statements that received applause (Bull, 2000a) In the second study, an analysis was conducted of mistimed applause, of instances where applause was not synchronized with speech (Bull & Noordhuizen, 2000).

In the first study, three speeches were selected for analysis: those delivered by the leaders of the principal British political parties (Conservative, Labour and Liberal Democrat) to their respective autumn conferences in 1996. Fifteen statements that received collective applause but did not employ any of the seven rhetorical formats reported by Atkinson, Heritage and Greatbatch were identified. These statements were analysed in terms of both speech content and of whether collective applause occurred at completion points.

The content analysis of all fifteen statements shows one highly distinctive feature: in every instance they constituted a statement of policy. For example, no rhetorical device preceded a policy proposal from Tony Blair for 'A directly elected authority for London our capital city'. In fact, this statement was greeted not only with rapturous applause but also with cheers from the audience. It should be noted that, in the early 1980s, the Greater London Council (GLC) had been a focal point of Labour opposition to the government of Margaret Thatcher; she eventually abolished the GLC in 1986. Hence, the commitment to the restoration of a directly elected authority for London was immensely popular with the Labour Party. Indeed, this policy seemed so popular with the conference audience that it needed no rhetorical formatting to evoke applause. The content of these fifteen non-rhetorically formatted statements contrasts strikingly with that of rhetorically formatted statements that receive collective applause. In the latter case, Atkinson (1984a) found that applaudable forms of content were predominantly favourable references to persons, favourable references to 'us' and unfavourable references to 'them' – in short, praising your own party and attacking the others.

A further analysis of these fifteen non-rhetorically formatted statements showed a marked lack of synchrony between speech and applause. In 40 per cent of cases, the applause started well before a completion point. In the following example from Tony Blair, the applause started a clear 3 seconds before he actually reaches the completion point:

We will put a roof over the heads of the homeless
    by releasing those capital receipts from the sale of
    council houses and let homes be built for our people
                    xxxxxxxxxxxxxxxxxxxxxxxxXXXXXXXXXXXX
                        (CHEERS)   (3 seconds)

Over all six examples, there was a mean 2.5 seconds of applause before Tony Blair reached his completion point. On every occasion the applause reached its full intensity only after the completion point has been reached, a considerably longer duration than the 1 second observed by Atkinson (1984a, p. 24).

In a further 20 per cent of examples, Tony Blair was actually interrupted by the applause, for example:

We will be part of the European Social Chapter
    as every other government Tory or Labour is in the rest of Europe.
    And there will be a right for any individual to join a trade union
    and if . . .
            xxxxXXXXXXXXXXXXXXXxxxxxx
                              . . . and if a majority
    of the workforce want it for the union to represent
    those people
            xxxxxxxxxXXXXXXXXXXXX

In this example, the audience interrupted to applaud the commitment for an individual to join a trade union, although it is clear from the transcript and the video recording of the speech that Tony Blair intended to continue at this point.

Thus, the majority of the examples of collective applause (60 per cent) to these fifteen non-rhetorically formatted statements showed a lack of synchrony between speaker and audience. This was quite contrary to the pattern observed by Atkinson in response to rhetorically formatted statements. As a consequence of the lack of synchrony found between speech and applause in this study, it was decided to conduct a second analysis, in this instance focused on incidences of mistimed applause (referred to as 'mismatches'). This study was based on six speeches delivered by the three leaders of the principal British political parties to their respective party conferences in 1996 and 1997 (Bull & Noordhuizen, 2000).

Three principal types of audience mismatch were identified: isolated applause, delayed applause and interruptive applause. An example of the speaker being interrupted by audience applause has already been given above. Isolated applause refers to claps by one or two people as distinct from collective applause by all of the audience or a substantial section of it, hence can also be seen as a failure in synchronization. In delayed applause, there is a discernible silence between the end of speech and the onset of applause. Silence suggests that the speaker was expecting applause but, for some reason, the audience failed to respond appropriately. Hence, there was a failure of synchronization between speaker and audience, just as an extended silence in conversation might be considered 'awkward'.

Over all six speeches, a mean of only 61 per cent of applause incidences were found to be fully synchronized with speech. This contrasts with Atkinson's statement that '. . . displays of approval are seldom delayed for more than a split second after a completion point, and frequently just before one is reached . . .' (Atkinson, 1984a, p. 33). Of the three principal types of audience mismatch identified in this study, only one (isolated applause) is discussed in any detail by Atkinson, Heritage and Greatbatch. Given that isolated applause occurred the least frequently of the three types of mismatch (with a mean of 4.6 per cent of all applause incidences), it is perhaps not surprising that Atkinson's research underestimates the frequency of mismatches.

Thus, the results of these two studies (Bull, 2000a; Bull & Noordhuizen, 2000) show that applause at political rallies is often not synchronized with speech and that collective applause occurs in response to non-rhetorically formatted statements, especially to statements of policy. Hence, the concept of rhetorical devices cannot be used to provide a comprehensive theory to account for all the incidences of applause that occur in political speeches, nor even for all the incidences of collective applause.

Invited and uninvited applause

A more comprehensive theory of audience applause can be derived from the work of Steven Clayman (1993), who proposed that there are two principal ways in which an audience can co-ordinate its behaviour, referred to as independent decision-making and mutual monitoring. In independent decision-making, individual audience members might act independently of one another yet still manage to co-ordinate their actions, for example, by applauding in response to rhetorical devices. However, in mutual monitoring, individual response decisions might be guided (at least in part) by reference to the behaviour of other audience members. Thus, once it becomes evident that some people are starting to applaud, this drastically alters the expected payoff for other audience members: fear of responding in isolation will be reduced, while not applauding can increasingly become an isolating experience.

Clayman points out that responses organized primarily by independent decision-making should begin with a 'burst' that quickly builds to maximum intensity, as many audience members begin to respond together. Mutual monitoring, in contrast, should result in a 'staggered' onset as the initial reactions of a few audience members prompt others to respond. In fact, staggered onset was typical of much of the applause to the non-rhetorically formatted statements analysed by Bull (2000a). Clayman's analysis was actually based on booing, and he concluded (Clayman, 1993, p. 124) that '. . . clappers usually act promptly and independently, while booers tend to wait until other audience behaviours are underway'. The staggered onset of clapping (Bull, 2000a) suggests that mutual monitoring could also be involved in applause. Given that all the fifteen non-rhetorically formatted statements from the 1996 speeches involved substantive policy issues, applause might have been initiated by some members of the audience specifically in response to the content of the speech, its take-up by other members of the audience being facilitated by mutual monitoring.

From the occurrence of staggered clapping, it was proposed that there are not one but two processes whereby applause occurs in political speeches (Bull, 2000a). There is the process analysed by Atkinson, in which the speaker indicates through the rhetorical structure when and where applause is appropriate. As this process is in effect initiated by the speaker, it could be referred to as 'invited applause'. There is also the process whereby applause occurs in the absence of rhetorical devices seemingly as a direct response to specific aspects of speech content. As this process appears to be initiated by the audience (or certain sectors of it), it might be referred to as 'uninvited applause'. Whereas invited applause is typically closely synchronized with speech, this is not necessarily the case with uninvited applause, which can occur through the process of mutual monitoring. This concept of uninvited applause not only provides an account of how collective applause occurs in response to nonrhetorically formatted statements, it can also be used to provide an account of how isolated applause occurs. In effect, isolated applause can be seen as a direct response to the content of the speech, but one that fails to win enough support to produce collective applause.

The distinction between invited and uninvited applause has a number of interesting implications. It would certainly suggest that Atkinson both overestimated the importance of synchronization between speaker and audience, and underestimated the significance of speech content. That is to say, collective applause can occur in an unsynchronized fashion in response to specific aspects of speech content through the process of mutual monitoring described by Clayman. Furthermore, there might be certain political statements that are so popular with the audience that they will be applauded irrespective of whether they employ rhetorical devices to invite applause.

A further implication concerns the role of spontaneous applause, which is regarded with considerable scepticism by Atkinson (1984a, pp. 45–6). 'Professional politicians', he writes 'would no doubt prefer us to think of displays of approval as wholly spontaneous responses to the depth and wisdom of their words. Unfortunately, however, the available evidence provides few grounds for so doing'. In fact, uninvited applause (Bull, 2000a) does appear to be much more spontaneous than invited applause and might be seen as more reflective of genuine audience enthusiasm. Of course, it would be naive to assume that uninvited applause is invariably spontaneous: the existence of claques, for example, in nineteenth century French theatre is well documented, and there is no reason why political activists should not collude in similar ways. Nevertheless, it is interesting to note that most of the uninvited applause (87 per cent) identified by Bull (2000a) occurred in the speech by Tony Blair, who went on to win a landslide Labour victory in the 1997 general election. Hence, the high proportion of uninvited applause to his speech might simply reflect his greater popularity.

In short, Atkinson has made a number of penetrating observations about the role of rhetorical devices in inviting applause to political speeches. Nevertheless, his theory is clearly not the whole story. A central weakness is a failure to analyse negative instances that might be inconsistent with the theory, especially mismatches and collective applause in relation to non-rhetorically formatted statements. From an analysis of such negative instances, it is proposed that applause is not invariably orchestrated by political speakers but might also be initiated independently by the audience. It would thus appear that a substantial revision of their respective roles in political speech-making could now be overdue.

Political interviews

It is now widely acknowledged that modern elections are essentially fought out on televison. As a consequence, the traditional political speech has greatly declined in significance. Televised political interviews have become an important means of political communication and have also become the focus of a substantive research literature, concentrating in particular on the nature of the interaction that takes place.

To some extent, this interaction is a kind of illusion: what appears to be a conversation is in fact a performance, transmitted to an overhearing audience that could number millions (Heritage, 1985). It is also a performance governed by its own special set of rules, in which the type of conversation that takes place is quite distinctive. Characteristic features include the pattern of turn-taking, the frequent occurrence of both interruptions and equivocation, and the central role of self-presentation and face management. Analysis of these features also has a number of interesting implications for the evaluation of the interview performance of both interviewers and politicians.

Turn-taking

A number of observers have commented on the distinctive nature of turn-taking in political interviews. Typically, the interviewer both begins and ends the interview and is also expected to ask questions; the interviewee is expected to provide replies (e.g. Greatbatch, 1988; Heritage *et al.*, 1988; Clayman, 1989). Even when the interviewer departs from the question/answer format, for example by making a statement, that statement will typically be followed with a question or concluded with a tag in the form of 'isn't it?' or 'wasn't it?'. Thus, the question/answer format is the principal means of interaction used by the participants, although interviewers might engage in non-questioning actions in order to open and close interviews (Heritage & Greatbatch, 1991).

The way in which news interviews are terminated is significantly affected by the pattern of turn-taking (Clayman, 1989). Given that interviewees are not expected to speak unless the interviewer has asked them to do so, termination can be accomplished in a unilateral fashion by the interviewer; this is in contrast to ordinary conversation, where it is managed jointly by the participants. The opening sequence of a news interview also differs from ordinary conversation in a number of important respects. In particular, the primary task of the opening is to project the agenda for the interview, whereas topics in ordinary conversation are not predetermined but developed during the course of the interaction (Clayman, 1991).

Turn-taking in political interviews can break down if interruptions are excessive. A detailed analysis was conducted of interruptions in two political interviews from the 1979 British general election (Beattie, 1982a). One interview was between Denis Tuohy and Margaret Thatcher (at that time Leader of the Conservative Opposition), the other was between Llew Gardner and James Callaghan (at that time Labour Prime Minister). Whereas Margaret Thatcher was interrupted by her interviewer almost twice as often as she interrupted him, the pattern for James Callaghan was the reverse: he interrupted his interviewer more than he was interrupted. Margaret Thatcher, it was claimed, was often interrupted following the display of turn-yielding cues, in particular at the ends of clauses associated with drawl on the stressed syllable and a falling intonation pattern. These turn-yielding cues were in effect misleading, giving the interviewer the impression that she had completed her utterance. The interviewer would then attempt to take over the turn, whereupon Margaret Thatcher would continue speaking. This, it was proposed, was why Margaret Thatcher was excessively interrupted in political interviews (Beattie, 1982a).

This interpretation was disputed in an analysis of eight political interviews from the 1987 British general election (Bull & Mayer, 1988). In this study, Margaret Thatcher (by this time Prime Minister) was compared with Neil Kinnock (Leader of the Labour Opposition, 1983–92). No significant difference was found between the two party leaders in the extent to which they either interrupted the interviewers or were interrupted by them. Indeed, the pattern of interruptions between the two leaders was markedly similar and correlated at a highly significant level. Thus, there was no objective evidence to suggest that Margaret Thatcher was interrupted excessively. Where the two party leaders did differ was in their response to interruptions. Margaret Thatcher objected much more frequently to interruptions than did Neil Kinnock, with comments such as '. . . please let me go on' or '. . . may I now and then say a word in my own defence'. On at least two occasions she objected to interruptions even when none seemed to have occurred. Indeed, on one occasion, the interviewer (Jonathan Dimbleby) openly protested that he was not about to interrupt! Margaret Thatcher's frequent objections might have given the misleading impression that she was being excessively interrupted, although the objective evidence showed that the two politicians received remarkably even-handed treatment in this respect.

Another feature of Margaret Thatcher's interview style was a tendency to personalize issues, as well as a tendency to take questions and criticisms as accusations (Bull & Mayer, 1988). Both these features can be illustrated in the following excerpt from the interview with Jonathan Dimbleby:

Jonathan Dimbleby: . . . if the National Health Service is only safe in your hands wouldn't it be a good idea to demonstrate that and a way of demonstrating that might be to use it some people would say

Margaret Thatcher: don't you think that you'd have **got at me very much** had I said look I've got to be in on a certain day and I've got to be out on a certain day **you'd accuse me of queue jumping and you'd have been the first to have done so**

Jonathan Dimbleby: certainly not

Thus, in all these ways Margaret Thatcher gave the impression that she was badly treated by the interviewers: claiming that she was excessively interrupted, taking questions as accusations, implying that interviewers had some personal hostility towards her. Furthermore, the way in which she addressed the interviewers formally by title and surname suggested that they needed to be called to account for these misdemeanours. On two occasions she actually addressed the interviewer (Sir Robin Day) incorrectly, calling him Mr Day (rather than Sir Robin): 'Mr Day I think you're asking me I think you're I'm so sorry I made that mistake last time I won't do it again Sir Robin . . .'; she then repeated the mistake on a subsequent occasion in the middle of one of her answers with '. . . but Mr Sir Robin . . .' These 'mistakes' could very easily be construed as some kind of put-down, especially given that it was Margaret Thatcher who had been responsible for awarding Sir Robin Day the knighthood in the first place (in 1981). All these stylistic features, it was concluded, had the effect of wrong-footing interviewers and putting them on the defensive, making it difficult for them to ask Margaret Thatcher tough and challenging questions.

Equivocation

In the study reported above (Bull & Mayer, 1988), a content analysis of interruptions was also conducted, which showed that the most frequent reason for interrupting was to reformulate a question. This suggested that there might be a close link between interruptions and equivocation: if an interviewee talks at length while failing to answer a question, the interviewer must be able to interrupt effectively in order to pursue an appropriate reply. Hence, further analysis was conducted of these eight interviews from the 1987 British general election, but this time focused on equivocation (Bull & Mayer, 1993).

Results showed that Margaret Thatcher replied to only 37 per cent of the questions put to her, Neil Kinnock to only 39 per cent (Bull & Mayer, 1993). These findings are remarkably similar to the results of a completely independent study of a different set of interviews with Margaret Thatcher and Neil Kinnock (Harris, 1991), in which it was found that the two politicians gave direct answers to just over 39 per cent of questions. In contrast, it is interesting to consider reply rates in televised interviews with people who are not politicians. The late Diana, Princess of Wales, in her interview with Martin Bashir (20 November 1995), replied to 78 per cent of the questions put to her (Bull, 1997). Louise Woodward, the British au pair who was convicted in the United States of the manslaughter of 8-month-old Matthew Eappen, in an interview with Martin Bashir (22 June 1998), replied to 70 per cent of the questions (Bull, 2000b). Monica Lewinsky replied to 89 per cent of questions posed by Jon Snow (4 March 1999) in an interview concerning her affair with President Clinton (Bull, 2000b). The mean reply rate of 79 per cent across three of these interviews is effectively double that reported for interviews with Margaret Thatcher and Neil Kinnock (Harris, 1991; Bull & Mayer, 1993). It would appear that the popular view that politicians do not reply to a large proportion of questions in political interviews is well supported by the evidence!

There are many different ways of not replying to a question. Thirty ways were identified in the interviews with Margaret Thatcher and Neil Kinnock (Bull & Mayer, 1993). These thirty forms of non-reply were regarded as subordinate categories, which could also be grouped into eleven superordinate categories. For example, 'attacking the question' is a superordinate category that has a number of subordinate categories, such as 'the question is hypothetical or speculative', 'the question is based on a false presupposition' or 'the quotation in the question is taken out of context'. At the subordinate category level, it was possible to discern stylistic differences between the two politicians. Whereas Margaret Thatcher inhibited awkward questions by making personal attacks on the interviewers, Neil Kinnock's style was much more defensive. He would sometimes answer in the negative (stating at length the policies that the Labour Party would not follow), thereby simply inviting further questioning on the same topic, while also making himself appear evasive.

However, at the superordinate category level, a striking degree of similarity was found between the two politicians, with a highly significant correlation of 0.93 across the eleven superordinate categories. Thus, not only did the two politicians not reply to a similar proportion of questions, they also tended not to reply in similar kinds of ways. These findings might be taken as supportive of the popular view that one politician is very much like another, in effect that politicians are in some way intrinsically evasive. However, an alternative view comes from the theory of equivocation discussed in Chapter 3 (pp. 68–70). According to Bavelas *et al.* (1990), equivocation occurs in response to 'avoidance–avoidance' conflicts; furthermore, such conflicts are deemed to be especially prevalent in interviews with politicians. In these terms, the high degree of equivocation shown by politicians in interviews can be seen not so much as a reflection of their intrinsic evasiveness, but rather as a response to the communicative situation in which they find themselves.

In fact, a number of different types of 'avoidance–avoidance' conflict have been identified in the context of political interviews (Bavelas *et al.*, 1990). For example, there are many controversial issues on which there is a divided electorate. Politicians often seek to avoid direct replies supporting or criticizing either position, which would offend a substantial number of voters. Another set of conflicts is created by the pressure of time limits. If the politician is under pressure to respond briefly to a complex question, he or she has to make a choice between two unattractive alternatives: reducing the issue to a simple, incomplete answer, or appearing long-winded, circuitous and evasive. A further set of conflicts can occur if the politician lacks sufficient knowledge of the political issue being addressed. In this circumstance, he or she has to make the unfortunate choice between acknowledging ignorance, or improvising, even fabricating, an answer.

It is important to note that with the exception of being well-prepared on every conceivable issue, politicians can do little about the other sources of conflict. Inevitably, voters will be divided; parties, candidates and constituencies will disagree; there will always be occasions when brief replies are required in political interviews; politicians will have to keep secrets and reporters will ask aggressive questions. Most important of all, the public and press are waiting to seize on any mistake. Over and over again, politicians told the researchers that the goal of a campaign was to avoid making mistakes. They told familiar horror stories of the one highly publicized mistake that ended a political career; in short, that elections are lost, not won (Bavelas *et al.*, 1990).

Issues of face

As noted above in Chapter 3 (pp. 68–70), Bavelas *et al.*, in their theory of equivocation, do not present any unifying theoretical explanation for what it is that people are seeking to avoid. In the context of political interviews, it has been proposed that an important source of 'avoidance–avoidance' conflicts is the danger of losing face (Bull *et al.*, 1996). For example, if politicians equivocate on controversial issues, they protect their own face by not supporting opinions that a substantial body of voters may find offensive or unacceptable. Conflicts created by the pressure of time limits can also be seen to threaten face, because a politician will not wish to appear either incompetent (by reducing the issue to a simple, incomplete answer) or devious (by appearing long-winded, circuitous or evasive). In conflicts created by a lack of sufficient knowledge of the issue being addressed, the risk to face is of either appearing incompetent (by admitting ignorance), or of putting face at risk in the future, if subsequently it can be shown that the answer was less than adequate. Indeed, not only can threats to face be seen as an important factor underlying equivocation, they can also be seen to influence when and why politicians *do* reply to questions in political interviews. Thus, if a politician is asked to justify a specific policy, failure to offer an appropriate rationale can raise doubts either about the politician's professional competence, or about the validity of the policy, or both.

A detailed analysis of face-threats in political interviews was conducted in the context of the theory of equivocation (Bull *et al.*, 1996). The study was based on a set of eighteen interviews with the leaders of the three main political parties in the 1992 British general election. A new typology of questions was devised, based on their face-threatening structure. The typology distinguishes between nineteen different types of face-threat, divided into three superordinate categories of face that politicians must defend – their own personal face, the face of the party they represent and the face of significant others. From this analysis, two types of question were distinguished: those where each of the principal modes of response were considered to present some kind of threat to face and those where a non-threatening response was considered possible.

Some questions (40.8 per cent of all questions) were so tough that each of the principal modes of response open to the politician was considered to present some form of face-threat, and hence to create an 'avoidance–avoidance' conflict. For example, Sir Robin Day posed this kind of problem to Neil Kinnock when he asked him whether, under a Labour Government, the trade unions would recover much of their pre-Thatcher power. If he answered yes to this question, Neil Kinnock would run the risk of offending that proportion of the electorate that was opposed to trade unions and fearful of their excessive influence. If he replied no, he would risk offending that proportion of the electorate that favoured trade unions, as well as offending the trade unions themselves and their supporters within his own party. If he failed to reply, he might simply be seen as evasive. Thus, each of the principal response options presented some kind of threat to face; in the event, Neil Kinnock made the best of a bad job by simply stating Labour Party trade union policy, without indicating whether or not this meant they would recover much of their pre-Thatcher power under a Labour Government.

However, not all questions pose the politician with this kind of dilemma. It was considered that there were some questions to which the politician could respond without necessarily threatening face, in the sense that it was possible to produce a response that did not incur any of the nineteen face-threats specified in the coding system. Where it was considered that such a response could be made, that response option was coded as 'no necessary threat'. It is important to note that this coding was used, regardless of whether or not such a response actually occurred. It is also important to note that a 'no necessary threat' response can take the form either of a reply or of a non-reply.

Some questions are so favourable that they give the politician an open invitation to make positive statements about him- or herself and the party the politician represents. So, for example, Day asked John Major: 'Why do you deserve . . . why does the Conservative Party deserve under your leadership what the British people have never given any political party in modern times – a fourth successive term of office?'. In replying to this question, John Major can present both himself and the Conservative Party in a favourable light. Failure to reply would be extremely face-threatening because it would imply that neither he nor the Conservative Party deserved a fourth term of office.

Questions where a 'no necessary threat' response was judged possible comprised 59.2 per cent of the questions in all eighteen political interviews. This latter type of question is of particular importance because it allows a direct test of hypothesis that politicians, in responding to questions, will opt for a 'no necessary threat' response if one is available. The results of the analysis provided overwhelming support for this hypothesis, in that in most cases where it was possible to choose a 'no necessary threat' response, this was the response the politicians chose, either directly or by implication. For example, the most frequently occurring type of question was couched in a 'yes–no' format (Quirk *et al.*, 1985; see Chapter 3, p. 64). Given that there are three principal modes of responding to such questions (confirm, deny, equivocate), the probability of a 'no necessary threat' response occurring by chance is 33 per cent; in fact, the total proportion of 'no necessary threat' responses to 'yes–no' questions was 87 per cent.

Evaluating the interview performance of interviewers

The face model has interesting implications for evaluating the interview performance both of interviewers and politicians. In this respect, the distinction between 'avoidance–avoidance' and 'no necessary threat' questions is of particular significance. Those questions where all the principal modes of response open to the politician present some kind of face-threat can be seen as 'tougher' than those that allow at least one type of response that is not intrinsically face-threatening. Specifically, it is proposed that the relative proportion of 'avoidance–avoidance' questions in an interview can be used as a measure of toughness, which is referred to as 'level of threat'. 'Level of threat' can also be compared across interviews with politicians from different political parties as a means of assessing interviewer neutrality (Bull & Elliott, 1998).

The concept of 'level of threat' is based on the proposition that politicians will tend to find 'avoidance–avoidance' questions problematic; this is borne out by the finding that politicians typically respond with equivocation. Most of the 'avoidance–avoidance' questions (87 per cent) in the study of the 1992 British general election (Bull *et al.*, 1996) were couched in a 'yes–no' format. Given that there are three principal modes of responding to such questions (confirm, deny, equivocate), the probability of an equivocal response occurring by chance is 33 per cent; in fact, the total proportion of equivocal responses to yes–no questions was 66 per cent. The fact that equivocation occurs at twice the rate expected by chance alone would suggest that politicians found difficulty with these questions, and were unsure how to tackle them. A high proportion of 'avoidance–avoidance' questions would therefore constitute a tough form of interview, and make the politician appear evasive.

'Level of threat' can be used as a means of evaluating the performance of interviewers with respect to both toughness and neutrality. Of the six interviewers studied in the 1992 British general election, Brian Walden emerged as the toughest, with almost half (49.4 per cent) of his questions carrying a threat in every direction, almost twice as many as those for Sir David Frost, who emerged as the softest interviewer with only 28.9 per cent of 'avoidance–avoidance' questions (Bull & Elliott, 1998). Brian Walden came out highest on the face-threats of 'creating/confirming a negative statement about the party' (72 per cent) and 'loses credibility' (42 per cent) (Elliott & Bull, 1996). Often, these face-threats occurred in combination, when he posed highly critical questions that could not easily be rebutted because they contained some obvious truth (face threat of 'loses credibility'), but could not be confirmed because they put the politician's party in a negative light.

For example, Brian Walden asked John Major, in connection with the poll tax (a flat-rate charge for local services that aroused widespread popular hostility):

Brian Walden: What did you choose to do? You chose to have a tax where everybody except the very poor had to pay at exactly the same level – the dustman and the duke alike and moreover of course you were wildly out in your estimates of what the bills would be. Even your own reckoning showed that they'd be comfortably over £200, er you told the House of Commons that it was going to be £224 per person. Now people say that is a monstrously uncaring thing to do isn't it?

If John Major confirmed this statement, he would be making a negative statement about his party, but it would have been hard to deny it without losing credibility; by not replying, he would simply appear evasive. (N.B. poll tax bills were often greatly in excess of the £224 stated by John Major.) This type of question poses real problems for the politician, and confirms the impression of Brian Walden's toughness as an interviewer.

'Level of threat' also provides a means of evaluating differential reply rates to questions. For example, it was found that Paddy Ashdown answered significantly more questions than John Major. Was this because he was simply asked easier questions? In fact, his reply rate was much greater, irrespective of whether he was responding to 'no necessary threat' or 'avoidance–avoidance' questions, which would suggest this was not the case. The results also showed an interesting trend where most of the interviewers gave the toughest interviews to John Major, in terms of the relative proportion of avoidance–avoidance questions. The one exception to this trend was Sir David Frost, who gave his softest interview to John Major, and was also markedly the softest of all the interviewers in terms of the relative proportion of avoidance–avoidance questions. In both respects, therefore, he was atypical of the other interviewers.

Evaluating the interview performance of politicians

Politics in the United Kingdom is essentially adversarial, it has for centuries been based on a system of competing political parties. In this context, politicians must seek to present the best face both for themselves and the party they represent. In the setting of a political interview, the problems of face management can be seen as particularly acute. Interviewers can ask repeated questions, challenge equivocal responses and draw attention to contradictions in policy. These potential face-threats are, of course, only intensified by the transmission of the interview directly to the electorate through the medium of television. How well politicians cope with the needs of face management in political interviews can be seen as an important element of skill in political communication.

The social skills model (see Chapter 1, pp. 16–19) has played a prominent role in research on social interaction for over 30 years (e.g. Argyle & Kendon, 1967). However, one of its major limitations has been the need to specify what are the skills appropriate for different social situations. Given that the face model provides a theoretical analysis of one of the central communicative features of the political interview, it can also provide a set of criteria whereby the interview performance of politicians can be appraised. In particular, the distinction between 'no necessary threat' and 'avoidance–avoidance' conflict questions has a number of significant implications for evaluating the interview skills of politicians.

'No necessary threat' questions

'With regard to 'no necessary threat' questions, one means of assessing interview performance is in terms of what have been called 'avoidable face-damaging responses' (Bull, 1998b). That is to say, given an adversarial political system in which a politician must seek to present the best possible face, interview performance can be regarded as unskilled to the extent that a politician produces a face-damaging response where a 'no necessary threat' response was possible. On this basis, an evaluation was conducted of the interview performance of the leaders of the three principal parties in the 1992 British general election (Bull & Elliott, 1995).

For example, Sir Robin Day asked Paddy Ashdown 'You promised to put an extra penny on the standard rate of tax for education and training. Can you call this courageous and honest when very few people think you're ever going to be in a position to do that?'. Ashdown did not reply to this question, instead he attacked it; in fact, he could have given a reply in the affirmative. He could have argued for the possibility of a hung Parliament, maintaining that in such circumstances the Liberal Democrats would use all their influence to try and get this measure through the House of Commons. By not replying to the question, Paddy Ashdown left the impression that he didn't really believe that he could substantiate the stance that this policy was courageous and honest, thereby undermining the face of his party.

In the eighteen televised interviews from the 1992 British general election, John Major produced the lowest proportion of avoidable face-damaging responses, Neil Kinnock the highest. Where a 'no necessary threat' response was possible, John Major nearly always selected this option (90.4 per cent of questions), in comparison to Neil Kinnock (83.0 per cent of questions) and Paddy Ashdown (87.2 per cent of questions) (Bull & Elliott, 1995). This was interesting, given the extensive criticism that John Major's communicative style attracted at that time in the media; however, the analysis presented here would suggest that critics might have underestimated his communicative skills in terms of the actual content of what he said.

'Avoidance–avoidance' questions

With regard to 'avoidance–avoidance' questions, equivocation theory would of course predict that politicians will equivocate, but is equivocation always the optimal response? An important issue here is that there are many different ways of not replying to a question. The thirty types of non-reply identified by Bull and Mayer (1993) are by no means equally effective: some forms of equivocation can be quite skilled, others transparently evasive. But these different interactional advantages and disadvantages are not represented in the existing theory of equivocation, it simply predicts that equivocation is the most likely form of response to an 'avoidance–avoidance' conflict. Thus, in considering what is the optimal response to an 'avoidance–avoidance' question, it is essential to take the form of equivocation into account.

John Major, for example, in televised interviews broadcast soon after his appointment as Prime Minister in 1990, used one particularly ineffectual form of equivocation: namely, that of pleading ignorance (Bull & Mayer, 1991). The problem here is two-fold. As Prime Minister, he must be expected to give intelligent comments on the nation's affairs. If he really did not know the answer to a question, then he ran the risk of being seen as naive or incompetent, which clearly would be extremely face-damaging. On the other hand, if the response was disingenuous and he actually did know the answer to a question but simply did not wish to reply, then he was at risk of being seen as deceitful. Furthermore, pleading ignorance might not deter a persistent interviewer, who could repeat the question on a number of occasions, or even dispute a politician's aired lack of knowledge (Bull & Mayer, 1991).

Highly skilled use of equivocation, in contrast, was observed in televised interviews given by Tony Blair during the 1997 British general election campaign (Bull, 2000b). The analysis was set in the context of the so-called 'modernization' of the British Labour Party, the dramatic policy changes that took place in the years following the Labour's disastrous electoral defeat in 1983 and which culminated in its landslide victory in 1997. The 1983 manifesto was memorably dubbed by Gerald Kaufman (a leading member of Labour's front bench at the time) as 'the longest suicide note in history'. It called for unilateral nuclear disarmament, withdrawal from the Common Market, massive nationalization and renationalization with much greater planning of the economy, exchange controls and trade barriers. By 1997, the manifesto had explicit commitments to retaining the Trident nuclear deterrent, to the rapid completion of the European Union single market, to the retention of the Conservative trade union legislation of the 1980s, and a 5-year pledge to no increases in income tax: in short, a complete reversal of what the Labour Party stood for in 1983.

Such dramatic changes typically pose political parties with a major problem of presentation. A complete about-turn inevitably reflects badly on what has gone before: there is a clear implication that the previous policies were ill-judged and inappropriate. Presenting the new policies also creates a problem; they could be depicted as cynical, opportunist and unprincipled, simply a means of currying support with the electorate. Nowhere is this problem of presentation more pronounced than in the context of a political interview, where interviewers can ask repeated questions, challenge equivocal responses and draw attention to contradictions in policy.

In an analysis of five televised political interviews from the 1997 general election campaign (Bull, 2000b), it was hypothesized that questions about these policy changes would pose Tony Blair with a classic 'avoidance–avoidance' conflict, and that his responses would be characterized by equivocation. It was in fact in the general election of 1983 that Tony Blair was first elected to Parliament, as a member for what has come to be known as Old Labour. Thus, if he condemned the old Labour Party, he would, at the very least, be open to the charge of inconsistency; if he was to admit to any lack of belief in the manifesto of 1983 then he would be open to the further charge of hypocrisy. In addition, if he was too critical of Old Labour, it might also make his party look bad and he might well alienate support within his own party. Conversely, as the man pre-eminently associated with the 'modernization' of the Labour Party, if he failed to acknowledge criticisms of Old Labour, then it would naturally invite the question as to why all the changes to what has become known as New Labour had taken place.

Just as predicted, it was found that Tony Blair equivocated to questions about policy changes judged as creating an 'avoidance–avoidance' conflict and replied to those questions judged as not creating such a conflict. However, his use of the term 'modernization' enabled him to do much more than just avoid replying to awkward questions. In particular, it had the advantage of enabling him to emphasize both continuity and change. For example, with regard to Old Labour, he stated 'I believed in the values of the Labour Party', whereas the process of modernisation has been '. . . to keep [the Labour Party] true to its principles but put those principles properly in a modern setting . . .'. This allowed him not only to acknowledge the changes that had taken place, but also to present them as principled – as representing an adaptation of the traditional values of the Labour Party to the contemporary political situation. In this way, he could claim a positive face for his party, as both principled but also moving with the times. At the same time, change could be acknowledged without condemning or criticizing the old Labour Party, in order to minimize the risk of alienating traditional Labour support. Although in almost half the questions about policy changes Tony Blair was invited to criticize or condemn Old Labour, it is notable that he never did so.

Equivocation has been defined as the 'intentional use of imprecise language' (Hamilton & Mineo, 1998). In these terms, Tony Blair's strategic use of the imprecise language of 'modernization' can certainly be regarded as a highly skilled form of political communication. Not only does it provide a means of avoiding the risks of making face-damaging remarks, it also enabled him to present the best possible face for himself and the party he represents, by striving to create a highly inclusive identity for New Labour. In fact, the very name 'New Labour' could be seen to project this inclusive identity, emphasizing change while still preserving the link with the Labour Party of old. New Labour certainly had a new rhetoric, but it should not be dismissed as 'just rhetoric'. Tony Blair's use of this 'rhetoric of modernization' can be seen as representing a high level of communicative skill, which arguably played a crucial role in the Labour Party's stunning landslide victory in the British general election of 1997 (Bull, 2000c).

Conclusions

Microanalytic studies of political speeches and interviews have thus identified a number of key interactional features of these particular forms of political communication. Characteristic of political interviews are the distinctive pattern of turn-taking, the high frequency of interruptions and equivocation, and the importance of face management and self-presentation. To a large extent the direction of a politician's response to a question is predictable from its face-threatening structure and it has been argued that the concept of face management can be used to evaluate the interview skills of both interviewers and politicians.

Studies of political speeches have identified the rhetorical devices that are used by speakers to invite applause and have also provided some compelling insights into the nature of 'charismatic' oratory. However, it has also been argued that greater attention needs to be given to the phenomenon of audience-initiated or 'uninvited' applause in order to acquire a fuller understanding of how applause occurs in response to political speeches, although our understanding of both these forms of political communication has been greatly enhanced through the kinds of microanalytic studies reviewed above.

6 Practical applications

There is no doubt that the microanalysis of communication does have considerable practical significance. Even the very act of carrying out such research, of disseminating results, both through the narrow confines of academic publications and the broader spectrum of books, newspapers, radio and television could be influential. By highlighting the fine details of social interaction, it becomes much easier for people to change their behaviour, if they so desire. Changes can also occur in the way in which people actually think about communication. In addition, formal training procedures have been developed specifically intended to improve how people communicate. This chapter is divided into two sections: the first is intended as a review of communication skills training, the second as a discussion of the wider practical implications of microanalytic research. Each of these two sections is summarized below:

Section 1. Communication skills training:
　　　　　　forms of training:
　　　　　　　　microtraining
　　　　　　　　assertiveness training.
　　　　　　social contexts:
　　　　　　　　job interviews
　　　　　　　　intercultural communication
　　　　　　　　medical communication.

Section 2. Practical implications of microanalytic research:
　　　　　　nonverbal communication
　　　　　　speech:
　　　　　　　　conversation analysis
　　　　　　　　the Linguistic Category Model
　　　　　　　　Communication Accommodation Theory
　　　　　　　　theory of equivocation
　　　　　　　　face and face management
　　　　　　gender and communication
　　　　　　political communication.

Communication skills training

In Chapter 1, a number of different approaches to communication research were considered. The one most explicitly concerned with practical applications is the social skills model. If communication can be regarded as a skill, there is the clear implication that it can be taught, learned and improved like any other skill. This is what communication skills training is intended to achieve.

As a formal means of instruction, communication skills training does have a number of advantages (Ellis & Whittington, 1981). It is a relatively short, inexpensive intervention strategy that has proved viable across a wide range of trainees and settings. Its credibility with trainees is good. Their attitudes towards the experience are positive and improvements can occur quickly. It is also good for stimulating discussion between theorists, practitioners and trainees about the nature of communication.

Communication skills training is an umbrella term, which can refer to a variety of procedures. Two of its most well-known forms are what are called 'microtraining' and 'assertiveness training'. These are discussed in further detail below as illustrative examples of what the procedure involves.

Forms of training

Microtraining

Microteaching was first introduced at Stanford University, California, in 1963 as a novel technique for training teachers (Hargie, 1997b). In many other contexts, complicated skills are taught by breaking them down into their basic components. For example, stage actors will rehearse different scenes in private, until the whole play is judged ready for public performance. Tennis players in training will concentrate on specific aspects of the game, such as the serve, smash, lob, volley and backhand in order to improve their overall performance. Similarly, the learner driver might learn to use the various controls separately before taking the car on the public highway. The rationale in all of these instances is to analyse a complex act in terms of its simpler component parts and to practise these elements separately, with a view to improving the overall performance (Hargie, 1997b).

By the same token, teaching can be seen as a complex skill that can be broken down into a number of manageable elements. In microteaching, the trainee teaches a small group of pupils for a short period of time with a focus on one particular skill, such as using questions. This 'microlesson' can be videotaped, and the trainee receives feedback on the skill under review in the form of a video replay coupled with tutorial guidance. This procedure can be repeated for a number of different teaching skills and is designed to prepare students more systematically for actual classroom practice. In this way, not only is the complexity of teaching broken down into manageable elements but it is also possible to provide students with a gentler introduction to teaching through learning in a safe, controlled environment (McGarvey & Swallow, 1986).

As a training technique, microteaching has become extremely popular. Indeed, it became firmly established in teacher education programmes throughout the world (McGarvey & Swallow, 1986). Its principles have also been adapted to other occupations, leading to the introduction of the term 'microtraining' (Hargie *et al.*, 1981). In microtraining, the aim is to improve communicative ability. Thus, core skills involved in professional interactions are identified and training is provided through analysis, discrimination, practice and focused feedback sessions (McGarvey & Swallow, 1986). Analysis is provided in lectures, which describe and examine skills critically. Discrimination training takes place in workshops where videotaped models are viewed and discussed, while attention is drawn to key aspects of the model's behaviour. Observation schedules and rating scales help in the critical analysis of behaviour components and their effectiveness. Feedback is provided by the replay of videotaped practice sessions in conjunction with rating scales and discussions with the tutor. Evaluation takes place in the subsequent period of fieldwork placement, in which trainees are encouraged by their tutors to make a critical evaluation of their skills in action (McGarvey & Swallow, 1986).

One extensively used form of microtraining is 'microcounselling'. This has been used in the training of counsellors: for example, by focusing on skills such as asking questions, observing clients, encouraging clients to talk and paraphrasing what the client has said (Daniels *et al.*, 1997). More than 300 empirical investigations of microcounselling have been conducted, including both narrative and meta-analytic reviews (Daniels *et al.*, 1997). In one meta-analysis (Baker & Daniels, 1989), eighty-one studies were examined, showing an overall effect size on counselling skills of 0.85. A second meta-analysis of nineteen microcounselling studies showed an overall effect size of 1.41 (Van der Molen *et al.*, 1995). Effect sizes of this magnitude indicate substantial experimental effects (Cohen, 1979); hence, the counselling skills of trainees seem to benefit significantly from this training procedure.

Microteaching, in contrast, emerged less favourably from a review of forty-nine studies of different forms of teacher training (Rose & Church, 1998). Of the procedures examined, microteaching was actually considered to produce the weakest training effects. Conversely, practice with feedback emerged as the procedure producing the strongest effects. Feedback combined with practice, praise or goal setting sometimes had an even stronger effect. However, an odd feature of this review is that practice with feedback is considered independently from microteaching. Given that feedback is actually an integral part of microtraining procedures, and that the feedback employed in these studies was often very specific and focused, the results would actually seem to support the value of microteaching as a training procedure.

Assertiveness training

Probably the most well known – and most controversial – form of communication skills training is assertiveness training. Social skills training and assertiveness training were at one time regarded as virtually synonymous but this is misleading; skills in self-assertion are only one aspect of social competence.

Assertiveness trainers stress that assertion should not be confused with aggression. Whereas aggression involves hostile behaviour, which may in turn evoke hostility from the other person, this is not the purpose of assertion. The intent of an assertive response is to communicate one's own position effectively and provide the other person with specific feedback about how he or she should behave in the future. While an assertive response should be firm, clear and convincing, it should not be hostile in tone, style or content. An assertive response should also be direct, specific and respectful (Rakos, 1990). To be direct and specific means focusing explicitly on the problem behaviour and avoiding generalities; statements that lack directness are likely to be seen as non-assertive. To be respectful is to avoid blaming, attacking or demeaning the other person.

The following example (from Rakos, 1990) illustrates the difference between an assertive and unassertive response. A sales rep. comes to your door selling a product you do not want. An effective response might be 'No, thanks, I'm not interested'. An ineffective response might be 'No, thanks, I'm not interested. I already have one [or 'I don't need one'].' The effective response treats the rep. politely but offers little with which to continue the discussion. If the rep. does attempt to continue, perhaps by inquiring why you're not interested, the refusal might be escalated into 'I'm sorry, I'm *simply* not interested' (in a firmer, louder voice and with a very serious face). Conversely, the ineffective response increases the chance of a lengthy interaction because it offers the rep. the opportunity to prolong the conversation. If you say you already have the product, the rep. might ask which one and then offer you a whole variety of reasons why the new product is superior. If you say you don't need one, the rep. might offer you a whole variety of reasons why it would be useful to you. If you say it's too expensive, the rep. will point out a number of reasons why it's good value or offer you alternative ways of payment.

Assertion can vary according to the nature of the relationship. Assertion that might be entirely appropriate when dealing with a stranger may be quite inappropriate for a continuing relationship. In non-continuing relationships, explanations, expressions of understanding and apologies are not effective; they are socially unnecessary and can blur the focus of the problem. Thus, in refusing to purchase something from a sales rep., no explanation, apology or expression of understanding is necessary; indeed, they should be avoided because they can give the wily rep. a chance to prolong the interaction. Conversely, assertion in a continuing relationship can present particular problems. When an individual begins to behave more assertively and less submissively, existing expectations are challenged and people are likely to react with feelings of hurt, anger, depression or even vengeance. In such circumstances, what has been called empathic assertion (Rakos, 1986) will be appropriate. Protecting the relationship in these circumstances can require increased empathic reflection of the underlying feelings.

There are many situations in which assertion will be required. Refusing an unwelcome request is one; trying to persuade someone to change an objectionable behaviour is another; expressing an unpopular or different opinion is a third. In assertiveness training, instruction is given in how to deal with such situations. One of the most important skills is referred to as refusal assertion. Its purpose is to deal with situations in which someone else attempts to impose demands, take advantage or otherwise unreasonably seek to exert control. If a person is continually unable to assert themselves in such situations, this can result in feelings of helplessness, loss of control, lowered self-esteem and even depression. Conversely, when a person learns to behave more assertively, a number of desirable consequences may follow. Most importantly, the person might be able to bring about changes in the behaviour of others. This can also result in improved feelings of effectiveness and self-worth (Kelly, 1982).

One of the key elements in refusal assertion has been termed the 'minimal effective response' (Rimm & Masters, 1979). The basic idea is to use the least amount of assertion necessary to achieve an objective. This might in itself be sufficient. On many occasions, violations of an individual's rights are quite unintentional or accidental. In such circumstances, a highly assertive response can be seen as excessive, as an over-reaction, as 'going over the top'. Consequently, excessive assertion can be counter-productive, producing hostility rather than compliance.

However, there might be other instances where the minimal response may, in itself, be insufficient. In such instances, persistence will be necessary; it is also essential to be able to increase the degree of assertion. Take the following example (from Rakos, 1990). A sales rep. who has just sold a television tries to sell the customer an extended warranty:

Customer: No, thanks, I'm not interested in the extended warranty.
Sales rep: Are you sure? It's a small investment to protect your much larger investment.
Customer: [1st escalation] Yes, I'm sure, I'm not interested in it.
Sales rep: You are buying a very good product, but a complicated electronic one. You know that problems can occur after the manufacturer's 1-year warranty expires.

Customer: [2nd escalation] I am not interested in the extended warranty.
Sales rep: The extended warranty will mean you will not have to spend anything on this television in the next 5 years. I think that such peace of mind is worth the slight cost of the warranty. Haven't you ever had a TV go on the blink just when it's most inconvenient?
Customer: [3rd escalation] I told you I do not want the extended warranty. If you persist in trying to sell it to me, I will buy the TV from another store and also inform your supervisor of your behaviour.

Assertiveness training has been given to a wide variety of populations. Often these groups might be described as unassertive or socially passive, but one interesting exception is the use of this kind of treatment for highly aggressive individuals. It appears that some people explode in violent rage because they lack the assertive skills to deal with conflict in a more appropriate fashion. It is possible that if such individuals are taught assertive skills, then their extremes of social passivity and violent rage could be moderated (Kelly, 1982, p. 176).

Women are one social group that has been particularly targeted by the assertiveness training literature. Many mass-market books have been aimed specifically a female audience, far fewer at adolescents, old people, ethnic minorities or other social groups (Crawford, 1995). Assertiveness training was considered especially appropriate for women because of the effects of gender socialization (Crawford, 1995). Traditionally, sex-role stereotypes have associated assertiveness with men; submissiveness and nurturance with women. The socialization of girls and later sex-role expectations restrict many females' opportunities to learn skills in assertiveness because, traditionally, this is not a female value. Assertiveness training was thus put forward as a way of directly counteracting the effects of gender socialization.

Not surprisingly, this view proved extremely controversial. It has been extensively criticized for its simplistic and stereotyped portrayal of women (Crawford, 1995). Furthermore, the prototype of assertiveness is arguably synonymous with the stereotype of masculinity. In that sense, assertiveness training could be seen as no more than training women in masculine social behaviour. Furthermore, instead of directing energy towards social change through collective action, women's position in society is blamed on their lack of assertiveness (Crawford, 1995). Thus, at a more fundamental level, it can be seen as an example of 'blaming the victim'.

Another important criticism of assertiveness training is the lack of outcome studies to investigate its effectiveness in everyday situations or to investigate the impact of assertive speech on its recipients (Crawford, 1995). There have been plenty of studies in which groups of clients have been pretested on questionnaire measures of self-esteem, depression or assertiveness. After attending training sessions for several weeks, post-tests on the same measures typically show self-rated improvement (Crawford, 1995). People do seem to feel better about themselves after training, but this does not provide any direct information on the social impact of assertiveness.

For example, social consequences might differ according to gender: a woman using an assertive response might be evaluated very differently from a man. Thus, when a woman behaves less assertively, such behaviour may well be an adaptive choice rather than a deficiency (Crawford, 1995). In one experiment, a number of scenarios were described in which either a woman or a man behaved assertively (Crawford, 1988). For example, one scenario takes place in an office where a supervisor habitually refers to an employee as 'kid' or 'kiddo' in front of the customers. The employee expresses mild dissatisfaction and requests the employer uses his/her name. Each scenario involved assertion either by a man or a woman, and was rated by a group of students and by a group of older adults. Analysis of the ratings showed a significant interaction, whereby assertive females received the lowest likability ratings of all from the older male judges and the highest likability ratings from the older female judges.

This experiment is one of the few to attempt any appraisal of the social consequences of assertiveness training. The lack of this kind of evaluation study is a serious omission in the research literature. It also has important implications for clinical practice. It is now more widely recognized that assertiveness training needs to be made much more sensitive to social context (Wilson & Gallois, 1993). To achieve this, two approaches have been recommended: one educational, the other through the analysis of social situations (Wilson & Gallois, 1993). The educational approach seeks to make clients better informed about relevant social rules, hence they can make more informed choices about the possible consequences of different behavioural options. Situational analysis seeks to develop clients' awareness of what kind of behaviours could be appropriate in particular situational contexts (Wilson & Gallois, 1993). If the social impact of assertion is to be better understood, these kinds of approach are important. It may be that assertiveness training is a highly effective procedure for training people in appropriate communication skills for certain kinds of problems in certain kinds of social contexts, but this still needs to be demonstrated through much more systematic investigation.

Social contexts

Communication skills training has been used with a wide variety of populations for many different problems. Thus, it has been used as a way of improving people's ability to handle conversations, to improve their perceptiveness of others and to improve their performance in job interviews. It has been used as a form of therapy for psychiatric patients experiencing a range of different problems. In addition, it has been used as a form of occupational training with, for example, teachers, doctors, nurses and policemen. Indeed, it would be impossible to consider in any detail the many different social contexts of communication skills training. Hence, in this section, three contrasting illustrative examples are discussed: employment interviews, inter-cultural communication and medical communication.

Job interviews

How best to handle a job interview has been taught through communication skills training in just the same way as people acquire other skills, for example, learning to play tennis. Thus, a tennis coach, when instructing a pupil in the art of serving, might demonstrate how to serve and might also get the pupil to practise the service. In the latter case, the coach would almost certainly give the pupil feedback on their performance. This might take the form of some kind of verbal comment; if videotape equipment was available, the coach might also videorecord the service and replay it to the pupil.

Similarly, in job interview training the instructor might demonstrate how best to answer a difficult question. The instructor might get the trainee to take part in a practice interview and might make comments on the interview, or indeed, make a videorecording of the interview and play it back to the trainee. The more explicit the feedback the better. Thus, comments such as 'I think you could do a little better' do not represent effective feedback because the behaviour to which they refer is unclear. Conversely 'You maintained a lot of eye contact, much more than last time. It made you more believable' or 'You spoke loud enough to be heard well, just as we'd been working on' give much more specific feedback and encourage the client with appropriate praise. The client is explicitly told that he or she performed well, and is also told why the performance has improved (Kelly, 1982).

Job interviews lend themselves particularly well to communication skills training for a number of reasons. For one thing, it is a situation of which most people have relatively little learning experience. Job interviews usually also take place in private, so there is little opportunity to observe skilled models in action. Furthermore, people typically do not receive specific feedback on their performance; the feedback they do receive is only of the most general kind, that is, whether or not they were successful. Because the outcome of such interviews can have significant implications for a person's life, they can also be a considerable source of anxiety.

A number of behaviours have been identified as important for good interview performance (Kelly, 1982). Appropriate affect is one. Poor affect might be characterized by an absence of lively voice intonation, by a bored or disinterested demeanour and by little emotional responsiveness to the interviewer. Other important elements are speech loudness, clarity and fluency. Positive statements about past experience, training or education also matter, as well as positive statements about personal hobbies, interests and pursuits. The client should also make statements demonstrating a clear interest in the job. Questions directed to the interviewer are important for two reasons: they show interest, and they may be a source of useful information.

A good example of job interview training is reported in a case study of a thirty-year-old college graduate who experienced extreme anxiety in interviews (Hollandsworth *et al.*, 1978). Although the client had good academic credentials, he had been unable to obtain a job after more than sixty unsuccessful interviews. Before the training programme began, the client was asked to take part in a role-played interview. This identified a number of problems. In particular, it showed that the client had a tendency to make rambling and disorganized responses to the interviewer's questions. It also showed that he needed to direct relevant questions to the interviewer, and to maintain eye contact and verbal composure. With the identification of these problematic behaviours, training could begin.

Each session began with a brief discussion of the particular aspect of interview technique to be trained that day. The client was then asked to focus on that skill while watching a videotape of good interview performance. Immediately after this demonstration, the client was asked to practise the particular skill in a role play. The practice interview was in turn video recorded and replayed to both client and trainer. In order to help the client in his replies, the trainer developed what was termed a 'Pause–Think–Speak' approach, whereby the client was advised to break eye contact with the interviewer whenever he asked a question during the role play. This was in order to think about the key elements in his reply before giving a response which should be both direct and clear. Training sessions continued until all the problematic aspects of the client's interview technique had been improved. The client was then encouraged to use these newfound skills in real interviews. The story has a happy ending: the client was offered jobs during the first three interviews following the completion of training!

The effects of interview training were systematically evaluated in the police and fire departments of a large American city (Maurer *et al.*, 1998). Interviewees were candidates for promotion to the ranks of police sergeant, police lieutenant, fire lieutenant, or fire captain. Those who had already passed a written knowledge test were offered the opportunity to participate in interview coaching. Those who volunteered were given instruction on interview procedures, advice on preparation and tips on appropriate interview behaviour. They also participated in role plays and were given feedback on their performance. The actual promotion interviews were conducted by four-member panels, who rated the performance of each candidate; the panel was blind as to who had received coaching. Attendance at a coaching session resulted in significantly better ratings of interview performance for candidates for three of the four ranks (police sergeant, police lieutenant and fire captain), even when controlling both for the candidates' job knowledge and their motivation to succeed. Thus, real interview candidates vying for real jobs have been shown to benefit from the effects of communication skills training.

Intercultural communication

A totally different social context is that of communication between members of different cultures. The term 'culture shock' has now passed into the common language but it was initially introduced to refer to the distress experienced by people in a foreign culture (Oberg, 1960). 'Culture shock' was simply ascribed to a lack of familiarity with the new culture but, as an analysis, this tends to be rather vague: the lack of familiarity could be with almost any aspect of the new society. Furthermore, no particular remedial action was recommended.

An alternative formulation of 'culture shock' was proposed in terms of social learning (Furnham & Bochner, 1982). People who are new to a particular culture will not have been socialized in the rules and behaviours of that society. As a consequence, they will, at least initially, be socially unskilled. Individuals in this predicament will include foreign students, businessmen, diplomats and visiting academics. Many of them will be perfectly competent – indeed highly skilled – in their own culture, but find their inadequacy in the new culture acutely frustrating and embarrassing (Furnham & Bochner, 1982). A particular problem is created by the uncertainty of handling unfamiliar situations. This requires increased cognitive effort, which might well be responsible for the fatigue that frequently plagues foreign travellers.

Communication skills training provides one technique for helping with difficulties in intercultural interaction. In practice, it has taken a variety of forms. Some investigators have stressed that simply being given information about other cultures is insufficient, some sort of explicit behavioural training is also required (Furnham & Bochner, 1986). For example, in one classic experiment, a group of male English students were trained in the nonverbal behaviour of Arabs (Collett, 1971). Specifically, they were instructed to shake hands on meeting, on parting and just before parting; to allow the Arab through the door, first touching him on the shoulder as he passed through; to sit close enough to touch his chest with arm outstretched; to look and smile as much as possible; and in no circumstances to point to the soles of an Arab's feet, because this would be taken as meaning 'You are worth as much as the dirt on the soles of my feet'. Conversations were arranged, in pairs, between Arab and English male students. Each Arab conversed with one English student who had been trained and with one who had not been trained in Arab nonverbal behaviour. After the conversation, the students filled in a questionnaire about each other. Arab students showed a significant preference for sharing a flat, being friends with and trusting the English students who had been trained in Arab nonverbal behaviour.

Other researchers have pointed out that problems in intercultural communication often stem from an inability to understand what causes the behaviour of the member of the different culture, that is to say, the attributions people make are inappropriate. Attribution training is often done through what is called the culture assimilator. This is based on a booklet that describes critical incidents where interactions between members of different cultures result in embarrassment, misunderstanding or even interpersonal hostility. Four or five different perspectives on each incident are presented and the reader is asked to select the one that best explains the problem from the viewpoint of someone who is not from the reader's own culture (Cushner & Brislin, 1996). At least twenty studies have been conducted, intended to evaluate the effectiveness of the culture assimilator. These have consistently shown that those trained with this technique are better able than untrained groups to interpret critical incidents from another cultural perspective (Cargile & Giles, 1996).

A more broadly based approach to intercultural communication is provided in a practical guide by Cynthia Gallois and Victor Callan (1997), who seek to present general principles that people can use in managing intercultural interactions. They stress the importance of social rules. Members of a culture share social rules that influence communication in many contexts. These rules are not necessarily explicit, rather they are shared expectations about the ways in which people should or should not behave. Gallois and Callan also stress that cultural bias is inevitable, given that cultures and other groups are important sources of self-esteem, as well as of knowledge, values and beliefs. People feel loyalty to the cultures to which they belong, as they do to other important social groups; hence, it is important to respect that loyalty. At the same time, cultural differences are not the only differences that matter: people within a culture can vary at least as much as the extent to which people vary between cultures.

Thus, rather than seeking to impart specific skills, Gallois and Callan's approach is intended to make people more aware of cultural differences, to stress the importance of what has been referred to elsewhere as 'mindfulness' (e.g. Gudykunst & Kim, 1992; Gudykunst & Nishida, 1994). People are said to act 'mindlessly' if they behave unreflectively or just according to habit (Langer, 1978), which can pose serious risks for intercultural interaction (Cargile & Giles, 1996). Indeed, miscommunication is almost inevitable if people interact with culturally different others as though culturally similar to themselves, or if they unreflectively judge strangers by their own norms and standards (Cargile & Giles, 1996). Thus, the purpose of training is not only to raise awareness of culture but, more especially, to encourage the consideration of potential difficulties during interaction. In effect, the aim of intercultural communication training is to encourage intercultural mindfulness.

The development of mindfulness and the acquisition of appropriate communication skills are regarded by Stella Ting-Toomey in her book *Communicating Across Cultures* (1999) as two important components of what she has termed 'transcultural communication competence'. Ting-Toomey also stresses the importance of a third component, the value of knowledge, which of the three she regards as the most important. Without culture-sensitive knowledge, she argues, communicators cannot become aware of the implicit 'ethnocentric lenses' that they use to evaluate behaviour in an intercultural situation. Furthermore, without accurate knowledge, communicators cannot reframe their interpretation from the other's cultural standpoint. 'To act competently across a wide range of cultures' Ting-Toomey concludes (1991, p. 271) 'individuals have to increase their knowledge and heighten their mindfulness in practising adaptive interaction skills in a variety of intercultural situations'.

Intercultural communication training is still very much in its infancy but its potential importance is immense. Rapid developments in technology have brought unprecedented numbers of people from different groups and cultures into increasing contact. Such relationships can present novel social and economic opportunities, and they also present huge opportunities for miscommunication. Furthermore, intercultural interaction is important not only for travellers visiting foreign countries, but also within societies as they become ethnically and culturally more heterogenous. Within the United Kingdom, a good practical example of a new intercultural awareness is the increasing recognition by the police of the importance of cultural diversity. The Metropolitan Police now has its own Diversity Training Support Unit and, in 2000, produced a handbook called *Policing Diversity* for serving officers, giving guidance and practical information on London's different religions, cultures and communities. In the broadest sense of the term, this can be seen as a form of intercultural skills training.

Medical communication

Communication skills training has been used extensively in a variety of occupations. Doctors are one such group for whom it has now become a recognized part of formal training. There is now an extensive research literature concerned with its effectiveness in this context; hence, medical communication is discussed in some detail as an illustrative example of occupational skills training.

Doctors traditionally learned to communicate with their patients through what was sometimes called the 'traditional apprenticeship method' (Maguire *et al.*, 1986). This typically consisted of asking students to interview several patients followed by a discussion of these histories either in seminars or on ward rounds. This approach was criticized on the grounds that it often failed to teach the students sufficient interviewing skills to enable them to obtain a full and accurate account of their patients' problems (Maguire *et al.*, 1986).

More recently, the trend in the United Kingdom has been for communication skills to be explicitly taught in medical schools. A survey was conducted of all the twenty-seven medical schools in British universities. Of the twenty-four schools who replied to the survey questionnaire, all reported providing courses with formal training in interpersonal communication (Frederikson & Bull, 1992). However, a more recent survey of the same medical schools reported considerable variability in the training offered in such areas as course content, timing, duration and assessment (Hargie *et al.*, 1998). Foremost amongst the difficulties encountered in implementing communication skills training appeared to be a lack of adequate physical resources and suitably trained staff.

The use of communication skills training in medical training can be justified by a series of evaluation studies, which have demonstrated its effectiveness over other approaches. In one experiment, the effects of different types of interview training were compared on four groups of medical students (Maguire *et al.*, 1978). All the students received training in taking a patient's history by the traditional apprenticeship method. In addition, three of the groups received one of three types of feedback training: they saw video recordings of their practice interviews, heard audio recordings of their practice interviews or received ratings from their tutors on their performance. The fourth group, whose only training was through the traditional apprenticeship method, was intended to serve as a control against which to assess the effectiveness of the different forms of feedback training. Care was taken to ensure that both 'feedback' and control students conducted the same number of interviews in their clinical firms during the period of the experiment.

To evaluate the different procedures, videotape recordings of interviews conducted by the students before and after training were rated in terms of the techniques used and the information obtained. This assessment was carried out by raters who were blind as to which training method the students had been assigned. The results showed little difference between the four groups before training, nor did the control group show any significant improvement during the course of the experiment. However, all three feedback groups showed a significant improvement in the amount of information they obtained from the patients. The groups who received video or audiotape feedback also showed a significant improvement in interview techniques. These techniques included assessment of skill in asking questions: for example, using open questions that do not direct the patients' answers, and avoiding long, complex questions. Other techniques measured included the interviewer's sensitivity to topics that might be disturbing or embarrassing to the patient, and the avoidance of jargon and repetition. Differences in interview technique between the audio and video feedback groups were not significant, but the group who received video feedback performed best overall.

A follow-up study was then conducted to assess whether the benefits of training were maintained 5 years later (Maguire *et al.*, 1986). Two groups of young doctors were compared. As medical students, they had either received video feedback training or conventional teaching through the traditional apprenticeship method. Each doctor interviewed one patient with a psychiatric illness and two with a physical illness. All the interviews were videotaped and assessed by a psychologist who did not know which form of interview training the doctors had received. The interview techniques of both groups had improved since their fourth year of training, but those given feedback training maintained their superior performance. The control group did as well as the video feedback group on only one skill – avoiding the use of jargon. In the other ten skills assessed, the interview technique of the video feedback group was still judged as superior (e.g. noticing verbal clues to patients' problems, preventing needless repetition, getting precise information).

Thus, the effects of this kind of video feedback training appear to be both significant and long-lasting. This is important in the context of other research on doctor–patient consultations. In one major study, the authors reached the conclusion that general practitioners become fixed in their style of interviewing soon after qualifying (Byrne & Long, 1976). Hence, the benefits of feedback training for medical students should persist throughout a doctor's professional life. Furthermore, studies of communication skills training with clinically experienced doctors have shown the effects to be rather limited (Hulsman *et al.*, 1999). Hence, it would seem better included as part of basic medical training.

A related issue is whether patients are more satisfied with doctors who have had some training in communication skills. This is an important question because quite high levels of patient dissatisfaction are often reported. For example, in two studies patients were asked to evaluate their consultations and an average of 40 per cent reported some dissatisfaction (Korsch *et al.*, 1968; Ley, 1972). Patients have criticized doctors for failing to treat them as people, by being insufficiently warm, friendly or caring (Friedson, 1961; Sanson-Fisher & Poole, 1979). Patients have also complained that doctors do not give them adequate information regarding their condition and its treatment (Fitzpatrick & Hopkins, 1981). These two aspects appear to be complementary, so that patient satisfaction could be best achieved by the doctor giving the fullest possible information regarding condition, treatment and prognosis in an atmosphere of warmth, friendliness and respect (DiMatteo & Taranta, 1979).

To investigate whether patient satisfaction could be enhanced by training doctors in communication skills, a study was conducted of general practitioners in the Melbourne metropolitan area in Australia (Evans *et al.*, 1987). Doctors were selected randomly from a list of general practitioners and invited by letter to participate in the study. Doctors who agreed to participate were then randomly allocated to one of two groups: either training (experimental) or control. Those in the training group attended two 3-hour seminars, at which they received the course booklet, as well as a lecture on patient satisfaction and compliance. The remaining time was spent in discussion within the group: on problems communicating with patients, on techniques suggested in the booklet and on techniques used by participating doctors. However, there was no opportunity for the doctors formally to practise skills in role play or other active learning situations.

Post-consultation interviews were held with ten patients from each participating doctor, which showed no difference in patient satisfaction between the two groups prior to training. Within four weeks of the seminar, data on patient satisfaction were collected from ten patients from each participating doctor in both experimental and control groups. Patients of doctors in the training group reported significantly greater overall satisfaction, especially with their doctors' information-sharing and concern during consultations.

In recent decades, there have been significant changes in the concept of the doctor–patient relationship. The old paternalistic, authoritarian style is giving way to one characterized more by mutual information exchange (e.g. Frederikson, 1993) and joint negotiation in medical decision making (e.g. Cegala *et al.*, 2000). In this context, it has been shown that clinical practice can also be improved by training patients in communication skills. In one study, patients who received communication skills training were compared with an untrained group; consultations of both groups were video recorded, although in each case the doctors did not know to which group the patient belonged (McGee & Cegala, 1998). Trained patients asked significantly more questions than untrained patients, especially questions in which patients checked their understanding of the information that had been given to them. Trained patients also had significantly better recall of the medical and treatment information they had received. However, there was no significant difference between the two groups in the duration of their consultations. This last finding is important, because the improved information exchange achieved between doctors and trained patients seemingly had no adverse effect on the overall efficiency of health care delivery. In fact, virtually all the research on patient communication skills training has shown no effect on the duration of consultations, which suggests that it is a highly cost-effective means for improving clinical practice (Cegala *et al.*, 2000).

Taken together, these evaluation studies show that training doctors in communication skills can be highly effective. Not only were the interview techniques of medical students judged to have significantly improved; these improvements were sustained 5 years later, after the students had become qualified doctors. Patients are also more satisfied with doctors who have received communication skills training. Furthermore, it can be of benefit to patients, thereby improving the quality and efficiency of clinical consultations.

Communication skills training has been used with other health professionals besides doctors. For example, in one study, it was shown to improve the interviewing technique of nurses (Davis & Ternuff-Nyhlin, 1982). Another study demonstrated the ability of nurses to acquire (through training) key social and assessment skills necessary for patients who had undergone mastectomy (Maguire *et al.*, 1980a). A follow-up of those patients who had been seen by the specially trained nursing staff had a more favourable outcome than those who received the traditional level of care (Maguire *et al.*, 1980b). However, a more cautious conclusion was reached in a recent review of fourteen studies of nurse training (Kruijver *et al.*, 2000). Overall, the researchers concluded that at best only limited effects were shown on nurses' skills, behavioural changes in practice and on patient outcomes. On the other hand, the authors of the more wideranging book *Communication Skills Training for Health Professionals* conclude that 'The evidence suggests that skills training is effective in improving communication performance, clinical practice and patient satisfaction' (Dickson *et al.*, 1997, p. 48).

Practical implications of microanalytic research

The proposal that communication can be taught like any other skill was one of the distinguishing features of the microanalytic approach identified in Chapter 1. Formal training in communication skills dovetails well with the microanalytic approach. Because such research identifies key features of social interaction, it can be incorporated relatively easily into such procedures. But this is only one part of the story. Improving one's communication skills is not necessarily dependent upon receiving some kind of formal instruction. By its very nature, microanalytic research is potentially applicable to a wide range of social situations. To substantiate this point, practical implications of the research reported in the first five chapters are discussed below.

Nonverbal communication

In Chapter 2, it was proposed that nonverbal communication can take place both without an intention to communicate and without conscious awareness of the cues through which communication is taking place. What we intend to communicate is not necessarily the message that others receive. Furthermore, we are not always aware of the nonverbal messages that we transmit to others, nor are they necessarily aware of the specific cues that are responsible for creating a particular impression.

This theoretical analysis has important practical implications for the significance we ascribe to nonverbal cues. One way in which this can be illustrated is through use of the rather picturesque term 'nonverbal leakage' (Ekman & Friesen, 1969b). This concept was developed in the context of studies of deception. It was based on the proposal that different parts of the body vary in their capacity to send messages. Three indices of sending capacity were proposed – average transmission time, number of discriminable patterns and visibility. According to these criteria, the face is the best sender, the legs/feet the worst. Facial muscle changes are rapid, they allow for a wide variety of expressions and they are usually clearly visible; the feet and legs move much less quickly, they are capable of only a limited number of movements and they are often screened from view by articles of furniture. Paradoxically, it was proposed that because of the greater sending capacity of the face, it may be a poorer source of information about deception, precisely because people are more careful to control their facial movements. Hence, attempts at deception might often be 'leaked' through movements of the legs and feet (Ekman & Friesen, 1969b).

However, research evidence shows no particular nonverbal behaviours specific to deception (Vrij, 2000). There is no 'Pinocchio's nose' which automatically indicates that someone is lying. All that can be said from a substantive review of relevant research is that some nonverbal behaviours are more likely than others to occur when people are lying (Vrij, 2000). But the concept of nonverbal leakage has broader implications than the analysis of deception. In Chapter 2, it was argued that one of the main social functions of nonverbal cues is to communicate emotion. It was further argued that an important distinction can be made between spontaneous and voluntary expressions of emotion. If what we intend to communicate is inconsistent with our spontaneous nonverbal expressions of emotion, then we might be said to 'leak' information about our underlying feelings. This can be important both for decoding and for encoding. In judging the sincerity of an apology, the warmth of an invitation, the interest of a potential customer or the intensity of interpersonal attraction, the nonverbal style can be as, or more, important than what is actually said. It is also of comparable importance in communicating effectively to others. Teachers who wish to convey enthusiasm to their pupils, doctors who wish to convey sympathy and understanding to their patients, politicians who wish to convey conviction in the justice of their cause, all need to appreciate the importance of consistency between nonverbal style and the spoken message.

In Chapter 2, it was pointed out that there are significant individual differences in both the decoding and encoding of nonverbal cues. The highest score ever obtained on one test of decoding (PONS: the Profile of Nonverbal Sensitivity) was achieved by a group of students studying nonverbal communication, although this was *before* they had actually taken the course! (Rosenthal *et al.*, 1979). Conversely, studies of marriage have found that unhappy couples are poor at decoding each other's nonverbal cues; this was especially true of husbands (Noller, 1980). One study showed that unhappy couples were actually significantly worse at decoding messages from their spouses than from strangers (Noller, 1981). Encoding is also important: if the partners show facial expressions of disgust and contempt, this appears to be predictive of subsequent physical illness and separation (Gottman, 1994).

Nonverbal communication thus appears to be important in marital difficulties, hence the attention it is given in marriage guidance and counselling would appear to be well justified. In this context, communication skills training is now a well established form of intervention. An example of this is the Couple Communication programme, developed initially in the late 1960s in the United States at the University of Minnesota Family Centre (Miller & Sherrard, 1999). The Couple Communication programme is described as a system for equipping partners to talk, listen and resolve conflicts effectively. It uses brief didactic presentations, directed practice or role playing, and homework exercises. It includes instruction in specific talking and listening communication skills, both verbal and nonverbal. A recent meta-analysis of sixteen studies showed that the Couple Communication programme is effective in improving marital communication, although not substantially more so than other comparable training procedures (Butler & Wampler, 1999).

Nonverbal cues have been considered of particular importance in the communication of emotion and interpersonal relationships. However, nonverbal cues are also closely synchronized with speech. In Chapter 2, it was argued that gesture should not be seen just as an alternative to speech, but as an additional resource, as part of a multichannel system of communication. For example, when something is too delicate to be put into words, gesture could be used instead as a form of tact. Gesture could also be used to comment on what is being said, to indicate how seriously it should be taken, or indeed whether it should be taken seriously at all (as when an accompanying smile indicates that an apparent criticism is meant as a joke). Gesture can be used to make speech more entertaining. The appearance of an action can never be as adequately described in words as it can be represented through bodily movement, hence its role in mimicry. Gestures are of particular value to the orator at a public meeting, because of their high visibility. Orators can use gesture to stress important parts of their speech or to stress a particular point where they are inviting applause. Thus, as a visual form of communication, gesture allows the skilled speaker further options through which to convey meaning. From this perspective, nonverbal cues should be seen not as an alternative form of communication to speech but rather as integral part of 'face-to-face dialogue' (Bavelas & Chovil, 2000).

Speech

One of the most influential approaches to the study of speech in naturally occurring situations has been that of conversation analysis (e.g. Sacks,

1992), discussed in Chapter 1. In Chapter 3, a number of techniques for content analysis were also considered, namely, the Linguistic Category Model (Semin & Fiedler, 1988, 1991), Communication Accommodation Theory (Giles *et al.*, 1987), equivocation theory (Bavelas *et al.*, 1990) and theories of face management (e.g. Goffman, 1955/1967; Brown and Levinson, 1978, 1987), Each of these theories and techniques has considerable practical significance.

Conversation analysis

Conversation analysis has some interesting clinical applications. A major consequence of brain damage can be severe difficulties in interpersonal communication. Conversation analysis has been advocated both as a way of advancing our understanding of these problems and as a means of giving practical advice to carers and speech therapists. One such technique is the Conversation Analysis Profile for People with Cognitive Impairment (CAPPCI). This was developed for people with generalized cognitive disabilities, arising, for example, from dementia in Alzheimer's disease (Perkins *et al.*, 1997). The same authors have also developed a comparable technique specifically for people with aphasia, the Conversation Analysis Profile for People with Aphasia (CAPPA; Whitworth *et al.*, 1997). (Alzheimer's disease is by far the most common cause of dementia. It is caused by massive loss of nerve cells in the brain and is characterized by progressive memory loss, disorientation and confusion. Aphasia is an acquired speech disorder resulting from brain damage. It affects the understanding and production of language and can be a common consequence of stroke.)

Both techniques comprise a method for analysing a 10-minute sample of conversation between carer and patient, and a structured interview with the carer. These are then combined to provide an overall profile of the interaction between patient and carer, from which intervention can proceed (Perkins *et al.*, 1998). Specific objectives are: to determine the carer's perceptions of the patient's current conversational abilities, to determine the strategies being employed in interaction and their success, to assess change from styles and opportunities of interaction before the onset of illness, and to assess the relationship between the carer's perceptions of interaction and what actually occurs in the sample of conversation (Perkins *et al.*, 1998).

The application of this technique to the case of a person suffering from aphasia is reported by Booth and Perkins (1999), who describe how an intervention programme was devised from the detailed insights provided by conversation analysis. Specific issues in interaction were addressed, which, according to the authors, would not have been covered by generalized advice leaflets. Furthermore, by analysing behaviour before and after the intervention it was possible to show that improvements in communication had occurred.

The Linguistic Category Model

The Linguistic Category Model focuses on the choice of words that people use. This is also a central concern of assertiveness training: an assertive response, it is recommended, should be direct, specific and respectful (Rakos, 1990). In particular, it should focus on the problem behaviour and avoid blaming, attacking or demeaning the other person. In the terminology of the Linguistic Category Model, it is better to use words that are concrete, rather than abstract. But studies of intergroup relations have shown a tendency for people to do precisely the opposite: socially undesirable behaviours by outgroups are typically described in terms that are both negative and abstract (e.g. Maass *et al.*, 1989). From the perspective of assertiveness training, this can make such behaviour harder to change; such language tends either to implicitly or explicitly blame, attack or demean the other person, rather than to focus on the actual behaviour itself.

Thus, on the basis of both these approaches, the following practical recommendation might be made. In seeking to change socially undesirable behaviours by outgroup members, a person needs to be aware of this tendency to use terms that are abstract and negative, and to counteract it by using words that are direct, concrete and specific. This proposal has interesting implications both for assertiveness training and for the Linguistic Category Model. Assertiveness training has typically been highly individualistic in its orientation but this analysis shows how it can be understood and applied in an intergroup context. The Linguistic Category Model has been essentially theoretical in its orientation; this analysis shows how it can be used in applied settings, through a more formal linguistic analysis of what is involved in an assertive response.

Communication Accommodation Theory

Communication Accommodation Theory is also theoretical in its orientation but lends itself more readily to specific, practical recommendations. Thus, speech convergence might be advisable for those who seek to make a favourable impression on others. This can take place through both speech content and style, and through features such as accent, pronunciation, speech rate, pauses and length of utterance. Convergence can also take place through nonverbal behaviour such as postural mirroring (see Chapter 2, pp. 39–40). This can be done strategically, as was shown in one experiment in which pairs of students conducted interviews with someone who (unknown to the students) was a trained actor (Dabbs, 1969). The actor was instructed by the experimenter to mimic the postures and gestures of one of each pair of students, who both completed a questionnaire at the end of the 'interview'. Students showed no awareness of the mimicry but the mimicked students did evaluate the actor more favourably; they also said the actor 'thought more like they did' and that they 'identified' with the actor.

However, it is possible to be overaccommodating. The shop assistant who invariably agrees with whatever the customer says might simply be perceived as obsequious. The politician who seeks to be 'all things to all men' might be perceived as unscrupulous and devoid of principle, with no interest beyond currying votes. Overaccommodation can also be perceived as patronizing. People sometimes accommodate excessively in speaking to the elderly. Although this speech style can facilitate their cognitive processing, the elderly do not necessarily like it (Gould & Dixon, 1997). In Chapter 3, the concept of an optimal level of convergence was discussed, and this would also appear to be a practical recommendation. Although failure to accommodate can be seen as impolite, rude or even downright hostile, excessive accommodation can be counterproductive.

Theory of equivocation

Communication Accommodation Theory has developed in complete independence from equivocation theory but, in Chapter 3, it was argued that their possible interrelationships might be well worth further consideration. This is particularly true with regard to practical implications. The theory of equivocation analyses the circumstances under which equivocation occurs (Bavelas *et al.*, 1990), it was not intended necessarily to evaluate its effectiveness as a communication style. To do this, consideration needs to be given to the consequences as well as to the causes of equivocation (Bull, 1998a). Traditionally, people have been enjoined to communicate in a way that is effective, clear, persuasive or efficient (Bavelas *et al.*, 1990). But if this means upsetting the feelings of others, it might be that in certain circumstances equivocation is preferable to clarity. In terms of Communication Accommodation Theory, equivocation can be seen as a form of speech convergence, a means of adapting the content of speech to the perceived opinions and evaluations of others. As such, equivocation can be seen as a form of tact.

One particularly interesting form of equivocation is the use of implicit replies. In the author's analysis of the interview with the late Diana, Princess of Wales, it was argued that her use of implicit responses could be seen as strategic (Bull, 1997). If, on the one hand, Diana had failed to answer any questions at all, she would have looked foolish for having agreed to give the interview at all, and would have be unable to put her side of the story. If on the other hand, her criticisms had been too direct, she might have been seen as strident, embittered or aggressive, indeed, she might have been frightened of some form of retaliation (Bull, 1997).

This use of hints or implicit responses, according to Tannen (1991), is one of the characteristic feature of women's speech. Women might find it optimal for dealing with what they experience as an 'avoidance–avoidance' conflict comparable to the one analysed in the interview with the Princess of Wales. In seeking to express a particular point of view, or get something done, women could be fearful that, if they express themselves too directly or explicitly, they will be seen as bossy or domineering. Hence, the use of hints or implicit responses might be seen as more appropriate. Something similar might also occur in the context of hierarchical organizations. In this setting, people might find it preferable to express a point of view indirectly. Too direct or explicit a statement could be seen as potentially challenging to the structure of authority within that organization.

Face and face management

In the above examples, equivocation can be understood at least in part in terms of theories of face and face management. Women might use implicit communication in order not to damage their own face by being seen as bossy or domineering. People of lower status in hierarchical organizations might use implicit communication in order not to seem disrespectful to others of higher status. Threats to face can arguably be seen as an important source of 'avoidance–avoidance' conflicts. Questions can be seen as having a 'face-threatening structure' (Bull *et al.*, 1996), that is to say, the structure of a question projects certain kinds of replies, which might in turn pose certain kinds of threats to face. If all the principal replies to a question are potentially face-threatening, then it is likely that, in responding, a person will equivocate. In many cases, people might see equivocation as preferable to losing face or threatening the face of others. This analysis has implications for those who ask questions, as well as for those who respond to them. For example, counsellors, social workers, doctors or researchers seeking to encourage their clients to talk freely and openly might need to structure their questions in such a way that people feel they can reply without damaging face; otherwise, they are more likely to equivocate.

The significance of theories of face and face management is not just confined to equivocation. Disagreements were discussed in Chapter 3 as an example of a speech act that is potentially face-threatening, because it shows a lack of positive approval or regard for the other person's opinions. Strategies have been identified whereby people soften the force of disagreement to make it less face-threatening, for example, through qualifying or 'hedging' disagreement, seeking common ground or through some form of self-deprecation (Holtgraves, 1997). From the perspective both of theories of face management and Communication Accommodation Theory, such strategies can seem advisable as a means both of reducing the threat to face in disagreements and of fostering convergence while reducing divergence.

It is noteworthy that this analysis of equivocation and face management makes recommendations that are directly contrary to those of assertiveness training. Whereas assertiveness trainers recommend that a response should be direct, specific and explicit, the analysis above suggests that under certain circumstances people might be more able to achieve their objectives through implicit communication. Furthermore, assertive responses can be highly face-threatening. Under certain circumstances they can be successful, under other circumstances assertive responses might be completely counterproductive and an implicit, less face-threatening approach might be more appropriate. Clearly, there is still much research to be done on the effectiveness of implicit and explicit styles of communication.

Gender and communication

According to politeness theory (Brown & Levinson, 1978, 1987), almost everything we do (which includes what we say) is potentially face-threatening. Politeness is regarded as showing a concern for people's face, which can either be negative or positive. In Chapter 4, gender differences in politeness were discussed. According to Holmes (1995), women tend to be more polite than men, in particular they are likely to express more positive politeness or friendliness in the way in which they use language. In a broader sense, gender differences in politeness can be seen to reflect differences in communicative style, which in turn can be seen as reflecting differences in culture. According to one perspective, men and women can be seen as coming from two cultures, who as a consequence communicate in different ways (Tannen, 1991). According to another perspective, gender differences in communication can be seen as reflecting differences in societal power. Although an explanation in terms of culture does not preclude one in terms of power (Tannen, 1994), the emphasis is still markedly different.

This is important with regard to the practical significance of research on gender. For those who emphasize power, microanalysis can lead to a greater awareness of the communicative patterns through which men have traditionally exerted and sustained their dominance in society. A fuller understanding of this process can in turn lead to greater possibilities for social change – to less discrimination and greater equality. For those who emphasize culture, the analysis of stylistic differences can lead to improved communication between the sexes. According to this approach, miscommunication reflects the different ways in which men and women use language (Tannen, 1991). Misunderstandings occur because they use language in different ways to mean different things. More importantly, they are often not aware of this process. The immense popularity of best-selling self-help books such as *Men are from Mars, Women are from Venus* (Gray, 1995) suggests that this approach has struck a significant chord with the wider public.

While Tannen (1991) takes the view communication can be improved if men and women get a better understanding of their different styles of communication, Holmes (1995) argues that men could learn a great deal from women's communicative style. According to her research, an important difference between men and women is in the amount of facework that they do, particularly with regard to the role of positive face (Holmes, 1995). But much public discourse (according to Holmes) is conducted according to male norms, which are more competitive and pay less attention to the role of positive face. Holmes' argument is that a greater use of female norms in public discourse could lead to more satisfying and rewarding interactions for all those involved (Holmes, 1995). Interestingly, her proposal is precisely the opposite of those who have argued that women can benefit from assertiveness training.

Political communication

Power is of course a topic in its own right, not just at issue in communication between men and women. In Chapter 5, detailed consideration was given to two particular forms of political communication – speeches and interviews. The practical significance of such research can be approached from a variety of perspectives – from that of the electorate, the politicians and also the political interviewers.

From the perspective of the politicians, it is not difficult to see how such analyses might be turned to their advantage. In the United Kingdom, politicians in recent decades have become far more sensitive to issues of presentation and media management. According to a recent analysis of political campaigning in the United Kingdom 'Media work has increased in importance more than any other aspect of party political campaigning over the past fifty years' (Rosenbaum, 1997, p. 120).

The presentation of the annual party conferences, for example, has changed out of all recognition. Speeches by the party leaders are now broadcast, in full, on nationwide television, thus reaching a far wider audience than ever before. The microanalysis of such speeches has provided politicians with easy tips on how to improve their oratory. Atkinson's (1984a) book *Our Masters' Voices* virtually provides a manual on how to script applause points through the use of appropriate rhetorical devices. Delivery, though, is important too. Delivery – in terms for example of gaze, posture, gesture, tone of voice – can indicate not only when a rhetorical device is intended to invite applause, but also when it is *not* intended to invite applause (Bull & Wells, 2001). Hence, a mastery of appropriate and effective delivery is an essential skill for a politician if rhetorical devices are to work to full effect. But incidences of uninvited applause can also be extremely revealing. If the audience interrupts the speaker with uninvited but enthusiastic applause, this can be a useful barometer of popular feeling, indicating a high (and possibly unexpected) level of support on a particular issue.

The analysis of interviews can be instructive. In this setting, a politician can be posed with any number of tough and challenging questions. In Chapter 5, it was argued that, given the adversarial nature of United Kingdom politics, face management is an essential skill for any elected politician. If the analysis of face management can be used to evaluate the interview performance of politicians, it can also be used to make practical recommendations as to what might be considered the optimal response. This will certainly not always be to equivocate. Equivocation in response to certain questions can be potentially more face-threatening than giving a reply, as was discussed in Chapter 5. But when presented with an 'avoidance–avoidance' conflict, equivocation may be the least face-threatening option. However, not all forms of equivocation are necessarily equivalent. In Chapter 5, a number of examples of ineffectual forms of equivocation were discussed, such as pleading ignorance and giving negative replies. Conversely, analysis of televised interviews with Tony Blair during the 1997 general election campaign showed not only how he used a 'rhetoric of modernization' to equivocate skilfully in response to questions about the volte-face in Labour Party policy between 1983 and 1997, but also to present a more positive, socially inclusive face for New Labour.

Microanalytic studies have practical implications for those who conduct interviews. Excessive equivocation by politicians can present a serious threat to the viability of the interview, if politicians make no real attempt to address questions or engage in any substantive dialogue with the interviewer. This was the view taken by the celebrated political interviewer Sir Robin Day in his memoirs (Day, 1989), when he cited communication research by Bull and Mayer (1988) in support of his argument. 'What deeply concerns me' he wrote 'is that the very principle of the television interview – the ancient Socratic method of imparting or gathering information by the process of question and answer – has been deliberately devalued' (Day, 1989, p. 292).

However, there are ways in which interviewers can counter this. If the interviewer asks a high proportion of 'avoidance–avoidance' conflict questions, this can make for a tough and challenging interview but will also increase the tendency of politicians to equivocate. Softer questions might in fact encourage a politician to talk more freely, especially if couched in such a way that not to reply is the most face-threatening option. In this context, a tough question can also be more effective, precisely because it is less expected. For example, in the 1992 British general election it was found that, out of five interviewers, Sir David Frost asked the smallest proportion of 'avoidance–avoidance' conflict questions (29 per cent; compared with 49 per cent asked by Brian Walden) (Bull & Elliott, 1998). But this does not make Frost ineffectual as an interviewer, as was explicitly commented on by John Prescott (Deputy Leader of the Labour Party since 21 July 1994): 'I find [David] Frost one of the most deadly [interviewers] myself, because he talks to you in such an easy manner but then slips in the difficult question – the one which gets you into trouble if you're not watching out for it' (*The Guardian*, 6 February 1995). Thus, equivocation by politicians can sometimes be countered through the use of skilled questioning by interviewers.

The microanalysis of political communication has implications for the electorate, as well as for politicians and interviewers. From the perspective of the electorate, such analyses can give greater awareness of the political process. The identification of rhetorical devices used by politicians to invite applause can give a much greater understanding of how political speeches can be stage-managed. The thirty different types of non-reply identified by Bull and Mayer (1993) can make it easier to identify how politicians equivocate. At the same time, an awareness of 'avoidance–avoidance' conflicts and the face-threatening structure of questions can lead to a deeper insight into how and why equivocation occurs. It can also provide a means of evaluating the performance of interviewers. An ability to recognize 'avoidance–avoidance' conflict questions can give a greater understanding of the relative toughness of interviewers, as well as of their fairness. An interviewer who consistently asked a much greater proportion of 'avoidance–avoidance' conflict questions to members of one political party rather than another might be seen as open to accusations of bias.

Conclusions

In this final chapter, consideration has been given both to communication skills training and to the wider practical implications of microanalytic research.

Communication skills training is an umbrella term that covers a variety of procedures; microtraining and assertiveness training were described as two examples of what it involves. Communication skills training has been used in many different social contexts: employment interviews, inter-cultural communication and medical communication were discussed as three illustrative examples. There is now a substantial body of research evidence drawn from a variety of different social contexts to support the value of this procedure. In a recent book *The Handbook of Communication Skills*, the editor, Owen Hargie, concluded: 'There is overwhelming evidence that, when used in a systematic, co-ordinated and informed fashion, communication skills training is indeed an effective training medium' (Hargie, 1997b, p. 481).

In the second half of this chapter, practical implications of microanalytic research were discussed. Research on nonverbal communication and speech is easily applicable to a wide variety of social settings. Similarly, research on gender and on political communication can be seen to have many practical implications. At a more profound level, microanalysis can also be seen to have affected the way in which we think about inter-personal communication. The fine details of communication are no longer necessarily regarded as trivial, irrelevant or unimportant. Terms like 'body language' and 'communication skills' have passed into everyday language. Politicians pay far greater attention to their media performances, doctors and other health professionals are given training in communication, the police produce handbooks that give practical guidance on religious and cultural diversity.

Thus, communication has now become an object of study in its own right, the video recorder the means whereby it can be dissected in the finest detail. To review this distinctive intellectual and social movement has been the principal theme of *Communication under the Microscope*.

References

Abramovitch, R. (1977). Children's recognition of situational aspects of facial expression. *Child Development*, *48*, 459–463.

Ambady, N., Hallahan, M. and Conner, B. (1999). Accuracy of judgements of sexual orientation from thin slices of behavior. *Journal of Personality and Social Psychology*, *77*, 538–547.

Anderson, K.J. and Leaper, C. (1998). Meta-analyses of gender effects on conversational interruption: who, what, when, where, and how. *Sex Roles*, *39*, 225–252.

Argyle, M. (1978). *The Psychology of Interpersonal Behaviour* (3rd edition). Harmondsworth: Penguin.

Argyle, M. (1988). *Bodily Communication* (2nd edition). London: Methuen.

Argyle, M. (1994). *The Psychology of Interpersonal Behaviour* (5th edition). London: Penguin.

Argyle, M. (1999). The development of social coping skills. In E. Frydenberg (ed.), *Learning to Cope: Developing as a Person in Complex Societies*, pp. 81–106. Oxford: Oxford University Press.

Argyle, M. and Kendon A. (1967). The experimental analysis of social performance. *Advances in Experimental Social Psychology*, *3*, 55–97.

Argyle, M., Salter, V., Nicholson, H., Williams, M. and Burgess, P. (1970). The communication of inferior and superior attitudes by verbal and nonverbal signals. *British Journal of Social and Clinical Psychology*, *9*, 222–231.

Argyle, M., Alkema, F. and Gilmour, R. (1972). The communication of friendly and hostile attitudes by verbal and nonverbal signals. *European Journal of Social Psychology*, *1*, 385–402.

Aries, E. (1987). Gender and communication. In P. Shaver and C. Hendrick (eds), *Sex and Gender*, pp. 149–176. Newbury Park, CA: Sage Publications.

Aries, E. (1996). *Men and Women in Interaction: Reconsidering the Differences*. New York: Oxford University Press.

Aries, E. (1997). Women and men talking: are they worlds apart? In M.R. Walsh (ed.), *Women, Men & Gender: Ongoing Debates*, pp. 91–100. New Haven: Yale University Press.

Aries, E. (1998). Gender differences in interaction: a re-examination. In D.J. Canary and K. Dindia (eds), *Sex Differences and Similarities in Communication: Critical Essays and Empirical Investigations of Sex and Gender in Interaction*, pp. 65–81. Mahwah, New Jersey: Lawrence Erlbaum Associates.

Atkinson, J.M. (1983). Two devices for generating audience approval: a comparative study of public discourse and text. In K. Ehlich and H. van Riemsdijk (eds), *Connectedness in Sentence, Text and Discourse*, pp. 199–236. Tilburg, The Netherlands: Tilburg Papers in Linguistics.

Atkinson, J.M. (1984a). *Our Masters' Voices*. London: Methuen.

Atkinson, J.M. (1984b). Public speaking and audience responses: some techniques for inviting applause. In J.M. Atkinson and J.C. Heritage (eds), *Structures of Social Action: Studies in Conversation Analysis*, pp. 370–409. Cambridge: Cambridge University Press.

Atkinson, J.M. and Drew, P. (1979). *Order in Court: The Organisation of Verbal Interaction in Judicial Settings*. London: Macmillan Press Ltd.

Austin, J.(1962). *How to do Things with Words*. Cambridge, MA: Harvard University Press.

Baker, S.B. and Daniels, T.G. (1989). Integrating research on the microcounselling program: a meta-analysis. *Journal of Counselling Psychology*, 36, 213–222.

Bartlett, M.S. (2001). *Face Image Analysis by Unsupervised Learning*. Boston, MA: Kluwer Academic Publishers.

Barlett, M.S., Hager, J.C., Ekman, P. and Sejmanski, T.J. (1999). Measuring facial expressions by computer image analysis. *Psychophysiology*, 36, 253–263.

Bateson, G. and Mead, M. (1942). *Balinese Character: A Photographic Analysis*. New York: Special Publications of the New York Academy of Sciences, Vol. 2.

Bavelas, J.B. (1998). Theoretical and methodological principles of the equivocation project. *Journal of Language and Social Psychology*, 17, 183–199.

Bavelas, J.B. and Chovil, N. (1997). Faces in dialogue. In J.A. Russell and J.M. Fernàndez-Dols (eds), *The Psychology of Facial Expression*, pp. 334–346. New York: Cambridge University Press.

Bavelas, J.B. and Chovil, N. (2000). Visible acts of meaning: an integrated message model of language in face-to-face dialogue. *Journal of Language and Social Psychology*, 19, 163–194.

Bavelas, J.B., Black, A., Chovil, N. and Mullett, J. (1990). *Equivocal Communication*. Newbury Park, CA: Sage.

Baxter, J.C. (1970). Interpersonal spacing in natural settings. *Sociometry*, 33, 444–456.

Beattie, G.W. (1982a). Turntaking and interruption in political interviews – Margaret Thatcher and Jim Callaghan compared and contrasted. *Semiotica*, 39, 93–114.

Beattie, G.W. (1982b) 'Look, just don't interrupt!' *New Scientist*, 23, 859–860.

Beattie, G. and Doherty, K. (1995). 'I saw what really happened.' The discursive construction of victims and perpetrators in firsthand accounts of paramilitary violence in Northern Ireland. *Journal of Language and Social Psychology*, 14, 408–433.

Benjamin, G.R. and Creider, C.A. (1975). Social distinctions in nonverbal behaviour. *Semiotica*, 14, 52–60.

Berger, K.W. and Popelka, G.R. (1971). Extra-facial gestures in relation to speech-reading. *Journal of Communication Disorders*, 3, 302–308.

Bernieri, F. (1988). Coordinated movement and rapport in teacher–student interactions. *Journal of Nonverbal Behaviour*, 12, 120–138.

Bernieri, F., Reznick, J.S. and Rosenthal, R. (1988). Synchrony, pseudosynchrony, and dissynchrony: measuring the entrainment process in mother–infant dyads. *Journal of Personality and Social Psychology*, 54, 243–253.

Birdwhistell, R.L. (1971). *Kinesics and Context*. London: Allen Lane, The Penguin Press.

Bolinger, D. (1978). Yes–no questions are not alternative questions. In H. Hiz (ed.), *Questions*, pp. 87–105. Dordrecht, The Netherlands: D. Reidel.

Bonifacio, G. (1616). *L'arte dei cenni con la quale formandosi fauella visibile, si tratta della muta eloquenza, che non è altro che un facondo silentio*. Vicenza: F. Grossi.

Booth, S. and Perkins, L. (1999). The use of conversation analysis to guide individualized advice to carers and evaluate change in aphasia: a case study. *Aphasiology*, 13, 283–303.

Bourhis, R.Y. and Giles, H. (1977). The language of intergroup distinctiveness. In H. Giles (ed.), *Language, Ethnicity and Intergroup Relations*, pp. 119–135. London: Academic Press.

Britain, D. (1992). Linguistic change in intonation: the use of high rising terminals in New Zealand English. *Language Variation and Change*, 4, 77–104.

Brown, P. and Levinson, S.C. (1978). Universals in language usage: politeness phenomena. In E. Goody (ed.), *Questions and Politeness*, pp. 56–310. Cambridge: Cambridge University Press.

Brown, P. and Levinson, S.C. (1987). *Politeness: Some Universals in Language Use*. Cambridge: Cambridge University Press.

Brunner, L.J. (1979). Smiles can be back channels. *Journal of Personality and Social Psychology*, 37, 728–734.

Buck, R.W. (1977). Nonverbal communication of affect in pre-school children: relationships with personality and skin conductance. *Journal of Personality and Social Psychology*, 35, 225–236.

Buck, R.W. (1984). *The Communication of Emotion*. New York: Guilford Press.

Buck, R.W., Savin, V.J., Miller, R.E. and Caul, W.F. (1972). Communication of affect through facial expressions in humans. *Journal of Personality and Social Psychology*, 23, 362–371.

Bull, P.E. (1983). *Body Movement and Interpersonal Communication*. Chichester: John Wiley & Sons Ltd.

Bull, P.E. (1986). The use of hand gesture in political speeches: some case studies. *Journal of Language and Social Psychology*, 5, 103–118.

Bull, P.E. (1987). *Posture and Gesture*. Oxford: Pergamon Press.

Bull, P.E. (1994). On identifying questions, replies and non-replies in political interviews. *Journal of Language and Social Psychology*, 13, 115–131.

Bull, P.E. (1997). Queen of Hearts or Queen of the Arts of Implication? Implicit criticisms and their implications for equivocation theory in the interview between Martin Bashir and Diana, Princess of Wales. *Social Psychological Review*, 1, 27–36.

Bull, P.E. (1998a). Equivocation theory and news interviews. *Journal of Language and Social Psychology*, 17, 36–51.

Bull P.E. (1998b). Political interviews: television interviews in Great Britain. In O. Feldman and C. De Landtsheer (eds), *Politically Speaking: A Worldwide Examination of Language Used in the Public Sphere*, pp. 149–160. Westport, CT: Greenwood Publishing Group.

Bull, P.E. (2000a). Do audiences only applaud 'claptrap' in political speeches? An analysis of invited and uninvited applause. *Social Psychological Review*, 2, 32–41.

Bull, P.E. (2000b). Equivocation and the rhetoric of modernisation: an analysis of televised interviews with Tony Blair in the 1997 British general election. *Journal of Language and Social Psychology, 19*, 222–247.

Bull, P.E. (2000c). New Labour, New Rhetoric? An analysis of the rhetoric of Tony Blair. In C. De Landtsheer and O. Feldman (eds), *Public Speech and Democratic Citizenship East West*, pp. 3–16. Westport, CT: Praeger.

Bull, P.E. and Connelly, G. (1985). Body movement and emphasis in speech. *Journal of Nonverbal Behaviour, 9*, 169–187.

Bull, P.E. and Elliott, J. (1995). Is John Major a major face-saver? An assessment of televised interviews with the party leaders during the 1992 British general election. *Proceedings of the British Psychological Society, 3*, 65.

Bull, P.E. and Elliott, J. (1998). Level of threat: means of assessing interviewer toughness and neutrality. *Journal of Language and Social Psychology, 17*, 220–244.

Bull, P.E. and Mayer, K. (1988). Interruptions in political interviews: a study of Margaret Thatcher and Neil Kinnock. *Journal of Language and Social Psychology, 7*, 35–45.

Bull, P.E. and Mayer, K. (December, 1991). 'Is John Major as unremarkable as he seems? A comparison of three political leaders'. Paper presented at the London Conference of the British Psychological Society.

Bull, P.E. and Mayer, K. (1993). How not to answer questions in political interviews. *Political Psychology, 14*, 651–666.

Bull, P.E. and Noordhuizen, M. (2000). The mistiming of applause in political speeches. *Journal of Language and Social Psychology, 19*, 275–294.

Bull, P.E. and Wells, P. (2001). Why do audiences applaud political speeches? An analysis of invited and uninvited applause. *Proceedings of the British Psychological Society, 9*, 80.

Bull, P.E., Elliott, J., Palmer, D. and Walker, L. (1996). Why politicians are three-faced: the face model of political interviews. *British Journal of Social Psychology, 35*, 267–284.

Bulwer, J. (1644). *Chirologia; or the Naturell Language of the Hand, Whereunto is added Chironomia: or, the Art of Manual Rhetoricke*. London: Henry Twyford.

Burns, T. (1992). *Erving Goffman*. London: Routledge.

Butler, M.H. and Wampler, K.S. (1999). A meta-analytic update of research on the Couple Communication program. *The American Journal of Family Therapy, 27*, 223–237.

Byrne, D. (1969). Attitudes and attraction. *Advances in Experimental Social Psychology, 4*, 35–89.

Byrne, P.S. and Long, B.E.L. (1976). *Doctors Talking to Patients*. London: HMSO.

Camras, L.A. (1977). Facial expressions used by children in a conflict situation. *Child Development, 48*, 1431–1435.

Caporael, L., Lukaszewski, M. and Culbertson, G. (1983). Secondary baby talk: judgements by institutionalised elderly and their caregivers. *Journal of Personality and Social Psychology, 44*, 746–754.

Cappella, J.N. (1981). Mutual influence in expressive behaviour; adult–adult and infant–adult dyadic interaction. *Psychological Bulletin, 89*, 101–132.

Cargile, A.C. and Giles, H. (1996). Intercultural communication training: review, critique, and a new theoretical framework. In B.R. Burleson (ed.), *Communication Yearbook 19*, pp. 385–423. Thousand Oaks, CA: Sage.

Cegala, D.J., McClure, L., Marinelli, T.M. and Post, D.M. (2000). The effects of communication skills training on patients' participation during medical interviews. *Patient Education and Counselling, 41*, 209–222.

Chance, M.R.A. (1967). Attention structure as the basis of primate rank orders. *Man* (new series), *2*, 503–518.

Charny, E.J. (1966). Psychosomatic manifestations of rapport in psychotherapy. *Psychosomatic Medicine, 28*, 305–315.

Clayman, S.E. (1989). The production of punctuality: social interaction, temporal organization and social structure. *American Journal of Sociology, 95*, 659–691.

Clayman, S.E. (1991). News interview openings: aspects of sequential organization. In P. Scannell (ed.), *Broadcast Talk*, pp. 48–75. London: Sage.

Clayman, S.E. (1993). Booing: the anatomy of a disaffiliative response. *American Sociological Review, 58*, 110–130.

Coates, J. (1989). Gossip revisited: language in all female groups. In J. Coates and D. Cameron (eds), *Women in their Speech Communities*, pp. 94–122. London: Longman.

Coates, J. (1996). *Women Talk: Conversation between Women Friends*. Oxford: Blackwell Publishers.

Cohen, J. (1969). *Statistical Power Analysis for the Behavioural Sciences*. New York: Academic Press.

Cohen, J. (1979). *Statistical Power Analysis for the Behavioural Sciences* (revised edition). New York: Academic Press.

Collett, P. (1971). Training Englishmen in the nonverbal behaviour of Arabs. *International Journal of Psychology, 6*, 209–215.

Condon, W.S. (1975). Multiple response to sound in dysfunctional children. *Journal of Autism and Childhood Schizophrenia, 5*, 37–56.

Condon, W.S. and Ogston, W.D. (1966). Sound film analysis of normal and pathological behaviour patterns. *Journal of Nervous and Mental Disease, 143*, 338–347.

Condon, W.S. and Ogston, W.D. (1971). Speech and body motion synchrony of the speaker–hearer. In D.L. Horton and J.J. Jenkins (eds), *Perceptions of Language*, pp. 150–173. Columbus, OH: Charles E. Merrill.

Cooley, C.H. (1902) *Human Nature and the Social Order*. New York: Charles Scribner's Sons.

Costanzo, M. and Archer, D. (1989). Interpreting the expressive behaviour of others: the Interpersonal Perception Task. *Journal of Nonverbal Behaviour, 13*, 225–245.

Costanzo, M. and Archer, D. (1993). *Interpersonal Perception Task-15 (IPT): a guide for researchers and teachers*. Santa Cruz, CA: University of California.

Coupland, N. (1984). Accommodation at work: some phonological data and their implications. *International Journal of the Sociology of Language, 46*, 49–70.

Cowley, S.J. (1998). Of timing, turn-taking and conversations. *Journal of Psycholinguistic Research, 27*, 541–571.

Craig, K.D., Hyde, S.A. and Patrick, C.J. (1991). Genuine, suppressed and faked facial behaviour during exacerbation of chronic low back pain. *Pain, 46*, 161–172.

Crawford, M. (1988). Gender, age and the social evaluation of assertion. *Behaviour Modification, 12*, 549–564.

Crawford, M. (1995). *Talking Difference: On Gender and Language*. London: Sage.

Cushner, K. and Brislin, R.W. (1996). *Intercultural Interactions: A Practical Guide* (2nd edition). Thousand Oaks, CA: Sage.

Dabbs, J.M. (1969). Similarity of gestures and interpersonal influence. *Proceedings of the 77th Annual Convention of the American Psychological Association, 4*, 337–338.

Daniels, T.G., Rigazio-Digilio, S.A. and Ivey, A.E. (1997). Microcounselling: a training and supervision paradigm for the helping professions. In C.E. Watkins Jr (ed.), *Handbook of Psychotherapy Supervision*, pp. 277–295. New York: John Wiley & Sons.

Darwin, C. (1872). *The Expression of the Emotions in Man and Animals*. London: Murray.

Davis, P.J. and Gibson, M.G. (2000). Recognition of posed and genuine facial expressions of emotion in paranoid and non-paranoid schizophrenia. *Journal of Abnormal Psychology, 109*, 445–450.

Davis, B. and Ternuff-Nyhlin, K. (1982). Social skills training. The assessment of training in social skills in nursing, with particular reference to the patient profile interview. *Nursing Times, 78*, 1765–1768.

Day, Sir R. (1989). *Grand Inquisitor*. London: George Weidenfeld & Nicholson Ltd.

De Landtsheer, C. (1998). The political rhetoric of a unified Europe. In O. Feldman and C. De Landtsheer (eds), *Politically Speaking: A Worldwide Examination of Language Used in the Public Sphere*, pp. 129–145. Westport, CT: Greenwood Publishing Group.

De Landtsheer, C. and Feldman, O. (eds) (2000). *Beyond Public Speech and Symbols: Exploration in the Rhetoric of Politicians and the Media*. Westport, CT: Praeger.

Dickson, D., Hargie, O. and Morrow, N. (1997). *Communication Skills Training for Health Professionals* (2nd edition). London: Chapman & Hall.

DiMatteo, M. and Taranta, A. (1979). Nonverbal communication and physician–patient rapport: an empirical study. *Professional Psychology, 10*, 540–547.

Dittman, A.T. and Llewellyn, L.G. (1967). The phonemic clause as a unit of speech decoding. *Journal of Personality and Social Psychology, 6*, 341–349.

Duncan, S. (1969). Nonverbal communication. *Psychological Bulletin, 72*, 118–137.

Duncan, S. and Fiske, D.W. (1977). *Face-to-face Interaction: Research, Methods and Theory*. Hillsdale, NJ: Lawrence Erlbaum Associates.

Duncan, S. and Fiske, D.W. (1985). *Interaction Structure and Strategy*. New York: Cambridge University Press.

Duncan, S. and Niederehe, G. (1974). On signalling that it's your turn to speak. *Journal of Experimental Social Psychology, 10*, 234–247.

Dunne, M. and Ng, S.H. (1994). Simultaneous speech in small group conversation: all-together-now *and* one-at-a-time? *Journal of Language and Social Psychology, 13*, 45–71.

Eco, U. (1986). Eine Palette von Grautönen. *Die Zeit*, August 29, 51.

Edelsky, C. (1979). Question intonation and sex roles. *Language in Society, 8*, 15–32.

Edelsky, C. (1981). Who's got the floor? *Language in Society, 10*, 383–421.

Edwards, D. and Potter, J. (1992). *Discursive Psychology*. London: Sage.

Edwards D. and Potter J. (1993). Language and causation: a discursive action model of description and attribution. *Psychological Review*, *100*, 23–41.

Edwards D. and Potter J. (1999). Language and causal attribution: a rejoinder to Schmid and Fiedler. *Theory and Psychology*, *9*, 823–836.

Eibl-Eibesfeldt, I. (1972). Similarities and differences between cultures in expressive movements. In R.A. Hinde (ed.), *Nonverbal Communication*, pp. 297–314. Cambridge: Cambridge University Press.

Eibl-Eibesfeldt, I. (1973). The expressive behaviour of the deaf-and-blind born. In M. von Cranach and I. Vine (eds), *Social Communication and Movement*, pp. 163–194. London: Academic Press.

Ekman, P. (1972). Universal and cultural differences in facial expressions of emotion. In J.R. Cole (ed.), *Nebraska Symposium on Motivation 1971*, pp. 207–283. Lincoln, NE: University of Nebraska Press.

Ekman, P. and Friesen, W.V. (1969a). The repertoire of nonverbal behaviour: categories, origins, usage and coding. *Semiotica*, *1*, 49–98.

Ekman, P. and Friesen, W.V. (1969b). Nonverbal leakage and clues to deception. *Psychiatry*, *32*, 88–106.

Ekman, P. and Friesen, W.V. (1974). Nonverbal behaviour and psychopathology. In R.J. Friedman and M.M. Katz (eds), *The Psychology of Depression: Contemporary Theory and Research*, pp. 203–232. New York: John Wiley & Sons.

Ekman, P. and Friesen, W.V. (1975). *Unmasking the Face: A Guide to Recognising Emotions from Facial Clues*. Englewood Cliffs, NJ: Prentice Hall.

Ekman, P. and Friesen, W.V. (1978). Measuring facial movement. *Environmental Psychology and Nonverbal Behaviour*, *1*, 56–75.

Ekman, P. and Friesen, W.V. (1982). Felt, false and miserable smiles. *Journal of Nonverbal Behaviour*, *6*, 238–252.

Ekman, P. and Friesen, W.V. (1986). A new pan-cultural facial expression of emotion. *Motivation and Emotion*, *10*, 159–168.

Ekman, P. and Rosenberg, E.L. (eds) (1997). *What the Face Reveals: Basic and Applied Studies of Spontaneous Expression Using the Facial Action Coding System (FACS)*. New York: Oxford University Press.

Ekman, P., Friesen, W.V. and Malmstrom, E.J. (1970). *Facial behaviour and stress in two cultures*. Unpublished manuscript, Langley Porter Neuropsychiatric Institute, San Francisco.

Ekman, P., Friesen, W.V. and Ellsworth, P.C. (1972). *Emotion in the Human Face: Guidelines for Research and an Integration of Findings*. New York: Pergamon.

Ekman, P., Hager, J.C. and Friesen, W.V. (1981). The symmetry of emotional and deliberate facial actions. *Psychophysiology*, *18*, 101–106.

Elliott, J. and Bull, P.E. (1996). A question of threat: face threats in questions posed during televised political interviews. *Journal of Community and Applied Social Psychology*, *6*, 49–72.

Ellis, R. and Whittington, D. (1981). *A Guide to Social Skill Training*. London: Croom Helm.

Erickson, B., Lind, E.A., Johnson, B.C. and O'Barr, W. (1978). Speech style and impression formation in a court setting: the effects of 'powerful' and 'powerless' speech. *Journal of Experimental Social Psychology*, *14*, 266–279.

Evans, E.C. (1969). Physiognomics in the ancient world. *Transactions of the American Philosophical Society, 59*, 1–101.

Evans, B.J., Kiellerup, F.D., Stanley, R.O., Burrows, G.D. and Sweet, B. (1987). A communication skills programme for increasing patients' satisfaction with general practice consultations. *British Journal of Medical Psychology, 60*, 373–378.

Exline, R.V. (1963). Explorations in the process of person perception: visual interaction in relation to competition, sex, and need for affiliation. *Journal of Personality, 31*, 1–20.

Exline, R.V. (1972). Visual interaction: the glances of power and preference. *Nebraska Symposium on Motivation 1971*, 163–206.

Feldman, O. and De Landtsheer, C. (eds) (1998). *Politically Speaking: A Worldwide Examination of Language Used in the Public Sphere*, Westport, CT: Greenwood Publishing Group.

Ferguson, N. (1977). Simultaneous speech, interruptions and dominance. *British Journal of Social and Clinical Psychology, 16*, 295–302.

Fiedler, K. and Schmid, J. (1999). Implicit attributions and biases: an answer to Edwards' and Potter's rejoinder. *Theory and Psychology, 9*, 837–845.

Fiedler, K. and Semin, G.R. (1996). Language in applied contexts. In G.R. Semin and K. Fiedler (eds), *Applied Social Psychology*, pp. 91–109. London: Sage.

Fishman, P.M. (1983). Interaction: the work women do. In B. Thorne, C. Kramerae and N. Henley (eds), *Language, Gender and Society*, pp. 127–132. Rowley, MA: Newbury House.

Fitzpatrick, R. and Hopkins, A. (1981). Patients' satisfaction with communications in neurological outpatients' clinics. *Journal of Psychosomatic Research, 25*, 329–334.

Franco, F.M. and Maass, A. (1996). Implicit versus explicit strategies of out-group discrimination: the role of intentional control in biased language use and reward allocation. *Journal of Language and Social Psychology, 15*, 335–359.

Frank, M.G. and Stennett, J. (2001). The forced-choice paradigm and the perception of facial expressions of emotion. *Journal of Personality and Social Psychology, 80*, 75–85.

Frederikson, L.G. (1993). Development of an integrative model for medical consultation. *Health Communication, 5*, 225–237.

Frederikson, L.G. and Bull, P. (1992). An appraisal of the current status of communication skills training in British medical schools. *Social Science and Medicine, 34*, 515–522.

Freedman, N. and Hoffman, S.P. (1967). Kinetic behaviour in altered clinical states: approach to objective analysis of motor behaviour during clinical interviews. *Perceptual and Motor Skills, 24*, 527–539.

Freud, S. (1925). Instincts and their vicissitudes. In *Collected Papers*, vol. 4, pp. 60–83. London: Hogarth Press (originally published, 1915).

Fridlund, A.J. (1994). *Human Facial Expression: An Evolutionary View*. San Diego, CA: Academic Press.

Fridlund, A.J. (1997). The new ethology of human facial expressions. In J.A. Russell and J.M. Fernández-Dols (eds), *The Psychology of Facial Expression*, pp. 103–129. New York: Cambridge University Press.

Friedson, E. (1961). *Patients' View of Medical Practice*. New York: Russell Sage Foundation.

Furnham, A. and Bochner, S. (1982). Social difficulty in a foreign culture: an empirical analysis of culture shock. In S. Bochner (ed.), *Cultures in Contact: Studies in Cross-Cultural Interaction*, pp. 161–198. Oxford: Pergamon.

Furnham, A. and Bochner, S. (1986). *Culture Shock: Psychological Reactions to Unfamiliar Environments*. London: Methuen.

Gallois, C. and Callan, V. (1997). *Communication and Culture: A Guide for Practice*. Chichester: John Wiley & Sons Ltd.

Giesen, M. and McClaren, H.A. (1976). Discussion, distance and sex: changes in impressions and attraction during small group interaction. *Sociometry, 39*, 60–70.

Giles, H. (1973). Accent mobility: a model and some data. *Anthropological Linguistics, 15*, 87–105.

Giles, H. (1977). Social psychology and applied linguistics. *ITL: Review of Applied Linguistics, 33*, 27–42.

Giles, H. and Coupland, N. (1991). *Language: Contexts and Consequences*. Buckingham: Open University Press.

Giles, H. and Smith, P.M. (1979). Accommodation theory: optimal levels of convergence. In H. Giles and R. St. Clair (eds), *Language and Social Psychology*, pp. 45–65. Oxford: Blackwell.

Giles, H., Taylor D.M. and Bourhis, R.Y. (1973). Towards a theory of interpersonal accommodation through language: some Canadian data. *Language in Society, 2*, 177–192.

Giles, H., Mulac, A., Bradac, J.J. and Johnson, P. (1987). Speech Accommodation Theory: the first decade and beyond. In M.L. McLaughlin (ed.), *Communication Yearbook 10*, pp. 13–48. Newbury Park, CA: Sage.

Ginsburg, H.J., Pollman, V.A. and Wauson, M.S. (1977). An ethological analysis of nonverbal inhibitors of aggressive behaviours in male elementary school children. *Developmental Psychology, 13*, 417–418.

Goffman, E. (1955). On face-work: an analysis of ritual elements in social interaction. *Psychiatry, 18*, 213–231. Reprinted in E. Goffman (1967). *Interaction Ritual: Essays on Face to Face Behaviour*, pp. 5–45. Garden City, NY: Anchor.

Goffman, E. (1959). *The Presentation of Self in Everyday Life*. Harmondsworth: Penguin.

Goffman, E. (1961). *Encounters: Two Studies in the Sociology of Interaction*. Indianapolis, IN: Bobbs-Merrill.

Goffman, E. (1971). *Relations in Public: Microstudies of the Public Order*. London: Penguin Press.

Gottman, J.M. (1994). *What Predicts Divorce? The Relationship between Marital Processes and Marital Outcomes*. Hillsdale, NJ: Lawrence Erlbaum Associates.

Gould, O.N. and Dixon, R.A. (1997). Recall of medication instructions by young and elderly adult women: is overaccommodative speech helpful? *Journal of Language and Social Psychology, 16*, 50–69.

Graham, J.A. and Argyle, M. (1975). A cross-cultural study of the communication of extra-verbal meaning by gestures. *International Journal of Psychology, 10*, 57–69.

Graham, J.A. and Heywood, S. (1976). The effects of elimination of hand gesture and of verbal codability on speech performance. *European Journal of Social Psychology, 5*, 189–195.

Grahe, J.E. and Bernieri, F.J. (1999). The importance of nonverbal cues in judging rapport. *Journal of Nonverbal Behaviour*, 23, 253–269.

Gray, J. (1995). *Men are from Mars, Women are from Venus*. London: Thorsons.

Greatbatch, D. (1988). A turn-taking system for British news interviews. *Language in Society*, 17, 401–430.

Gudykunst, W.B. and Kim, Y.Y. (1992). *Communicating with Strangers: An Approach to Intercultural Communication*. New York: McGraw-Hill.

Gudykunst, W.B. and Nishida, T. (1994). *Bridging Japanese/North American Differences*. Thousand Oaks, CA: Sage.

Gumperz, J.J. (1982). *Discourse Strategies*. Cambridge: Cambridge University Press.

Gumperz (1992). Contextualization and understanding. In A. Duranti and C. Goodwin (eds), *Rethinking Context: Language as an Interactive Phenomenon*, pp. 229–252. Cambridge: Cambridge University Press.

Hadar, U., Steiner, T.J., Grant, E.C. and Rose, F.C. (1983). Head movement correlates of juncture and stress at sentence level. *Language and Speech*, 26, 117–129.

Hadar, U., Steiner, T.J., Grant, E.C. and Rose, F.C. (1984). The timing of shifts of head postures during conversation. *Human Movement Science*, 3, 237–245.

Hall, E.T. (1963). A system for the notation of proxemic behaviour. *American Anthropologist*, 65, 1003–1026.

Hall, J.A. (1978). Gender effects in decoding nonverbal cues. *Psychological Bulletin*, 85, 845–857.

Hall, J.A. (1979). Gender, gender roles and nonverbal communication skills. In R. Rosenthal (ed.), *Skill in Nonverbal Communication: Individual Differences*, pp. 32–67. Cambridge, MA: Oelgeschlager, Gunn and Hain.

Hall, J.A. (1984). *Nonverbal Sex Differences: Communication Accuracy and Expressive Style*. Baltimore, MD: The Johns Hopkins University Press.

Hall, J.A. (1996). Touch, status, and gender at professional meetings. *Journal of Nonverbal Behaviour*, 20, 23–44.

Hall, J.A. and Halberstadt, A.G. (1997). Subordination and nonverbal sensitivity: a hypothesis in search of support. In M.R. Walsh (ed.), *Women, Men & Gender: Ongoing Debates*, pp. 120–133. New Haven, CT: Yale University Press.

Hall, J.A. and Veccia, E.M. (1990). More 'touching' observations: new insights on men, women, and interpersonal touch. *Journal of Personality and Social Psychology*, 59, 1155–1162.

Halliday, M.A.K. (1970). *A Course in Spoken English: Intonation*. London: Oxford University Press.

Hamilton, M.A. and Mineo, P.J. (1998). A framework for understanding equivocation. *Journal of Language and Social Psychology*, 17, 3–35.

Hargie, O.D.W. (1997a). Interpersonal communication: a theoretical framework. In O.D.W. Hargie (ed.), *The Handbook of Communication Skills* (2nd edition), pp. 29–63. London: Routledge.

Hargie, O.D.W. (1997b). Training in communication skills: research, theory and practice. In O.D.W. Hargie (ed.), *The Handbook of Communication Skills* (second edition), pp. 473–482. London: Routledge.

Hargie, O.D.W. and Marshall, P. (1986). Interpersonal communication: a theoretical framework. In O.D.W. Hargie (ed.), *The Handbook of Communication Skills*, pp. 22–56. London: Croom Helm.

Hargie, O.D.W., Saunders, C.Y.M. and Dickson, D. (1981). *Social Skills in Interpersonal Communication*. London: Croom Helm.

Hargie, O.D.W., Dickson, D., Boohan, M. and Hughes, K. (1998). A survey of communication skills training in UK Schools of Medicine: present practices and prospective proposals. *Medical Education*, 32, 25–34.

Harling, P.A. and Edwards, A.D.N. (1997). *Progress in Gestural Interaction*. London: Springer-Verlag Ltd.

Harris, S. (1991). Evasive action: how politicians respond to questions in political interviews. In P. Scannell (ed.), *Broadcast Talk*, pp. 76–99. London: Sage.

Heath, C. (1986). *Body Movement and Speech in Medical Interaction*. Cambridge: Cambridge University Press.

Heider, F. (1958). *The Psychology of Interpersonal Relations*. New York: John Wiley.

Henley, N.M. (1973). Status and sex: some touching observations. *Bulletin of the Psychonomic Society*, 2, 91–93.

Henley, N.M. (1977). *Body Politics: Power, Sex and Nonverbal Communication*. New York: Prentice Hall.

Henley, N.M. (1995). Body politics revisited: what do we know today? In P.J. Kalbfleisch and M.J. Cody (eds), *Gender, Power and Communication in Human Relationships*, pp. 27–61. Hillsdale, NJ: Lawrence Erlbaum Associates.

Henley, N.M. and Kramarae, C. (1991). Gender, power and miscommunication. In N. Coupland, H. Giles and J.W. Wiemann (eds), *'Miscommunication' and Problematic Talk*, pp. 18–43. London: Sage.

Henley, N.M. and LaFrance, M. (1984). Gender as culture: difference and dominance in nonverbal behaviour. In A. Wolfgang (ed.), *Nonverbal Behaviour: Perspectives, Applications, Intercultural Insights*, pp. 351–371. Lewiston, NY: C.J. Hogrefe.

Heritage, J.C. (1985). Analyzing news interviews: aspects of the production of talk for an overhearing audience. In T. van Dijk (ed.), *Handbook of Discourse Analysis*, vol. 3, pp. 95–117. New York: Academic Press.

Heritage, J.C. (1989). Current developments in conversation analysis. In D. Roger and P. Bull (eds), *Conversation: An Interdisciplinary Perspective*, pp. 21–47. Clevedon, UK: Multilingual Matters.

Heritage, J. and Greatbatch D. (1986). Generating applause: a study of rhetoric and response at party political conferences. *American Journal of Sociology*, 92, 110–157.

Heritage, J.C. and Greatbatch, D.L. (1991). On the institutional character of institutional talk: the case of news interviews. In D. Boden and D. Zimmerman (eds), *Talk and Social Structure*, pp. 93–137. Cambridge, UK: Polity Press.

Heritage, J.C., Clayman, S.E. and Zimmerman, D. (1988). Discourse and message analysis: the micro-structure of mass media messages. In R. Hawkins, S. Pingree and J. Weimann (eds), *Advancing Communication Science: Merging Mass and Interpersonal Processes*, pp. 77–109. Newbury Park, CA: Sage.

Hess, E.H. (1965). Attitude and pupil size. *Scientific American*, 212, 46–54.

Hess, E.H. (1975). The role of pupil size in communication. *Scientific American*, 233, 110–119.

Hess, E.H. and Polt, J.M. (1960). Pupil size as related to interest value of visual stimuli. *Science*, 132, 349–350.

Hittelman, J.H. and Dickes, R. (1979). Sex differences in neonatal eye-contact time. *Merrill-Palmer Quarterly*, 25, 171–184.

Hofstede, G. (1980). *Culture's Consequences*. Beverly Hills, CA: Sage.

Hollandsworth, J.G., Glazeski, R.C. and Dressel, M.E. (1978). Use of social skills training in the treatment of extreme anxiety and deficient verbal skills in the job interview setting. *Journal of Applied Behaviour Analysis*, 11, 259–269.

Holmes, J. (1985). Sex differences and miscommunication: some data from New Zealand. In J.B. Pride (ed.), *Cross-cultural Encounters: Communication and Miscommunication*, pp. 24–43. Melbourne: River Seine.

Holmes, J. (1986). Functions of *you know* in women's and men's speech. *Language in Society*, 15, 122.

Holmes, J. (1995). *Women, Men and Politeness*. New York: Longman.

Holtgraves, T. (1997). Yes, but . . .: positive politeness in conversation arguments. *Journal of Language and Social Psychology*, 16, 222–239.

Holtgraves, T. (1998). Interpreting indirect replies. *Cognitive Psychology*, 37, 1–27.

Homans, G.C. (1961). *Social Behaviour: Its Elementary Forms*. New York: Harcourt, Brace & World.

Hulsman, R.L., Ros, W.J.G., Winnubst, J.A.M. and Bensing, J.M. (1999). Teaching clinically experienced physicians communication skills. A review of evaluation studies. *Medical Education*, 33, 655–668.

Huxley, J. (1914). The courtship habits of the great crested grebe (*Podiceps cristatus*); with an addition to the theory of natural selection. *Proceedings of the Zoological Society of London*, 35, 491–562.

Huxley, J.S. (1963). *Evolution: The Modern Synthesis* (2nd edition). Northampton: John Dickens & Co.

James, D. and Clarke, S. (1993). Women, men and interruptions: a critical review. In D. Tannen (ed.), *Gender and Conversational Interaction*, pp. 231–280. New York: Oxford University Press.

Jefferson, G. (1984). On the organisation of laughter in talk about troubles. In J.M. Atkinson and J.C. Heritage (eds), *Structures of Social Action: Studies in Conversation Analysis*, pp. 347–369. Cambridge: Cambridge University Press.

Jefferson, G. (1990). List-construction as a task and resource. In G. Psathas (ed.), *Interaction Competence*, pp. 63–92. Lanham, MD: University Press of America, Inc.

Jenni, D.A. and Jenni, M.A. (1976). Carrying behaviour in humans: analyses of sex differences. *Science*, 194, 859–860.

Jones, H.E. (1960). The longitudinal method in the study of personality. In I. Iscoe and H.W. Stevenson (eds), *Personality Development in Children*, pp. 3–27. Chicago, IL: University of Chicago Press.

Jones, S.E. (1994). *The Right Touch: Understanding and Using the Language of Physical Contact*. Cresskill, NJ: Hampton Press.

Jucker, J. (1986). *News Interviews: A Pragmalinguistic Analysis*. Amsterdam: Gieben.

Kalma, A. (1992). Gazing in triads: a powerful signal of floor apportionment. *British Journal of Social Psychology*, 31, 21–39.

Kauffman, L. (1969). Tacesics, the study of touch: a model for proxemic analysis. *Semiotica*, 4, 149–161.

Kelly, J.A. (1982). *Social Skills Training: A Practical Guide for Interventions*. New York: Springer Publishing Company.

Kelly, S.D., Barr, D.J., Church, R.R. and Lynch, K. (1999). Offering a hand to pragmatic understanding: The role of speech and gesture in comprehension and memory. *Journal of Memory and Language, 40*, 577–592.

Kendon, A. (1967). Some functions of gaze direction in social interaction. *Acta Psychologica, 26*, 22–63.

Kendon, A. (1982). Organization of behaviour in face-to-face interaction. In K.R. Scherer and P. Ekman (eds), *Handbook of Methods in Nonverbal Behaviour Research*, pp. 440–505. Cambridge: Cambridge University Press.

Kendon, A. (1985). Some uses of gesture. In O. Tannen and M. Saville-Troike (eds), *Perspectives on Silence*, pp. 215–234. Norwood, NJ: Ablex.

Kendon, A. (1988). Goffman's approach to face-to-face interaction. In P. Drew and A. Wootton (eds), *Erving Goffman: Exploring the Interaction Order*, pp. 14–40. Cambridge, UK: Polity Press.

Kendon, A. (1994). Do gestures communicate? A review. *Research on Language and Social Interaction, 27*, 175–200.

Kendon, A. and Ferber, A. (1973). A description of some human greetings. In R.P. Michael and J.H. Crook (eds), *Comparative Ecology and Behaviour of Primates*, pp. 591–668. London: Academic Press.

Kiritz, S.A. (1971). 'Hand movements and clinical ratings at admission and discharge for hospitalised psychiatric patients'. Unpublished doctoral dissertation, University of California, San Francisco.

Knapp, M.L. and Hall, J. (1997) *Nonverbal Communication in Human Interaction* (4th edition). Orlando, FL: Harcourt Brace College Publishers.

Korsch, B., Gozzi, E. and Francis, V. (1968). Gaps in doctor–patient communication; doctor–patient interaction and patient satisfaction. *Pediatrics, 42*, 855–871.

Kruijver, I.P.M., Kerkstra, A., Francke, A.L., Bensing, J.M. and van de Wiel, H.B.M. (2000). Evaluation of communication training programs in nursing care: a review of the literature. *Patient Education and Counselling, 39*, 129–145.

Labov, W. (1966). *The Social Stratification of English in New York City*. Washington, DC: Centre for Applied Linguistics.

LaFrance, M. (1979). Nonverbal synchrony and rapport: analysis by the cross-lag panel technique. *Social Psychology Quarterly, 42*, 66–70.

LaFrance, M. and Broadbent, M. (1976). Group rapport: posture sharing as a nonverbal indicator. *Group and Organisation Studies, 1*, 328–333.

LaFrance, M. and Hecht, M.A. (2000). Gender and smiling: a meta-analysis. In A.H. Fischer (ed), *Gender and Emotion: Social Psychological Perspectives*, pp. 118–142. Cambridge: Cambridge University Press.

LaFrance, M. and Henley, N.M. (1997). On oppressing hypotheses: or, differences in nonverbal sensitivity revisited. In M.R. Walsh (ed.), *Women, Men & Gender: Ongoing Debates*, pp. 104–119. New Haven, CT: Yale University Press.

Lakoff, R. (1973). Language and women's place. *Language in Society, 2*, 45–80.

Lakoff, R. (1975). *Language and Women's Place*. New York: Harper and Row.

Lakoff, G. and Johnson, M. (1980). *Metaphors We Live By*. Chicago, IL: Chicago University Press.

Lalljee, M. and Widdicombe, S. (1989). Discourse analysis. In A.M. Colman and

G. Beaumont (eds), *Psychology Survey 7*, pp. 76–97. Leicester: The British Psychological Society.

Langer, E. (1978). Rethinking the role of thought in social interaction. In J.Harvey, W. Ickes and R. Kidd (eds), *New Directions in Attribution Research*, vol. 2, pp. 35–58. Hillsdale, NJ: Lawrence Erlbaum Associates.

Lanzetta, J.T. and Kleck, R.E. (1970). Encoding and decoding of nonverbal affect in humans. *Journal of Personality and Social Psychology*, 16, 12–19.

LaRusso, L. (1978). Sensitivity of paranoid patients to nonverbal cues. *Journal of Abnormal Psychology*, 87, 463–471.

Lashley, K.S. (1951). The problem of serial order in behaviour. In L.A. Jeffress (ed.), *Cerebral Mechanisms in Behaviour*. New York: Wiley.

Levine, L. and Crockett, H.J. (1966). Speech variation in a Piedmont community: post-vocalic r-. In S. Lieberson (ed.), *Exploration in Sociolinguistics*, pp. 76–98. The Hague: Mouton.

Ley, P. (1972). Complaints made by hospital staff and patients: a review of the literature. *Bulletin of the British Psychological Society*, 25, 115–120.

Lindenfeld, J. (1971). Verbal and nonverbal elements in discourse. *Semiotica*, 3, 223–233.

Lippa, R. (1978). The naïve perception of masculinity–femininity on the basis of expressive cues. *Journal of Research in Personality*, 12, 1–14.

Maass, A., Salvi, D., Arcuri, L. and Semin, G. (1989). Language use in intergroup contexts: the linguistic intergroup bias. *Journal of Personality and Social Psychology*, 57, 981–993.

McClave, E.Z. (2000). Linguistic functions of head movements in the context of speech. *Journal of Pragmatics*, 32, 855–878.

McFadyen, R.G. (1996). Gender, status and 'powerless' speech: interaction of students and lecturers. *British Journal of Social Psychology*, 35, 353–367.

McGarvey, B. and Swallow, D. (1986). *Microteaching in Teacher Education and Training*. London: Croom Helm.

McGee, D.S. and Cegala, D.J. (1998). Patient communication skills training for improved communication competence in the primary care medical consultation. *Journal of Applied Communication Research*, 26, 412–430.

McNeil, N.M., Alibali, M.W. and Evans, J.L. (2000). The role of gesture in children's comprehension of spoken language: now they need it, now they don't. *Journal of Nonverbal Behaviour*, 24, 131–150.

McNeill, D. (1985). So you think gestures are nonverbal? *Psychological Review*, 92, 350–371.

McNeill, D. (1992). *Hand and Mind: What Gestures Reveal About Thought*. Chicago, IL: University of Chicago Press.

Magnusson, M.S. (1996). Hidden real-time problems in intra- and inter-individual behaviour: Description and detection. *European Journal of Psychological Assessment*, 12, 112–123.

Maguire, P., Fairbairn, S. and Fletcher, C. (1986). Consultation skills of young doctors: 1 – Benefits of feedback training in interviewing as students persist. *British Medical Journal*, 292, 1573–1578.

Maguire, P., Tait, A., Brooke, M. and Sellwood, R. (1980a). Emotional aspects of mastectomy: a conspiracy of pretence. *Nursing Mirror*, 10 January, 17–19.

Maguire, P., Tait, A., Brooke, M., Thomas, C. and Sellwood, R. (1980b). The effect of counselling on the psychiatric morbidity associated with mastectomy. *British Medical Journal*, *281*, 1454–1456.

Maguire, P., Roe, P., Goldberg, D., Jones, S., Hyde, C. and O'Dowd, T. (1978). The value of feedback in teaching interviewing skills to medical students. *Psychological Medicine*, *8*, 695–704.

Major, B., Schmidlin, A.M. and Williams, L. (1990). Gender patterns in social touch: the impact of setting and age. *Journal of Personality and Social Psychology*, *58*, 634–643.

Maltz, D.N. and Borker, R.A. (1982). A cultural approach to male–female miscommunication. In J.J. Gumperz (ed.), *Language and Social Identity*, pp. 196–216. New York: Cambridge University Press.

Marey, É.J. (1895). *Movement*. New York: D. Appleton.

Martin, R. (1997). 'Girls don't talk about garages!': perceptions of conversation in same- and cross-sex friendships. *Personal Relationships*, *4*, 115–130.

Matsumoto, D. (1990). Cultural similarities and differences in display rules. *Motivation and Emotion*, *14*, 195–214.

Matsumoto, D. (1992). American–Japanese cultural differences in the recognition of universal facial expressions. *Journal of Cross-Cultural Psychology*, *23*, 72–84.

Matsumoto, D. (1996). *Unmasking Japan: Myths and Realities about the Emotions of the Japanese*. Stanford, CA: Stanford University Press.

Matsumoto, D. and Ekman, P. (1989). American–Japanese cultural differences in intensity ratings of facial expressions of emotion. *Motivation and Emotion*, *13*, 143–157.

Maurer, T., Solamon, J. and Troxtel, D. (1998). Relationship of coaching with performance in situational employment interviews. *Journal of Applied Psychology*, *83*, 128–136.

Mead, G.H. (1934). *Mind, Self and Society: From the Standpoint of a Social Behaviourist*. Chicago, IL: University of Chicago Press.

Mehrabian, A. and Williams, N. (1969). Nonverbal concomitants of perceived and intended persuasiveness. *Journal of Personality and Social Psychology*, *13*, 37–58.

Metropolitan Police Diversity Training Support Unit (2000). *Policing Diversity: Metropolitan Police Service Handbook on London's Religions, Cultures and Communities*. London: Metropolitan Police Publication.

Miller, S. and Sherrard, P.A.D. (1999). Couple communication: a system for equipping partners to talk, listen and resolve conflicts effectively. In R. Berger and M.T. Hannah (eds), *Preventive Approaches in Couples Therapy*, pp. 125–148. Philadelphia, PA: Brunner/Mazel Inc.

Morris, D., Collett, O.P., Marsh, P. and O'Shaugnessy, M. (1979). *Gestures: Their Origins and Distribution*. London: Jonathan Cape.

Moscovici, S. (1967). Communication processes and the properties of language. *Advances in Experimental Social Psychology*, *3*, 226–270.

Mott, H. and Petrie, H, (1995). Workplace interactions: women's linguistic behaviour. *Journal of Language and Social Psychology*, *14*, 324–336.

Mulac, A. (1998). The gender-linked language effect: do language differences really make a difference? In D.J. Canary and K. Dindia (eds), *Sex Differences and Similarities in Communication: Critical Essays and Empirical Investigations of Sex and Gender in Interaction*, pp. 127–153. Mahwah, NJ: Lawrence Erlbaum Associates.

Mulac, A., Lundell, T.L. and Bradac, J.J. (1986). Male/female language differences and attributional consequences in a public speaking situation: toward an explanation of the gender-linked language effect. *Communication Monographs*, 53, 115–129.

Mulac, A., Erlandson, K.T., Farrar, W.J., Hallett, J.S., Molloy, J.L. and Prescott, M.E. (1998). 'Uh-huh. What's that all about?' Differing interpretations of conversational backchannels and questions as sources of miscommunication across gender boundaries. *Communication Research*, 25, 641–668.

Murray, S.O. and Covelli, L.H. (1988). Women and men speaking at the same time. *Journal of Pragmatics*, 12, 103–111.

Muybridge, E. (1899). *Animals in Motion*. Reprinted by Dover Publications, New York, 1957.

Muybridge, E. (1901). *The Human Figure in Motion*. Reprinted by Dover Publications, New York, 1957.

Nakane, C. (1970). *Japanese Society*. Berkeley, CA: University of California Press.

Noller, P. (1980). Misunderstandings in marital communication: a study of couples' nonverbal communication. *Journal of Personality and Social Psychology*, 39, 1135–1148.

Noller, P. (1981). Gender and marital adjustment level differences in decoding messages from spouses and strangers. *Journal of Personality and Social Psychology*, 41, 272–278.

Noller, P. (1984). *Nonverbal Communication and Marital Interaction*. Oxford: Pergamon Press.

Noller, P. and Feeney, J.A. (1994). Relationship satisfaction, attachment, and non-verbal accuracy in early marriage. *Journal of Nonverbal Behaviour*, 18, 199–221.

O'Barr, W.M. and Atkins, B.K. (1980). 'Women's language' or 'powerless language'. In S. McConnell-Ginet, R. Borker and N. Furman (eds), *Women and Language in Literature and Society*, pp. 93–110. New York: Praeger.

Oberg, K. (1960). Cultural shock: adjustment to new cultural environments. *Practical Anthropology*, 7, 177–182.

O'Connell, D.C., Kowal, S. and Kaltenbacher, E. (1990) Turn-taking: a critical view of the research tradition. *Journal of Psycholinguistic Research*, 19, 345–373.

Oster, H. and Ekman, P. (1977). Facial behaviour in child development. In A. Collins (ed.), *Minnesota Symposia on Child Psychology*, 11, 231–276.

Parker, I. (1992). *Discourse Dynamics: Critical Analysis for Social and Individual Psychology*. London: Routledge.

Parkinson, B. (1995). *Ideas and Realities of Emotion*. London: Routledge.

Perkins, L., Whitworth, A. and Lesser, R. (1997). *Conversation Analysis Profile for People with Cognitive Impairments* (CAPPCI). London: Whurr.

Perkins, L., Whitworth, A. and Lesser, R. (1998). Conversing in dementia: a conversation analytic approach. *Journal of Neurolinguistics*, 11, 33–53.

Pittenger, R.E., Hockett, C.F. and Danehy, J.J. (1960). *The First Five Minutes: A Sample of Microscopic Interview Analysis*. Ithaca, NY: Martineau.

Pomerantz, A. (1984). Agreeing and disagreeing with assessments: some features of preferred/dispreferred turn shapes. In J.M. Atkinson and J. Heritage (eds), *Structures of Social Action*, pp. 57–101. Cambridge: Cambridge University Press.

Potter J. and Wetherell M. (1987). *Discourse and social psychology: Beyond attitudes and behaviour*. London: Sage.

Power, R.D.J. and dal Martello, M.F. (1986). Some criticisms of Sacks, Schegloff and Jefferson on turn-taking. *Semiotica*, *58*, 29–40.

Prkachin, K.M. and Craig, K.D. (1995). Expressing pain: the communication and interpretation of facial pain signals. *Journal of Nonverbal Behaviour, 19*, 191–205.

Psathas, G. (1995) *Conversation Analysis: The Study of Talk-in-Interaction*. Thousand Oaks, CA: Sage.

Quirk, R., Greenbaum, S., Leech, G. and Svartvik, J. (1985). *A Comprehensive Grammar of the English Language*. London: Longman,

Ragan, S.L. (1989). Communication between the sexes: a consideration of sex differences in adult communication. In J.F. Nussbaum (ed.), *Life-span Communication: Normative Processes*, pp. 179–193. Hillsdale, NJ: Lawrence Erlbaum Associates.

Rakos, R.F. (1986). Asserting and confronting. In O. Hargie (ed.), *A Handbook of Communication Skills*, pp. 407–440. London: Croom Helm.

Rakos, R.F. (1990). *Assertive Behaviour: Theory, Research and Training*. London: Routledge.

Register, L.M. and Henley, T.B. (1992). The phenomenology of intimacy. *Journal of Social and Personal Relationships, 9*, 467–481.

Rekers, G.A. (1977). Assessment and treatment of childhood gender problems. In B.B. Lahey and A.E. Kazdin (eds), *Advances in Child Clinical Psychology, 1*, 267–306.

Rekers, G.A. and Rudy, J.P. (1978). Differentiation of childhood body gestures. *Perceptual and Motor Skills, 46*, 839–845.

Rekers, G.A., Amaro-Plotkin, H.D. and Low, B.P. (1977). Sex-typed mannerisms in normal boys and girls as a function of sex and age. *Child Development, 48*, 275–278.

Rimm, D.C. and Masters, J.C. (1979). *Behaviour Therapy: Techniques and Empirical Findings* (2nd edition). New York: Academic Press.

Rinn, W.E. (1991). Neuropsychology of facial expression. In R.S. Feldman and B. Rimé (eds), *Fundamentals of nonverbal behaviour*, pp. 3–30. Cambridge: Cambridge University Press.

Riseborough, M.G. (1981). Physiographic gestures as decoding facilitators: three experiments exploring a neglected facet of communication. *Journal of Nonverbal Behaviour, 5*, 172–183.

Roger, D.B. and Nesshoever, W. (1987). Individual differences in dyadic conversational strategies: a further study. *British Journal of Social Psychology, 26*, 247–255.

Roger, D.B. and Schumacher, A. (1983). Effects of individual differences on dyadic conversational strategies. *Journal of Personality and Social Psychology, 45*, 700–705.

Roger, D.B., Bull, P.E. and Smith, S. (1988). The development of a comprehensive system for classifying interruptions. *Journal of Language and Social Psychology, 7*, 2734.

Rogers, W.T. (1978). The contribution of kinesic illustrators toward the comprehension of verbal behaviour within utterances. *Human Communication Research, 5*, 54–62.

Rose, D.J. and Church, R.J. (1998). Learning to teach: the acquisition and maintenance of teaching skills. *Journal of Behavioural Education, 8*, 5–35.

Rosenbaum, M. (1997). *From Soapbox to Soundbite: Party Political Campaigning in Britain since 1945*. London: Macmillan Press.

Rosenthal, R. and DePaulo, B.M. (1979). Sex differences in accommodation in nonverbal communication. In R. Rosenthal (ed.), *Skill in Nonverbal Communication*, pp. 68–103. Cambridge, MA: Oelgeschlager, Gunn and Hain.

Rosenthal, R., Hall, J.A., DiMatteo, M.R., Rogers, P.L. and Archer, D. (1979). *Sensitivity to Nonverbal Communication: The PONS Test*. Baltimore, MD: Johns Hopkins University Press.

Ruesch, J. and Bateson, G. (1951) *Communication: The Social Matrix of Psychiatry*. New York: Norton.

Russell, J.A. (1991). Culture and the categorization of emotions. *Psychological Bulletin, 110*, 426–450.

Russell, J.A. (1994). Is there universal recognition of emotion from facial expression? *Psychological Bulletin, 115*, 102–141.

Ryan, E.B. and Cole, R.L. (1990). Evaluative perceptions of interpersonal communication with elders. In H. Giles, N. Coupland and J.M. Wiemann (eds), *Communication, Health and the Elderly*, pp. 172–191. Manchester: Manchester University Press.

Ryan, E.B., Giles, H., Bartolucci, G. and Henwood, K. (1986). Psycholinguistic and social psychological components of communication by and with the elderly. *Language and Communication, 6*, 1–24.

Sackeim, H.A. and Gur, R.C. (1978). Lateral asymmetry in intensity of emotional expression. *Neuropsychologia, 16*, 473–481.

Sacks, H. (1992) (ed. G. Jefferson) *Lectures on Conversation*. Cambridge, MA: Blackwell.

Sacks, H., Schegloff, E.A. and Jefferson, G. (1974). A simplest systematics for the organisation of turn-taking for conversation. *Language, 50*, 696–735.

Sanson-Fisher, R. and Poole, A. (1979). Teaching medical students communication skills: an experimental appraisal of the short and long-term benefits. In D. Oborne, M. Gruneberg and J. Eiser (eds), *Research in Psychology and Medicine. Volume 2, Social Aspects: Attitudes, Communication, Care and Training*, pp. 288–294. London: Academic Press.

Scheflen, A.E. (1964). The significance of posture in communication systems. *Psychiatry, 27*, 316–331.

Scheflen, A.E. (1966). Natural history method in psychotherapy: communicational research. In L.A. Gottschalk and A.H. Auerbach (eds), *Methods of Research in Psychotherapy*, pp. 263–289. New York: Appleton-Century Crofts.

Scheflen, A.E. (1973). *Communicational Structure: Analysis of a Psychotherapy Transaction*. Bloomington, IN: Indiana University Press.

Schegloff, E.A. (1989). Harvey Sacks – lectures 1964–1965. An introduction/memoir. *Human Studies, 12*, 187–209.

Schegloff, E.A. (2000). Overlapping talk and the organization of turn-taking for conversation. *Language in Society, 29*, 1–63.

Scherer, K.R. (1971). Randomised-splicing: a note on a simple technique for masking speech content. *Journal of Experimental Research in Personality, 5*, 155–159.

Schmid, J. and Fiedler, K. (1996). Language and implicit attributions in the

Nuremberg Trials: analysing prosecutors' and defence attorneys' closing speeches. *Human Communication Research*, 22, 371–398.

Schmid, J. and Fiedler, K. (1998). The backbone of closing speeches: the impact of prosecution versus defence language on juridical attributions. *Journal of Applied Social Psychology*, 28, 1140–1172.

Schmid, J. and Fiedler, K. (1999). A parsimonious theory can account for complex phenomena. A discursive analysis of Edwards' and Potter's critique of non-discursive language research. *Theory and Psychology*, 9, 807–822.

Schroeder, J.E. (1995a). Interpersonal perception skills: self-concept correlates. *Perceptual and Motor Skills*, 80, 51–56.

Schroeder, J.E. (1995b). Self-concept, social anxiety, and interpersonal perception skills. *Personality and Individual Differences*, 19, 955–958.

Schroeder, J.E. and Ketrow, S.M. (1997). Social anxiety and performance in an interpersonal perception task. *Psychological Reports*, 81, 991–996.

Semin, G.R. and Fiedler, K. (1988). The cognitive functions of linguistic categories in describing persons: social cognition and language. *Journal of Personality and Social Psychology*, 54, 558–568.

Semin, G.R. and Fiedler, K. (1991). The linguistic category model, its bases, applications and range. In W. Stroebe and M. Hewstone (eds), *European Review of Social Psychology*, vol. 2, pp. 1–50. Chichester: John Wiley and Sons Ltd.

Shuy, R.W., Wolfram, W.A. and Riley, W.K. (1967). *Linguistic Correlates of Social Stratification in Detroit Speech*. Cooperative Research Project 6-1347, East Lancing: U.S. Office of Education.

Simmel, G. (1908). *Soziologie*. Leipzig: Duncker & Humblot.

Simmel, G. (1950) (K. Wolff, ed. and Trans.). *The Sociology of Georg Simmel*. Glencoe, IL: Free Press.

Sinclair, J. McH. and Coulthard, R.M. (1975). *Towards an Analysis of Discourse*. London: Oxford University Press.

Skinner, M. and Mullen, B (1991). Facial asymmetry in emotional expression: A meta-analysis of research. *British Journal of Social Psychology*, 30, 113–124.

Slama-Cazacu, T. (1976). Nonverbal components in message sequence: 'Mixed syntax'. In W.C. McCormack and S.A. Wurm (eds), *Language and Man: Anthropological Issues*, pp. 217–227. The Hague: Mouton.

Smith, W.J. (1969). Messages of vertebrate communication. *Science*, 165, 145–150.

Smith, W.J. (1977). *The Behaviour of Communicating*. Cambridge, MA: Harvard University Press.

Smith, H.J., Archer, D. and Costanzo, M. (1991) 'Just a hunch': accuracy and awareness in person perception. *Journal of Nonverbal Behaviour*, 15, 3–18.

Starkweather, J.A. (1956). The communication value of content-free speech. *American Journal of Psychology*, 69, 121–123.

Stier, D.S. and Hall, J.A. (1984). Gender differences in touch: an empirical and theoretical review. *Journal of Personality and Social Psychology*, 47, 440–459.

Tajfel, H. (1972). Experiments in a vacuum. In J. Israel and H. Tajfel (eds), *The Context of Social Psychology: A Critical Assessment*. London: Academic Press.

Tannen, D. (1984). *Conversational Style: Analyzing Talk among Friends*. Norwood, NJ: Ablex Publishing Corporation.

Tannen, D. (1991). *You Just Don't Understand: Women and Men in Conversation*. London: Virago Press.

Tannen, D. (1994). *Gender and Discourse*. New York: Oxford University Press.

Thomas, A.P. and Bull, P.E. (1981). The role of prespeech posture change in dyadic conversations. *British Journal of Social Psychology, 20*, 105–111.

Thompson, L.A. and Massaro, D.W. (1986). Evaluation and integration of speech and pointing gestures during referential understanding. *Journal of Experimental Child Psychology, 42*, 144–168.

Thorpe, W.H. (1979). *The Origins and Rise of Ethology*. London: Heinemann Educational Books.

Tinbergen, N. (1953). *Social Behaviour in Animals, with Special Reference to Vertebrates*. London: Methuen.

Ting-Toomey, S. (1999). *Communicating Across Cultures*. New York: Guilford.

Tracy, K. (1990). The many faces of facework. In H. Giles and W.P. Robinson (eds), *Handbook of Language and Social Psychology*, pp. 209–222. Chichester: John Wiley & Sons Ltd.

Trager, G.L. (1958). Paralanguage: a first approximation. *Studies in Linguistics, 13*, 1–12.

Trager, G.L. and Smith, H.L. Jr (1951). *An Outline of English Structure*, (Studies in Linguistics: Occasional Papers, 3). Norman, OK: Battenberg Press. (Republished by American Council of Learned Societies, New York, 1965.)

Trimboli, A. and Walker, M. (1987). Nonverbal dominance in the communication of affect: a myth? *Journal of Nonverbal Behaviour, 11*, 180–191.

Trout, D.L. and Rosenfeld, H.M. (1980). The effect of postural lean and body congruence on the judgement of psychotherapeutic rapport. *Journal of Nonverbal Behaviour, 4*, 176–190.

Trudgill, P. (1983). *Sociolinguistics: An Introduction to Language and Society*. Harmondsworth, Middlesex: Penguin.

Turner, J. (1975). Social comparison and social identity: some prospects for intergroup behaviour. *European Journal of Social Psychology, 5*, 534.

van der Molen, H., Smit, G.N., Hommes, M.A. and Lang, G. (1995). Two decades of microtraining in The Netherlands: narrative and meta-analysis. *Educational Research and Evolution, 1*, 347–378.

van Dijk, T.A. (1997). *Discourse as Structure and Process. Discourse Studies: A Multidisciplinary Introduction, vol. 1*. London: Sage.

Vrij, A. (2000) *Detecting Lies and Deceit*. Chichester: John Wiley & Sons Ltd.

Walker, M. (1977). The relative importance of verbal and nonverbal cues in the expression of confidence. *Australian Journal of Psychology, 29*, 45–57.

Walker, M.B. (1982). Smooth transitions in conversational turn-taking; implications for theory. *The Journal of Psychology, 110*, 31–37.

Watzlawick, P., Beavin, J.H. and Jackson, D.D. (1968). *Pragmatics of Human Communication*. New York: W.W. Norton & Co.

Weakland, J.H. (1967). Communication and behaviour: an introduction. *American Behavioural Scientist, 10*, 1–4.

Weitz, S. (ed.) (1974). *Nonverbal Communication: Readings with Commentary*. New York: Oxford University Press.

West, C. (1984). Medical misfires: mishearings, misgivings and misunderstandings in physician–patient dialogues. *Discourse Processes, 7*, 107–134.

West, C. and Zimmerman, D. (1983). Small insults: a study of interruptions in cross-sex conversations between unacquainted persons. In B. Thorne, C.

Kramarae and N. Henley (eds), *Language, Gender and Society*, pp. 102–117. Rowley, MA: Newbury House Publishers Inc.

White, G.L. and Maltzman, I. (1978). Pupillary activity while listening to verbal passages. *Journal of Research in Personality*, 12, 361–369.

Whitworth, A., Perkins, L. and Lesser, R. (1997). *Conversation Analysis Profile for People with Aphasia*. London: Whurr.

Wiener, N. (1948). *Cybernetics; or Control and Communication in the Animal and the Machine*. New York: Technology Press/Wiley.

Wiener, M., Devoe, S., Robinson, S. and Geller, J. (1972). Nonverbal behaviour and nonverbal communication. *Psychological Review*, 79, 185–214.

Wilson, J. (1990). *Politically Speaking: The Pragmatic Analysis of Political Language*. Oxford: Basil Blackwell.

Wilson, K. and Gallois, C. (1993). *Assertion and Its Social Context*. Oxford: Pergamon Press.

Wood, L.A. and Kroger, R.O. (2000). *Doing Discourse Analysis: Methods for Studying Action in Talk and Text*. Thousand Oaks, CA: Sage.

Woodbury, H. (1984). The strategic use of questions in court. *Semiotica*, 48, 197–228.

Yik, M.S.M. and Russell, J.A. (1999). Interpretation of faces: a cross-cultural study of a prediction from Fridlund's theory. *Cognition and Emotion*, 13, 93–104.

Yngve, V.H. (1970). On getting a word in edgewise. *Papers from the Sixth Regional Meeting of the Chicago Linguistic Society*, pp. 567–578. Chicago: Chicago Linguistic Society.

Zimmerman, D.H. and West, C. (1975). Sex roles, interruptions and silences in conversation. In B. Thorne and N. Henley (eds), *Language and Sex: Difference and Dominance*, pp. 105–129. Rowley, MA: Newbury House.

Author index

Subject index